The United States Infantry

An Illustrated History, 1775–1918

1. Corporal, 14th Continental Regiment,
1775–6

3. Private, Colonel Bridge's
Massachusetts Battalion, 1775

2. Private, 2nd Rhode Island Regiment,
1775

4. Sergeant Major, 3rd New York
Regiment, 1775

The United States Infantry

An Illustrated History, 1775–1918

GREGORY J.W. URWIN
Color Illustrations by Darby Erd

BLANDFORD PRESS

LONDON NEW YORK SYDNEY

Dedicated to
Rev. Donald Smythe, S.J.
Priest, Teacher, Scholar, and Friend

Other books by Gregory J.W. Urwin

Custer Victorious: The Civil War Battles of General
George Armstrong Custer
The United States Cavalry: An Illustrated History

PLATE 1: THE BIRTH OF AN ARMY, 1775–6
*Raw recruits struggle to master the British Army's 1764 drill
manual.*
**1. Corporal, 14th Continental Regiment (Colonel Glover's
Marblehead Battalion), 1775–6:** *An eyewitness recalled that the
fishermen and sailors who composed this Massachusetts outfit took
great pride in 'their own round jackets and fisher's trousers.' A green
epaulette on the right shoulder denoted a corporal in the Continentals from 1775 to 1779. This man holds an American-made
Committee of Safety musket.* **2. Private, 2nd Rhode Island
Regiment, 1775:** *Rhode Island issued this unit British-style coats
with brass buttons and breeches of brown linen. This confused novice
is trying to fix his bayonet on a British Long Land Pattern ('Brown
Bess') musket.* **3 Private, Colonel Bridge's Massachusetts
Battalion, 1775:** *On 5 July 1775, the Massachusetts Provincial
Congress approved the order of 13,000 plain brown coats for its
troops besieging Boston. Red 'Liberty' caps and leather breeches were
popular among the rebellious New England rustics. On 15
December, General George Washington directed each of his
regiments to form a reserve of thirty pikemen to guard against
possible British sorties from Boston.* **4. Sergeant Major, 3rd
New York Regiment, 1775:** *The sergeant major, fife major, and
drum major of New York's first four infantry regiments wore silver
lace trim on their coats and hats, as well as buckskin breeches and
waistcoats in their unit's facing color. The 1st New York received
blue coats with crimson facings; the 2nd, light brown faced blue; the
3rd, gray faced green; and the 4th, brown faced scarlet or gray faced
blue.*

First published in Great Britain in 1988 by Blandford Press,
Artillery House, Artillery Row, London SW1P 1RT.

Distributed in the USA by Sterling Publishing Co. Inc.,
°2 Park Avenue, New York, NY 10016.

Distributed in Australia by Capricorn Link (Australia) Pty.
Ltd., P.O. Box 665, Lane Cove, New South Wales 2066,
Australia.

© Gregory J.W. Urwin, 1988

British Library Cataloguing in Publication Data:
Urwin, Gregory J.W.
The United States Infantry – an illustrated history, 1775-1918.
– (Uniforms and history).
1. United States. *Army – Infantry – History*
I. Title   II. Series
356'.11'0973   UA28

ISBN 0-7137-1757-2

Designed by Blandford Press; layout by DAG Publications
Ltd. Layout artist Anthony A. Evans. Typeset by Ronset
Typesetters, Darwen, Lancashire; camerawork by M & E
Graphics, North Fambridge, Essex; printed and bound in
Spain.

*Soldiers of the 27th U.S. Infantry fire their Krag rifles at Muslim
tribesmen during Captain John J. Pershing's brilliant attack on the
Moro fort at Bacolod, Mindanao Island, Philippine Archipelago, 6–8
April 1903.*

Contents

Preface

From 1775 to 1918, the infantry was the mainstay of the United States Army. The War of Independence, the War of 1812, the Mexican War, the Civil War, the Spanish-American War, and the Philippine-American War were, in their land phases, essentially infantry wars. On dozens of far-flung battlefields, the fortunes of the growing republic were shaped by foot soldiers—men who faced danger armed only with muskets or rifles and who killed their foes with bullets, bayonets, and gunbutts. Contrary to popular belief, the U.S. Cavalry did not tame the American West unassisted. Infantrymen were guarding the frontier long before the Army acquired a permanent mounted arm, and they remained in the thick of things until the wilderness was finally conquered. And in World War I, when machine guns, tanks, airplanes, poison gas, and improved artillery altered the face of battle, the U.S. Army still depended on the lowly infantry to handle its dirtiest fighting.

During the period covered by this book, the U.S. Infantry was the Army's largest combat branch, and it profoundly influenced the institution it served so well. No less an authority than General of the Army Omar N. Bradley (1893-1981), who began his illustrious military career in 1915 as a second lieutenant with the 14th U.S. Infantry Regiment, stated in his memoirs: 'We in the infantry soon learned that it is in that branch more than any other that a soldier learns the art of command and, ultimately, has the best chance of reaching the topmost positions.' Indeed, the U.S. Infantry served as a sort of military nursery for some of America's outstanding commanders, including William Henry Harrison, Samuel Houston, Zachary Taylor, Ulysses S. Grant, Philip H. Sheridan, George Crook, Nelson A. Miles, George C. Marshall, Mark Clark, and Dwight D. Eisenhower.

It would require volumes to do justice to a subject as broad as this. A concise pictorial history can deal only with the important highlights. This narrative focuses on organization, tactics, the changes produced by new weapons in American infantry doctrine, and—in recognition of the fascinating social approaches explored in recent years by leading military historians—the background and character of the officers and men who made up the U.S. Infantry. The uniforms, weapons, and equipment of the American foot soldier from George Washington's time to that of John J. Pershing are briefly described in the captions to the illustrations.

Wherever space permitted, I have recreated certain battles and campaigns with the aim of expanding upon the book's major themes. As well as exploring *how* the American infantryman fought, the text also attempts to explain *why*—touching on the diplomatic and political factors which determined America's military policy and pushed her into wars.

During the three years I labored over this book, I received an enormous amount of help from many kind and talented people. I would like to take this opportunity to thank them.

First on the list is Darby Erd. The scope and quality of his contributions are obvious. Patient, conscientious, and hard-working, he made this collaboration a source of joy and satisfaction. He is as fine a gentleman as he is an artist.

John P. Langellier, Assistant Curator of the Fort Bridger State Historic Site, put almost as much work into this volume as I did. An accomplished student of the U.S. Army's history and dress, he reviewed my manuscript with painstaking care, catching errors of fact and style. He also examined most of the color plates and generously supplied me with black-and-white illustrations culled from his extensive research files. Michael J. McAfee, Curator of the West Point Museum, accorded me every courtesy when I visited the U.S. Military Academy in June 1985 in search of illustrations and uniform data. He led me to some hidden treasures in the museum collection, consented to the reproduction of some of his exquisite Civil War photographs in Chapter 7, and helped in the preparation of the color plates. Stephen E. Osman, Program Manager at Historic Fort Snelling, provided a treasure trove of information on the U.S. Infantry's uniforms and gear in the 1820s, 1850s, and 1860s. Captain Fitzhugh McMaster, U.S. Navy (Retired), responded with promptness and warmth to my queries regarding uniforms and illustrations. Two good comrades in the reactivated 33rd Iowa Volunteer Infantry, Dennis R. Bowles and Calvin Clay Kinzer, volunteered information on flags and accoutrements.

The people who staff America's museums, libraries, historic sites, and historical societies are rightly renowned for their courtesy. The following went far out of their way to satisfy my numerous requests for pictures, information, and research materials: Michael J. Winey, Curator, U.S. Army Military History Institute; Michael E. Moss, Art Curator, West Point Museum;

Private Jesse Hepson of Company F, 108th Infantry Regiment, United States Colored Troops, 1864. This black unit was raised in Kentucky by the Union Army and armed with Enfield rifles imported from England.

Theodore F. Wise, Director/Curator, U.S. Army Signal Museum; Roger E. Stoppard, Curator of Rare Books, Houghton Library, Harvard University; Ellen G. Miles, Curator, Department of Painting and Sculpture, National Portrait Gallery; Richard B. Harrington, Curator, Anne S. K. Brown Military Collection, John Hay Library, Brown University; Thomas G. Kuhn, Museum Director, Warren County Historical Society; Richard H. Zeitlin, Director, Wisconsin Veterans Museum; John C. Curry, Photo Archivist, Michigan History Division, State Archives; Jennifer Bright, Photo Archives, Museum of the City of New York; Donna Quaresima, Audiovisual Librarian, Colonial Williamsburg Foundation; Ann B. Abid, Head Librarian, the Cleveland Museum of Art; Michael N. Morell, Curator, Fort Meigs State Memorial; Brian Leigh Dunnigan, Director, Old Fort Niagara; B. William Henry, Historian, Jefferson National Expansion Memorial National Historic Site; Linda Meyers, Visual Information Specialist, Branch of Graphics, Division of Publications, National Park Service, U.S. Department of the Interior; Dione Longley, Assistant Curator, the Connecticut Historical Society; Roy Kemp, Park Manager, Fort Clinch State Park; Bobby Roberts, Archivist, University of Arkansas at Little Rock; Mary Coleman, Library Technical Assistant, Torreyson Library, University of Central Arkansas; and Robert J. Dudek, Acquisitions/ Collection Development Librarian, also of the Torreyson Library.

Herb Peck, Jr., William Gladstone, Mrs. James Collins, Jr., Randy W. Hackenburg, Michael F. Bremer, George E. Bush, Jr., Greg Novak, Cliff Breidinger, and Roger O. Hunt graciously consented to the use of photographs and artwork from their private collections as illustrations in the text or as references for the color plates. Gary Zaboly, one of America's more gifted young military artists, cheerfully furnished, at his own expense, a photograph of his stirring painting, *Beaujeu's Signal,* for publication in Chapter 1. A similar service was performed by Tim Todish, the owner of two other Zaboly masterpieces, *Amherst's Review* and *On the Right Flank at the First Battle on Snowshoes.* Color prints of the last two works may be obtained from Suagothel Productions Ltd., P.O. Box 2083, Grand Rapids, Michigan 49501. James Offie Lites, Jr., University Photographer, University of Central Arkansas, assisted in the processing of several key illustrations.

Any book featuring U.S. Army uniforms must rely in large part on the research of the Company of Military Historians. Established in 1949, the Company has done more in recent years than any other organization or institution to preserve the material culture of the American military. Space restrictions prohibit the citing of every article and plate from the *Military Collector &*

Historian, the Company's outstanding journal, that was utilized in the preparation of this volume, but the following pioneers deserve recognition for their indispensable contributions: John R. Elting, Frederick P. Todd, Frederic E. Ray, Frederick T. Chapman, Ed Sharples, Peter F. Copeland, H. Charles McBarron, Jr., Eric I. Manders, James P. Simpson, Philip R. N. Katcher, Dennis Martin, Marko Zlatich, Detmar H. Finke, James T. Jones, George Woodbridge, Michael J. McAfee, Edward T. Vebell, H. Michael Madaus, John P. Severin, Harry T. Grube, Roger D. Sturcke, Alan T. Nolan, Randy Steffen, Fitzhugh McMaster, Lee A. Wallace, Jr., Gary Zaboly, John P. Langellier, Donna Neary, Francis A. Lord, Alan and Barbara Aimone, Raymond S. Johnson, Don Troiani, Paul Loane, William Emerson, Alan Archambault, David C. Cole, David C. Abbott, Anthony Gero, James L. Kochan, M. C. Bruun, Douglas C. McChristian, Joseph Hefter, Edward S. Milligan, Gilbert A. Sanow II, Harold L. Peterson, Rene Chartrand, Richard Warren, Allan J. Ferguson, Stephen E. Osman, James S. Hutchins, Mendel L. Peterson, William G. Gavin, Ray Riling, Thomas McGuir, Stanley J. Olsen, Richard Ceconi, and Frederick C. Gaede. Likewise, *Military Images,* a handsome magazine devoted to photographs of the American soldier from 1839 to 1939, was a tremendous aid in preparing the pictorial portions of this history.

Valued colleagues in the Department of History at the University of Central Arkansas responded unstintingly to my frequent pleas for assistance. Waddy W. Moore reviewed the manuscript with a critical eye, suggesting numerous improvements. W. Foy Lisenby, the department chairman when this project began, and Harry W. Readnour, the chairman when it ended, offered me the material aid, moral support, and extra time I needed to get the job done. Various graduate assistants, Cynthia D. Burnett, Barry M. Gunn, Joanne Lehmann, George R. Hoelzeman, Jacque M. Rowland, Alan D. Ogle, John Nunes, Mary Landreth, and Kevin Sanford, were pressed into service as proofreaders, and the department's incomparable secretary, Carol D. Griffith, performed a host of helpful errands.

Grateful acknowledgment is made for permission to quote short passages from the following: Henry Berry, *Make the Kaiser Dance* (Garden City, New York: Doubleday & Company, 1978).

I would like to offer my deepest thanks to my wife, Cathy Kunzinger Urwin, an historian in her own right and a helpmate in every sense of the word, who interrupted work on her dissertation whenever I had need of her time, judgment, and encouragement. Cathy's brother, Fred, and his charming wife, Jeanne, kindly allowed me to share their home near Washington, D.C., while I did research at the National Archives, Library of Congress, and Smithsonian Institution in July 1985. Likewise, Darby acknowledges his debt to his wife, Gloria, for all her support—particularly for taking over all the household chores while he toiled long into the night at his drawing board.

Finally, Darby and I wish to express our gratitude to our understanding and attentive commissioning editor, Michael Burns, and all the other fine folks at Blandford Press who had a hand in making this book such an attractive showcase for the work of the artist and author.

The special, giving people listed above are largely responsible for whatever success this book enjoys. I, on the other hand, take full responsibility for any errors or other shortcomings found in these pages.

Due to the space restrictions dictated by this popular format, it is impossible to list all the primary and secondary sources that were examined to produce this foray into the past. However, a select bibliography is appended to the text for those readers desiring to learn more about the fascinating history of the U.S. Infantry.

Gregory J. W. Urwin

Department of History
University of Central Arkansas
Conway, Arkansas

1 The Roots of the US Infantry

1607–1775

The first truly American army sprang to life only on the outbreak of the War of Independence, but the American military tradition was already more than 150-years-old by the spring of 1775. The English adventurers and religious zealots who laid the foundations for the United States in the 17th century were beset by enemies the moment they arrived in the New World. For many settlers, fighting was as much a part of the colonizing process as clearing a field or plowing a furrow.

Stripped of romantic embellishment, the English colonization of North America was an invasion. The multitudes who crossed the Atlantic in search of wealth or religious freedom found their promised land already occupied by another race, the American Indians. The Europeans simply took whatever land they wanted, evicting the natives through bribery, trickery, intimidation, or aggression.

The Indians were ill-equipped to defend themselves against this treatment. They were divided into dozens of small tribes, which often warred among themselves. Ancient hatreds kept them from presenting a single front against the white invaders, even after the full extent of the European threat became obvious. They had other handicaps, too. The colonists were generally better armed and organized. Then, the natives were highly susceptible to the diseases the whites carried with them

Stripped and painted like an Indian brave, Captain Liénard de Beaujeu leads his forces into the Battle of the Monongahela, better known as Braddock's Defeat, 9 July 1755. Employing wilderness tactics, Beaujeu's 108 French regulars, 146 Canadian militia, and 650 Indians defeated 1,400 Redcoats and American Provincials under Major General Edward Braddock, inflicting 977 casualties on the English column. Painting by Gary Zaboly.

from Europe. Whole tribes were brought to the brink of extinction by measles or smallpox. These epidemics, and the sheer numbers of immigrants who swarmed to America, meant that the English soon outnumbered the Indians.

Nevertheless, when the Indians did resist, they exacted a dreadful toll from their dispossessors. At one with his wilderness environment, the Indian brave outclassed the average colonist as a warrior. Indians favored surprise attacks and ambushes. They terrorized the settlers, killing men, women, and children without compunction. Whenever a few tribes joined together in short-lived confederations, their revenge was terrible. On a single day in March 1622, some Chesapeake tribes slaughtered 347 Englishmen in Virginia, a quarter of the colony's white population. The same bands outdid that grisly performance on 18 April 1644, when they cut down 500 colonists. During King Philip's War (1675-78), the Wampanoags and their allies destroyed or depopulated twenty Massachusetts towns, slaying one-sixteenth of the colony's white male population.

As the English colonies expanded, they encountered even more formidable opponents. To the north and west lay New France, and to the south stood the Spanish borderlands. Both the French and Spanish regarded the English settlers as unwanted interlopers, a sentiment the English heartily reciprocated. Religious differences intensified this hostility. France and Spain were Catholic countries, while England was Protestant. In the 17th century, Christians of different persuasions still killed each other in the name of the Prince of Peace. Imperial ambition, national pride, land hunger, the vagaries of the fur trade, and sectarian antagonism embroiled the English and their European rivals in four major wars to decide the fate of North America. In the English colonies, these conflicts were known as King William's War (1689-97), Queen Anne's War (1702-13), King George's War (1739-49), and the French and Indian War (1754-63).

Apart from a brief interval in Queen Anne's War, when 5,000 Redcoats participated in a feeble thrust at Quebec, England committed no significant body of regular troops to North America prior to 1755. The colonists had to shift for themselves during the first three imperial wars and the intervening periods of sporadic frontier raiding. Though the first colonizing bands sometimes hired soldiers of fortune to serve as military advisers, they possessed neither the means nor the inclination to support standing military forces.

The English settlers provided for their own defense by transplanting an institution from the mother country—the militia. With its origins stretching back to Anglo-Saxon times, the militia was a defense system based on the principle of universal military service. All of the

thirteen English colonies, except Quaker Pennsylvania, passed laws which turned their citizens into potential instant soldiers. All adult males aged sixteen to sixty were obliged to arm themselves with modern weapons, to meet regularly for training, and to hold themselves in readiness to repel attacks upon their own colonies. Early Massachusetts and Virginia required their militias to drill once a week.

The militia's primary unit of organization was the company, which might contain anything between sixty-five and 200 men. In New England, any town of consequence had one or two companies. In Virginia, Maryland and the rest of the sparsely populated South, the militia was organized on a county basis. In December 1636, Massachusetts grouped its fifteen militia companies into three permanent regiments. By 1622, Plymouth, Maryland, Virginia, and Connecticut had adopted regimental systems, and the other colonies soon followed suit.

Colonial militiamen were predominantly foot soldiers. The dense forests of eastern North America impeded the movement of horses and fieldpieces. Cavalry and artillery were viewed as needless extravagances. A few groups of willful urban gentlemen formed troops of horse and companies of artillery, bearing the extra expenses out of their own pockets, but colonial cavalrymen were chiefly employed in reconnaissance and in carrying dispatches, and artillery-men were confined to coastal defense and formal sieges.

Early in the 17th century, one-third of the men in the average militia company carried pikes, and the rest shouldered matchlock muskets. But polearms and the massed formations associated with their use proved unsuitable for Indian fighting. The individualistic nature of forest warfare made colonists yearn for a more reliable firearm. By 1675, all militiamen in English America were required to own a flintlock musket, a move that placed these part-time soldiers twenty-five years ahead of several European armies.

Some historians depict the colonial militia as a middle-class association essentially concerned with the defense of property. It took a considerable sum of money to purchase a sound musket, adequate ammunition, and a sword, hatchet, or bayonet for hand-to-hand fighting, and that made the militia the eventual province of free, white, adult, propertied males. Slaves, free blacks, indentured servants, apprentices, drifters, and Indians were excluded in practice if not by law. In parts of the South, militiamen were called out most frequently to chase runaway slaves.

The militia was primarily a local institution. Its members fought best when they were protecting their own homes and families. However, colonial officials saw that the surest way to safeguard their frontiers was to carry war to the enemy. Occasionally, the militia managed to massacre an isolated Indian village, but the colonists were less successful in their offensives against the French and Spanish.

If numbers alone were the decisive factor in war, the struggle for North America would have been a short one. By 1713, the English colonies contained 375,000 people, about twenty times as many as the white populations of Spanish Florida and New France. Ironically, the very size of the English settlements drove most native tribes into the arms of the French and Spanish. Unlike the English, who came as land-grabbing farmers, the French and Spanish moved among the Indians as traders, trappers, and missionaries. The French were particularly adept at cultivating Indian friendship. In time of war, mixed bands of French and Indian raiders spread fear and carnage along the English frontier. To further complicate things, the English colonies quarrelled incessantly among themselves. They could seldom unite for long on a course of action against their common foes.

As the English colonies grew in size, their militias should have become stronger. Instead, the late 17th century witnessed the progressive deterioration of colonial forces. A growing list of professions—government officials, clergymen, millers, college professors and students—were exempted from militia service. Farmers and merchants in the more settled areas grew reluctant to abandon their lucrative pursuits and risk their lives in the distant wilderness. Calling on society's most productive citizens to answer every

frontier alarm came to be portrayed as harmful to a colony's economy.

In the 1670s, colonies began to hire volunteers to garrison frontier posts. For extended defensive or offensive operations, colonial governments formed temporary 'Provincial' units. Provincial battalions were raised for set periods of time—ordinarily a campaign season or one year. The militia was meant to serve as a training depot and a manpower source for the Provincials. Militia officers invariably filled the command slots in Provincial corps, and militia companies were compelled to contribute a percentage of their men to the Provincial outfits. Quotas were met by volunteers or draftees. As the 18th century developed, however, Provincial units increasingly drew their rank and file from outside the militia system. Drafted militiamen were permitted to hire substitutes for Provincial service. Soon the colonies were actively recruiting the poor and the propertyless for the Provincials. Thus the very people barred from the militia became the most likely to face the French, Spanish, and Indians in battle.

Representing as they did the dregs of colonial society, the Provincials frequently made a poor showing as soldiers. General James Wolfe, the great British hero of

Walking-stick in hand, Major General Jeffrey Amherst reviews a detachment of Rogers's Rangers and Stockbridge Indians at Crown Point, New York, in September 1759. Major Robert Rogers is at Amherst's right. Most of the Rangers wear their famous green jackets and Balmoral bonnets. In the background are companies of the 1st Royal Regiment, the 27th Inniskilling Regiment, and a Provincial outfit— the New Jersey Regiment ('Jersey Blues'). Painting by Gary Zaboly.

the colonial wars, called Provincials 'the dirtiest, most contemptible, cowardly dogs you can conceive. There is no depending on them in combat.' General John Forbes, the conqueror of Fort Duquesne, described his colonial troops as 'an extream [*sic*] bad Collection of broken Innkeepers, Horse Jockeys, and Indian traders . . . a gathering from the scum of the worst people.'

Wolfe and Forbes were unfair. With proper training, motivation, leadership, and supplies, the Provincials could give a good account of themselves. In 1690, 736 Massachusetts troops captured Port Royal in French Acadia. Three thousand New Englanders repeated that feat in 1710. During King George's War, Massachusetts, New Hampshire, and Connecticut raised an army of 3,500 men and an armada of 100 ships, sending them in the spring of 1745 to seize the French fortress at Louisburg from its 1,300-man garrison.

Not all Provincial expeditions ended in victory. Lured by dreams of Spanish treasure, the 3,600 colonists of Gooch's American Foot joined 5,000 British regulars in a bungled effort to reduce Cartagena, Colombia, in March and April 1741. All but 600 of the Americans died of yellow fever.

During the French and Indian War, the British government decided to commit its military resources to ejecting the French from Canada. Ultimately, 20,000 British regulars were stationed in North America. Though the Redcoats bore the brunt of the decisive battles, the Provincials did their part. On 8 September 1755, 3,000 New Yorkers and New Englanders defeated 900 Frenchmen and 600 Indians at Lake George. Three thousand American boatmen and 5,900 Provincials participated in the disastrous 1758 campaign against Ticonderoga. That same year, 2,600 Virginians and 2,700 Pennsylvanians accompanied General Forbes on his march to Fort Duquesne. Moreover, many of the Redcoats who earned so much glory in the contest were actually colonists. The 44th, 48th, 50th, and 51st Regiments of Foot recruited heavily in America, as did the 60th 'Royal American' Regiment.

The most famous, and arguably the most valuable, 'British' unit in the French and Indian War was an all-American affair, Rogers's Rangers. When Robert Rogers made his military debut on the Lake George front in 1755, he was a strapping twenty-four-year-old captain commanding a company of New Hampshire Provincials. Earning a reputation as a woodsman and a scout, Rogers was commissioned on 23 May 1756 to recruit two lieutenants, one ensign, three sergeants, and sixty privates for 'an Independent Company of Rangers.' By June 1758, Rogers commanded four such companies, as well as a company of Stockbridge Indians and another of Mohegans. Trained to move, live, and fight like Indians, Rogers's Rangers conducted numerous raids and reconnaissances behind French lines. They were deemed so indispensable that six additional companies of American rangers went with Wolfe to attack Quebec in 1759. Three of Rogers's veterans, John Stark, Seth Warner, and William Hazen, would gain fame later fighting the British in the Revolutionary War.

Captain Robert Rogers deploys his Rangers at the First Battle on Snowshoes, 21 January 1757. While on a scout behind enemy lines, Rogers and seventy-three men were ambushed by 150 Frenchmen and Indians. Holding his antagonists at bay until nightfall, Rogers skillfully broke off the action and led his remaining fifty-four Rangers to safety. Such exploits made Rogers a living legend on the Lake Champlain frontier. Painting by Gary Zaboly.

At the close of the French and Indian War, Great Britain became the possessor of a vastly enlarged empire. Determined to administer their holdings economically and efficiently, Britain's rulers decided to station 8,000 to 10,000 Redcoats in North America to shield the frontier from Indian attacks. Parliament would tax the Thirteen Colonies to support this standing force. But with the French gone from Canada and the Spanish from Florida, the colonists saw no need for so many regulars. Moreover, Americans refused to accept any taxes levied by Parliament on the grounds that they were not directly represented there.

Eighteenth-century Americans equated property rights with the rights to life and liberty. Unless a man was secure in the ownership of his property, he could not be truly free. Theoretically, if he had no say in the composition of the government which taxed him, he could be impoverished and reduced to political slavery. Thus the colonists protested any taxes not passed by their own representative assemblies.

British politicians considered American fears preposterous and stubbornly asserted the principle of parliamentary supremacy. The colonists responded with petitions, inflammatory rhetoric, trade stoppages, mass demonstrations, and mob violence. After ten years of this, relations between the Thirteen Colonies and England reached the breaking point. Resolving to make an example of Massachusetts, long the hotbed of colonial agitation, King George III and his ministers had Parliament pass the Coercive Acts. This punitive legislation closed the port of Boston and placed Massachusetts under military rule. Lieutenant General Thomas Gage and 4,000 Redcoats arrived in Boston to frighten the Massachusetts 'Whigs' into submission.

Massachusetts was not cowed. The Whigs promptly rejuvenated the colonial militia to better defend their liberty and property, purging 'Tories' from the officer corps. Meeting in defiance of British law, on 26 October 1774 the Massachusetts Provincial Congress directed the field officers to organize a quarter of the militia into fifty-man 'minute companies.' These 'Minutemen' were to keep themselves ready to turn out the instant the King's regulars ventured out of Boston. All militiamen were ordered to drill more frequently. The Provincial Congress also sanctioned the gathering of military supplies, establishing a major magazine at Concord, a town about twenty miles west of Boston.

On the night of 18 April 1775, 700 of Gage's grenadiers and light infantry slipped out of Boston on an ostensibly secret mission to destroy the stores at Concord. Gage hoped to prevent a war, but he started one instead. Forewarned of the Redcoats' approach, the Whigs removed or hid most of their matériel at Concord and roused the militia. The British clashed briefly with citizen soldiers at Lexington and Concord's Old North Bridge on the morning of 19 April. When the Redcoats turned around to return to Boston, 4,000 inflamed Massachusetts farmers and tradesmen descended on the line of march to fire into the retreating column. Only the timely arrival of a relief party of 1,000 regulars saved the original British force from total annihilation. As it was, Gage lost seventy-three killed and two hundred wounded or missing. By nightfall, the British found themselves bottled up in Boston by thousands of armed Whigs. Within a week, 10,000 angry New Englanders were in the 'Rebel' camp at Cambridge.

Massachusetts acted at once to impose stability and order over this spontaneous army of observation. On 23 April 1775, the Provincial Congress voted to raise 13,800 troops and invited the neighboring colonies to contribute men to a New England army totaling 30,000. By 27 April, the assemblies of Rhode Island and Connecticut decided to furnish 1,500 and 6,000 soldiers, respectively. New Hampshire took nearly a month to commit itself, but on 20 May its legislators set the colony's quota at 2,000 men.

The overwhelming majority of the troops enlisted for the New England Army were destined for infantry service. Massachusetts raised twenty-seven regiments of foot and one of artillery by mid-June. Each infantry regiment had an authorized strength of 599 officers and men divided among ten companies. A company was supposed to contain one captain, two lieutenants, four sergeants, four corporals, one drummer, one fifer, and forty-six privates. A regiment was commanded by a colonel, a lieutenant colonel, and a major, assisted by the following staff: one adjutant, one quartermaster, one surgeon, two surgeon's mates, and one chaplain. Regiments with general officers as their titular colonels (a practice copied from the British) were allowed two majors. Following the lead of Massachusetts, New Hampshire and Connecticut formed ten-company infantry regiments, but theirs were larger. New Hampshire's three foot battalions★ were designed to hold 648 officers and men apiece. Connecticut's first six regiments each had an authorized strength of 1,046.

Early in July, Connecticut created two new 796-man infantry battalions. Rhode Island initially organized its troops into three infantry regiments and one artillery company. Two regiments were mustered with eight companies and the third with seven. Later Rhode Island raised six more companies, adding two to each regiment. At full strength, a company included one

---

★During the Revolutionary War, the terms 'regiment' and 'battalion' were often used interchangeably, as most British and American regiments were single-battalion units.

captain, one lieutenant, one ensign, three sergeants, three corporals, one drummer, one fifer, and forty-nine privates. On paper, a Rhode Island regiment was comprised of 547 to 607 men.

Of course, it took time to sort through the confusion at Cambridge and to form these new regiments. None of them attained their authorized size, but by July 1775 the thirty-five infantry battalions in the entrenchments around Boston had a total of 1,109 officers and 18,538 enlisted men—an impressive showing for an army raised from scratch. Like their Provincial forebears, the New England units were short-term affairs. The Massachusetts, Rhode Island, and New Hampshire troops enlisted to serve until 31 December, and the Connecticut men were due to go home three weeks earlier.

Eager to enlist the aid of the other colonies in its squabble with Britain, on 16 May 1775 the Massachusetts assembly asked the Continental Congress sitting at Philadelphia to take charge of the force besieging Boston. Originally convened to coordinate colonial opposition to British taxes, the Continental Congress was neither a law-making nor an executive body. But it was the only pan-colonial council in America, and it shouldered the awesome responsibility of acting as the *de facto* central government of the rebellious Thirteen Colonies.

On 14 June 1775, the Continental Congress adopted the New England troops as 'the American continental army.' That same day, Congress authorized the formation of ten companies of 'expert riflemen' to serve as light infantry around Boston. Each company's complement was fixed at one captain, three lieutenants, four sergeants, four corporals, a musician, and sixty-eight privates. Six companies were to come from Pennsylvania, two from Maryland, and two from Virginia. Pennsylvania actually raised nine rifle companies, and they operated together as the Pennsylvania Rifle Regiment. These Continental riflemen were intended to symbolize the opposition of all America to British tyranny.

On 15 June, Congress endowed one of its own members, George Washington of Virginia, with the rank of general and named him as commander-in-chief of 'all the Continental forces.' A prominent officer in the Virginia militia who had held several important Provincial commands during the French and Indian War, Washington had probably seen as much military action as any American-born colonist, but the main reason for his appointment was clearly political. Putting a Virginian in charge of the Continental Army would dispel the impression that the Revolution was simply a New England war.

For all his previous soldiering, Washington had never commanded a large a body of troops. Yet his natural dignity masked his inexperience, and he learned quickly from his mistakes. His resolution, integrity, energy, tact, and occasional flashes of military genius kept the Continental Army together for eight miserable years and eventually prevailed over the might of Great Britain. Without Washington, there is no telling whether Americans could have won their independence or erected a free form of government.

General Washington reached the Rebel camp at Cambridge on 2 July 1775. The next day he took command of his host of pugnacious New Englanders. On 4 July, Washington announced:

'The Continental Congress having now taken all the Troops of the several Colonies which have been raised, or which may be hereafter raised for the support and defence of the Liberties of America; into their Pay and Service. They are now the Troops of the UNITED PROVINCES of North America; and it is hoped that all Distinctions of Colonies will be laid aside; so that one and the same Spirit may animate the whole, and the only Contest be, who shall render, on this great and trying occasion, the most essential service to the great and common cause in which we are all engaged.'

Ready or not, the Continental Army was in business.

This German engraving of two Continental infantrymen in blue linen hunting dress trimmed with white fringe was based on the drawing of a Hessian officer who served with British forces in the Revolution. Both Continentals wear leather caps with red plumes and painted yellow bands bearing the motto, 'Congress,' in black letters.

2 Washington's Continental Line
1775–83

The army George Washington inherited had already proven its mettle. On 17 June 1775, 2,500 Redcoats attacked 1,600 New Englanders entrenched atop Breed's Hill, an eminence overlooking Boston Harbor. The Rebels repulsed two British assaults before they were driven off the hill, and they killed or wounded 42 per cent of their assailants.

Breed's Hill and the performance of the Massachusetts militia on 19 April left many Americans with the mistaken notion that raw irregulars were more than a match for England's paid, professional soldiers. Washington knew better. He knew his Continentals needed considerable training and discipline before they could meet the Redcoats on equal terms. The Commander-in-Chief did his best to teach his unruly Yankees and Southern riflemen to behave like European regulars, employing general orders, courts-martial, and corporal punishment to mold what sometimes resembled a mob into a respectable army.

To provide a clear chain of command, Washington grouped his regiments into three divisions by 22 July. Each division had two brigades, and a brigade normally contained six regiments. Whenever possible, units from the same colony were brigaded together. Washington's 'Main Army' retained a divisional system of organization—with minor modifications—for the rest of the war. Due to constant fluctuations in regimental strengths, Continental brigades and divisions often altered their composition. In 1776 and 1777, most brigades held four or five regiments, but nine weak regiments from North Carolina were brigaded together for the Battle of Brandywine. After the consolidations of 1781, Washington organized his New England regiments into six brigades, assigning three regiments to a brigade.

Washington's army at Cambridge did not begin to master its trade until December 1775, but by then the men's enlistments were about to expire and they were planning to return home. Anticipating this eventuality, Washington, his generals, and delegates from the Continental Congress had already formulated plans to extend the life of the Continental Army. On 4 November 1775, Congress ordered the creation of an army of 20,732 men organized into twenty-six infantry regiments, one rifle regiment, and one artillery regiment. Every infantry regiment now had a standardized structure and size—eight companies and

728 officers and men. A company was to contain one captain, two lieutenants, one ensign, four sergeants, four corporals, one drummer, one fifer, and seventy-six privates. A regiment was commanded by a colonel, a lieutenant colonel, and a major, assisted by a surgeon, a surgeon's mate, an adjutant, a paymaster, a sergeant major, a quartermaster sergeant, a drum major, and a fife major. Later, a chaplain joined the regimental staff.

The reorganization of the Continental Army was scheduled to go into effect on 1 January 1776. Still caught in the Provincial tradition, Congress set the term of enlistment for its new Continentals at one year ending 31 December 1776. Washington's infantrymen were still drawn primarily from New England. Massachusetts was responsible for sixteen regiments, Connecticut for five, New Hampshire for three, and Rhode Island for two. To create the appearance of a truly national army, the regiments were given simple titles, which made no reference to their colonies of origin. Thus the Pennsylvania Rifle Regiment became the 1st Continental Regiment, and Colonel John Glover's Massachusetts Battalion became the 14th Continental Regiment.

Eager to have his new army in place before the old one melted away, Washington started recruiting late in October 1775, hoping particularly to re-enlist veterans. The results were disappointing. The ardor that had impelled the 'embattled farmers' to take up arms in the spring had waned, a victim of Washington's rigorous discipline and the boredom of siege life. By 30 December, only 9,649 Continentals were signed up for the next year, and that total inched to no higher than 12,457 by 3 February 1776. With just three-fifths of the authorized number of Continentals on hand, Washington called out nearly 7,000 local militia to help man his siege lines.

A perennial shortage of Continentals would compel Washington to resort to this practice many times in the future. But the militia's unpredictable reaction to combat made the custom a risky one. Not until France entered the war in 1778 did Washington have a better-than-average chance of finding reliable auxiliaries. Of the 16,600 troops who caged Cornwallis's army at Yorktown in October 1781, 5,600 were Continentals, 3,000 were Virginia militia, and 7,800 were French regulars. Yorktown was the only time French aid led directly to a Rebel victory, but once was enough. Yorktown broke Britain's will to continue the war.

Nevertheless, the militia played a vital part in winning the Revolution. In their traditional role as home guards, Rebel militiamen patrolled the coastline, protected the countryside from British foragers and raiding parties, suppressed local Tories, and defended frontier settlements from Indian depredations. On rare occasions, when they were inspired and well led, militiamen surprised their severest critics by standing fast on the battlefield. At Saratoga in September and October 1777, a Patriot army of 11,000 twice defeated and finally captured nearly 6,000 Redcoats and Hessians. That triumph turned the tide of the War of Independence, for it persuaded France to intervene in the struggle. More than two-thirds of the Americans engaged at Saratoga were militiamen from New England and New York.

The winter of 1775-6 turned Washington into an opponent of short-term enlistments. He recognized that it made no sense to release soldiers just as they were properly trained to execute their duties. Short terms of service detracted from the army's efficiency in other ways. To induce veterans to re-enlist, officers had to

relax discipline. By February 1776, Washington was asking for a regular standing army, but Congress and most colonists ignored his pleas. Ever since Oliver Cromwell's day, Americans had identified the idea of a standing army with tyranny. George III's use of the British Army to enforce the Coercive Acts bolstered this prejudice. Besides, it was difficult to persuade the typical colonial farmer to go off to war for a lengthy or indefinite span of time.

Fortunately for the Rebels, the British, still stunned by the slaughter at Breed's Hill, declined to test Washington's thinned ranks. Then in mid-March 1776, Major General William Howe, Gage's successor, evacuated Boston, taking his army by sea to Nova Scotia. Washington knew that the British would be back in even greater force. He anticipated that they would probably head for New York City, the most strategically located port in the Thirteen Colonies, and he immediately shifted elements of the Main Army southward to defend the city.

Congress had taken an interest in New York's security virtually a year before it became Washington's concern. The issue arose after Benedict Arnold, Ethan Allen, and eighty-three 'Green Mountain Boys' (frontier ruffians

Bayonets poised, the veteran 1st Maryland Regiment plows into the grenadier company of the Brigade of Guards at the bloody Battle of Guilford Court House, 15 March 1781. Seasoned Continentals took great pride in their ability to exchange close-range volleys and bayonet charges with the cream of the British Army. Painting by Don Troiani.

from backwoods New York) seized the British fort at Ticonderoga on 10 May 1775. That impetuous coup invited retaliation from British regulars in Canada, but it also exposed the former French colony to an invasion. The idea of adding a fourteenth colony to their confederation tantalized Patriot leaders.

Prodded by Congress, New York's legislature created four 758-man infantry regiments on 27 June 1775. These short-term units had ten companies apiece, each to contain three officers and seventy-two other ranks. Congress also directed New York to recruit 500 Green Mountain Boys for a seven-company battalion under Lieutenant Colonel Seth Warner. When the enlistments of the 1st, 2nd, 3rd, and 4th New York expired early in 1776, Congress had the colony field four new regiments for the coming year. On 21 June 1776, Congress expanded Warner's command into a full regiment, enlisting the men for three years. On the same day, Congress approved the 5th Regiment of New York Continentals, specifying that its complement should be composed of three-year men.

After the Rebels inaugurated their ill-fated drive to conquer Canada, Congress sanctioned the creation of two Canadian regiments. The 1st Canadian was formed along orthodox Continental lines, but Moses Hazen's 2nd Canadian borrowed its structure from the French Army. It was designed to accommodate 1,000 men in four five-company battalions. This odd departure, no doubt meant to attract French Canadians, was not a resounding success. The 2nd Canadian never raised more than half its complement, but it kept its unique configuration to the war's end.

While Washington and Congress worried about the safety of New England and New York, the war put its mark on the rest of America. Within sixteen months of Lexington and Concord, every colony south of the Hudson River raised units that ultimately became part of the Continental establishment. Some colonies acted on their own initiative to thwart royal governors or Tories who sought to restore British rule. Others waited for Congress's invitation to support the common cause. New Jersey fielded three infantry regiments, Delaware one, and Pennsylvania eight. Maryland raised one foot regiment and seven independent companies: South Carolina's Continental Line included two infantry regiments, two rifle regiments, one artillery regiment, and one of mounted rangers. North Carolina added six regiments to the Continental Army by the summer of 1776, while sparsely populated Georgia undertook to

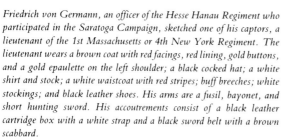

An American Officier

An American Soldier.

Friedrich von Germann, an officer of the Hesse Hanau Regiment who participated in the Saratoga Campaign, sketched one of his captors, a lieutenant of the 1st Massachusetts or 4th New York Regiment. The lieutenant wears a brown coat with red facings, red lining, gold buttons, and a gold epaulette on the left shoulder; a black cocked hat; a white shirt and stock; a white waistcoat with red stripes; buff breeches; white stockings; and black leather shoes. His arms are a fusil, bayonet, and short hunting sword. His accoutrements consist of a black leather cartridge box with a white strap and a black sword belt with a brown scabbard.

form one mounted-ranger and three infantry regiments. Virginia outdid its neighbors by producing nine regiments of foot.

The Delaware, New Jersey, North Carolina, and Georgia infantry regiments followed a table of organization similar to the one Congress had concocted in November 1775, but the other colonies followed their own whims. Seven of the Pennsylvania battalions contained the standard eight companies, but in at least six battalions one company was armed with rifles. Another Pennsylvania battalion counted only six companies. The 1st Maryland began life with one rifle and eight musket companies. The 1st and 2nd South Carolina were 750-man, ten-company regiments armed with muskets. The 5th South Carolina mustered seven companies of riflemen, and the 6th had five. Virginia

This 1778 von Germann watercolor depicts a Continental private in a black round hat with a brown plume; a gray coat with yellow facings and lining; a white shirt, stock, and waistcoat; brown breeches; light blue stockings; and black shoes. His buttons are of white metal and all his accoutrements are of black leather.

PLATE 2: SHAPING AN ARMY, 1777-80

5. Private, 2nd South Carolina Regiment, 1777-80: *Caps of beaver felt, coats with scalloped cuffs, canvas knapsacks, and white overalls gave this command a smart appearance. In December 1777, the men received Charleville muskets from France.* **6. Private, 5th Pennsylvania Regiment, 1780:** *During the first eight months of 1780, this organization received new coats, waistcoats, and white linen trousers. In August, the Pennsylvania Line refashioned its ragged cocked hats into handsome caps bedecked with white feathers and crests of white hair. This man is armed with a captured Hessian musket.* **7. Sergeant, 2nd Connecticut Regiment, 1777:** *Broad-brimmed hats turned up on one side, dark brown coats with white facings, and brown smallclothes made up this unit's uniform. To mark his rank, this non-commissioned officer wears a red cloth epaulette on his right shoulder and a British sergeant's Model 1751 hanger (short sword).* **8. Private, George Rogers Clark's Illinois Regiment, 1780:** *Established to guard the Ohio River frontier, this element of the Virginia State Forces received muskets, cartridge boxes, hats, coats, and smallclothes from the Spanish. The checked shirt is a civilian item.*

6. Private, 5th Pennsylvania Regiment,
1780

8. Private, George Rogers Clark's Illinois
Regiment, 1780

5. Private, 2nd South Carolina Regiment,
1777–80

7. Sergeant, 2nd Connecticut Regiment,
1777

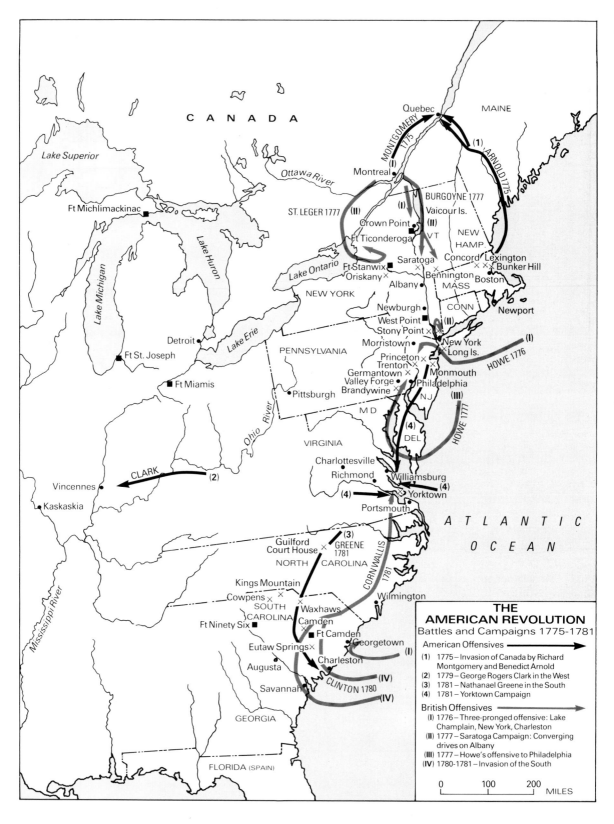

CANADA

MAINE

Lake Superior

Quebec

Ottawa River

Montreal

MONTGOMERY 1775

ARNOLD 1775

(1)

(I)

Ft Michlimackinac

ST. LEGER 1777

(II)

BURGOYNE 1777

Vaicour Is.

(I)

Lake Huron

Lake Michigan

Lake Ontario

Crown Point

Ft Ticonderoga

VT

NEW HAMP.

Concord Lexington

Bunker Hill

Ft Stanwix

Oriskany

Saratoga

Bennington

Albany

MASS

Boston

NEW YORK

Detroit

Lake Erie

Ft St. Joseph

PENNSYLVANIA

CONN

Newburgh

West Point

Stony Point

Morristown

Newport

New York

Long Is.

(II)

HOWE 1776

(I)

Ft Miamis

Pittsburgh

Princeton

Trenton

Germantown

Valley Forge

Brandywine

Monmouth

Philadelphia

NJ

(III)

HOWE 1777

Ohio River

MD

VIRGINIA

(4)

DEL

Charlottesville

Richmond

Williamsburg

(4)

CLARK

(2)

Vincennes

Yorktown

(4)

Kaskaskia

Portsmouth

ATLANTIC OCEAN

Mississippi River

(3)

Guilford

Court House

GREENE 1781

NORTH CAROLINA

CORNWALLIS 1781

Kings Mountain

Cowpens

SOUTH CAROLINA

Waxhaws

Camden

Ft Ninety Six

Ft Camden

Georgetown

Wilmington

Eutaw Springs

Charleston

(I)

Augusta

Savannah

CLINTON 1780

(IV)

(IV)

GEORGIA

FLORIDA (SPAIN)

THE AMERICAN REVOLUTION
Battles and Campaigns 1775-1781

American Offensives ⟶

(1) 1775 – Invasion of Canada by Richard
Montgomery and Benedict Arnold
(2) 1779 – George Rogers Clark in the West
(3) 1781 – Nathanael Greene in the South
(4) 1781 – Yorktown Campaign

British Offensives ⟶

(I) 1776 – Three-pronged offensive: Lake
Champlain, New York, Charleston
(II) 1777 – Saratoga Campaign: Converging
drives on Albany
(III) 1777 – Howe's offensive to Philadelphia
(IV) 1780-1781 – Invasion of the South

0   100   200
                              MILES

Captain John Haversham of the 1st Georgia Regiment sometime prior to his promotion to major in 1779. His dark blue regimental coat has yellow facings, gold buttons, and a gold epaulette on the right shoulder. His gold gorget is inscribed with a coiled rattlesnake and the motto: 'DON'T TREAD ON ME.' His black cocked hat is adorned with a gold cord and tassel, a gold button, and white feathers. He wears his crimson sash draped over his shoulder. His black stock is edged in white, and both his shirt and waistcoat are white.

A wealthy Philadelphian and a favorite of Anthony Wayne, Lieutenant Colonel Thomas Robinson of the 1st Pennsylvania Regiment posed for Charles Willson Peale soon after the Revolution. In conformance with George Washington's 1779 uniform regulations, the collar, cuffs, and lapels on Robinson's blue coat are red—the facing color for Pennsylvania, Delaware, Maryland, and Virginia regiments. As a field officer, Robinson sports a pair of plain silver epaulettes. The silver buttons of his coat are set in pairs, and he wears a handsome double-breasted waistcoat.

allotted ten companies (seven musket and three rifle) to a regiment. Carrying its singularity a step further, Virginia signed up its troops for three-year hitches. Similarly, North Carolina had the foresight to recruit troops for two-and-a-half years.

The Revolution had a radicalizing effect on the Thirteen Colonies. The longer the war lasted, the more it intensified American antagonism toward Great Britain. In July 1776, the Continental Congress transformed its struggle against British taxes into a crusade for American independence, and the United Colonies became a new nation, the United States.

The drift toward independence emboldened Congress to display an increasingly realistic attitude toward the war. On 25 May 1776, Congress authorized the enlistment of eight companies of German-Americans in Maryland and Pennsylvania for terms of three years.

This German Battalion, the Rebel response to the British use of Hessian mercenaries, later received a ninth company. On 17 June, with the discharge date for the original Continental riflemen fast approaching, Congress ordered them replaced with three-year men. Pennsylvanians continued to serve in the 1st Continental Regiment. Re-enlisted veterans from the Maryland and Virginia companies became the cadre for a new unit, the Maryland and Virginia Rifle Regiment.

Yet moves like these did not give the young United States an army capable of beating the British. In mid-August 1776, General Howe descended on New York City with 32,000 Redcoats and Hessians. To meet them, Washington scraped together an army of 28,500 men, but of these only 19,000 were effectives and more than half were skittish militia. Except for the 1st Maryland, the Delaware Regiment, and a sprinkling of 1775 veterans, the Continentals were half-trained recruits.

The outcome of Howe's offensive was a foregone conclusion.

In a series of deft flanking movements, Howe seized New York and chased the remnants of the Main Army into New Jersey. Rebel soldiers were killed, wounded, or captured in their thousands, and thousands more deserted as Washington retreated into Pennsylvania. By 22 December, the thirty-five battalions still with the Main Army mustered a mere 6,104 Continentals and militia 'present and fit for duty.' All but 1,400 of these stalwarts were scheduled for discharge on 31 December.

As the Main Army disintegrated—and the Patriot cause with it—the rebellion's leaders finally granted Washington's request for an army of long-term regulars. On 16 September 1776, Congress voted to raise eighty-eight infantry 'battalions' (i.e., eight-company regiments) 'to serve during the present war.' Congress assigned each state a quota of regiments based on population (see Table 1). Henceforth, Continentals would be recruited for the duration of the war. Enlisted recruits were promised a $20 bounty and a postwar land grant of 100 acres. On 27 December, Congress permitted Washington to raise sixteen additional infantry battalions, 3,000 light dragoons, three artillery regiments, and a corps of engineers. In all, Congress called for a standing force of 76,000 men in 110 battalions.

Table 1. State Quotas for Continental Infantry Regiments, 1777

New Hampshire	3 regiments	Pennsylvania	12 regiments
Massachusetts	15 regiments	Delaware	1 regiment
Rhode Island	2 regiments	Maryland	8 regiments
Connecticut	8 regiments	Virginia	15 regiments
New York	4 regiments	North Carolina	9 regiments
New Jersey	4 regiments	South Carolina	6 regiments
		Georgia	1 regiment

It was a simple matter to construct such a host on paper, but quite another thing to turn ambitious plans into reality. Washington's surprising victories at Trenton (26 December 1776) and Princeton (3 January 1777) resurrected Patriot morale and made it possible to recruit a new army. Nevertheless, fewer Americans than ever were now willing to face British volleys and bayonets. To stimulate enlistments, Congress offered prospective soldiers the option of serving three years instead of the duration. Recruits were also promised a free suit of uniform clothing each year. These perquisites lured men into Washington's ranks, but their numbers were hardly impressive. Two of the sixteen additional infantry battalions never took the field. Maryland raised only seven of the eight regiments in its quota. By May 1777, the forty infantry battalions attached to the Main Army totalled 10,003 officers and men, rather than the authorized 29,570. For the remainder of the Revolutionary War, Washington rarely counted more than 17,000 fit Continentals under his personal command.

According to the long-accepted myth, the Continental Army was composed of yeoman farmers and substantial

PLATE 3: CONTINENTAL ELITES: LIGHT INFANTRY AND RIFLEMEN, 1777-81

Continental light troops skirmish near a British redoubt at Yorktown, Virginia.

9. Private, Morgan's Rifle Corps, 1777: *Riflemen wore round hats and the fringed linen hunting dress associated with the colonial frontier. As the Pennsylvania long rifle was not designed to carry a bayonet, riflemen relied on tomahawks and knives for hand-to-hand combat.* **10. Private, Light Infantry Company, 2nd Virginia Regiment, 1779:** *In October 1778, the 2nd Virginia received French coats, red waistcoats, and brown linen overalls. By 1779, the light company was wearing leather caps with front plates and white trimmings. Around 1777, the French Charleville musket became the preferred arm of the Continental infantryman.* **11. Sergeant, Corps of Light Infantry (Lafayette's Light Division), 1781:** *When the Marquis de Lafayette took charge of two light infantry brigades in July 1780, he dipped into his own pockets to improve the appearance of his elite command. A Pennsylvania captain testified: 'Each non-commissioned officer received an elegant sword, feather, two bobs, and as much silver lace as would lace the front of their caps.' In the spring of 1779, infantry sergeants were directed to wear a pair of white worsted epaulettes. Later that year, white became the facing color of all New England regiments.*

If any man deserves to be called the 'Father of the U.S. Infantry,' it is Friedrich Wilhelm von Steuben, the gifted drillmaster of the Continental Army. Charles Willson Peale painted Steuben in the uniform Washington prescribed for Continental major generals on 18 June 1780, 'a blue coat, with buff facings and lining, yellow [gold] buttons, white or buff underclothes [waistcoat and breeches], 2 epaulettes, with 2 stars upon each, and a black and white feather in the hat.' Steuben's epaulettes are gold and his stars silver.

9. Private, Morgan's Rifle Corps, 1777

10. Private, Light Infantry Company, 2nd Virginia Regiment, 1779

11. Sergeant, Corps of Light Infantry (Lafayette's Light Division), 1781

tradesmen, amateurs in arms who gladly endured eight years of peril and privation for the cause of freedom. That may have been true in 1775, and to a lesser extent in 1776; but after 1777, aside from the handful who populated the officer corps, very few solid citizens followed Washington as regular soldiers. For the most part, Continentals came from the lower rungs of American society. They were vagrants, loafers, unemployed laborers, indentured servants, debtors, free blacks, and even slaves—desperate men who felt there was more to gain from military service than civilian life. Most were attracted by the promise of free land at the war's end.

Of course, the majority of the country's poor and transient were reluctant to face the dangers, diseases, and other hardships associated with Continental service. The inability of Congress properly to feed, clothe, and pay its troops also discouraged potential regulars. As a last resort, Continental recruiters solicited enemy deserters, prisoners of war, and ordinary criminals. Tories facing execution could save their lives if they enlisted for the war. According to eyewitnesses, a noticeable number of the 'able-bodied and effective' recruits rounded up for

Redcoats of the 26th Regiment of Foot overrun a band of Rebel riflemen near Montreal on 25 September 1775. Though more accurate and possessing a much greater range than the smoothbore musket, the American long rifle was slower to load and did not carry a bayonet— serious disadvantages on the 18th century battlefield. Painting by H. Charles McBarron, Jr.

Grasping his spontoon, a lieutenant forms a platoon of Continental infantry into the shoulder-to-shoulder line of battle described by Steuben's 'Blue Book.' The men deployed in two ranks one pace apart. A captain took his post with the company's first platoon, a lieutenant with the second. Each officer stood in the front rank, covered by a sergeant in the second. Painting by Don Troiani.

the Main Army were over-aged men and young boys. As long as a man could carry a musket, there was room for him in the Continental Line.

When not enough long-term recruits were forthcoming, Congress asked the states to draft militiamen for nine or twelve months of Continental service. It was hoped this expedient would enable Washington's regiment to make a respectable showing during the annual campaign season (spring, summer, and fall). But state conscription laws contained too many loopholes to net a sufficient number or a better class of Continentals. Draftees could avoid soldiering by paying a fine or hiring a substitute.

Foiled in its efforts to force upstanding citizen-soldiers into the Continental Army, Congress increased its bounties. On 15 May 1778, every non-commissioned officer and private who enlisted for the duration was promised $80. A paltry response motivated Congress to raise the bounty to $200 on 23 January 1779. Paradoxically, the states competed with Congress by raising independent forces of regulars to defend their own borders. Some of these state armies grew quite large. For example, between 1777 and 1782, Virginia raised seven infantry regiments, one of artillery, one of light dragoons, three legions (mixed commands of foot and horse), and several separate companies. The states offered extravagant bounties to fill their private armies, ranging from $86²/₃ in Massachusetts and New Hampshire to Virginia's $750, and thus they snatched away a significant proportion of the nation's available military manpower. Why should a fellow starve and go ragged in the Continentals when he received more money to serve close to home? Some state troops were ordered out of state from time to time, and during invasions of their home soil they were all expected to fight alongside the Continentals, but many state units went the entire war without seeing a major battle.

The year 1777 did not pass happily for Washington's Main Army. The recently knighted Sir William Howe thrashed Washington at Brandywine, mauled the Pennsylvania Line at Paoli, captured the Rebel capital at Philadelphia, and beat Washington again at Germantown. The Continentals fought much better than they had the previous year, but not well enough to stop the Redcoats. Only the Northern Army's victory at Saratoga gave the Patriots something to cheer about that year.

On 20 December 1777, the Main Army went into winter quarters at Valley Forge, Pennsylvania. There, 11,000 of Washington's soldiers were subjected to an epic of misery. At the start of the encampment, 2,898 men were unfit for duty due to lack of shoes or clothing. About 2,500 soldiers died from exposure, malnutrition, and disease by June 1778. In March, 1,134 disgruntled

Continentals deserted and joined the British at Philadelphia.

Valley Forge was a severe test, but it did not break the Main Army. In fact, the Continentals emerged from the ordeal as first-rate fighting men. This miracle was accomplished by a professional soldier from Germany named Friedrich Wilhelm von Steuben. Passing himself off falsely as a baron and a former lieutenant general in the Prussian Army, Steuben joined the Main Army in February 1778. Steuben had belonged to the staff of Frederick the Great, but he had been forced to retire from the Prussian service as a captain. Nonetheless, the 'Baron' was a seasoned campaigner, a skilled drillmaster, and a talented administrator. Shortly after his arrival at Valley Forge, Washington directed Steuben to train the Continentals to fight like European regulars.

Steuben's task was not a simple one. During the first two years of the war, Rebel troops drilled from at least three separate British manuals, a situation that generated much confusion when troops trained under different systems were brigaded together. Steuben gave the Continental Army a single manual by simplifying and improving the latest British drillbook, *The Manual Exercise, as Ordered by His Majesty, in 1764*. Published in 1779 as *Regulations for the Order and Discipline of the Troops of the United States, Part I*, Steuben's 'Blue Book' remained for the next thirty-three years the official manual of the U.S. Army.

A charismatic and energetic officer, Steuben taught his troops how to deploy quickly from column into line, to fire scything volleys, and to deliver or receive bayonet charges. Acting as his own drillmaster, Steuben insisted that all Continental officers do the same, repudiating the decadent British custom of consigning such drudgery to sergeants or enlisted 'fuglemen.' This innovation promoted closer bonds between the commissioned and enlisted ranks, while encouraging a greater degree of professionalism among the officers.

Steuben's methods were vindicated at the Battle of Monmouth, 28 June 1778. Hundreds of Washington's troops entered the fray dressed like paupers, but they fought like tigers, trading volleys with the cream of the British Army and fending off repeated bayonet attacks. The battle ended in a draw, but it was a moral victory for the Continental Line.

Curiously, the true magnitude of Steuben's contribution to the Rebel cause is unappreciated today. Most Americans believe their ancestors won the Revolution by sniping from behind rocks and trees at Redcoats who stupidly advanced across open ground in long, cumbersome formations. In reality, the smoothbore flintlock musket, the weapon carried by the bulk of the troops on *both* sides, was a primitive and often unreliable arm. Because the bore was unrifled, a musket could not shoot very far. Its killing range was eighty to 100 yards. Since a musket ball had to fit loosely in the bore for easy loading, it would go bouncing up and down the barrel when it was fired. Whether the ball flew straight and true or veered off course depended on the last bounce it took before it exited the muzzle. Moreover, the further the shooter stood from his mark, the less likely he was to hit it.

Sound tactics capitalize on the strengths of an army's weapons and compensate for their weaknesses. During the first half of the 18th century, European officers learned that the best way to utilize the musket was to line their men up in three to four ranks, have them point their muskets at the enemy, and then fire all at once in a volley. The idea was to propel a wall of lead into an opposing line. Some European armies did not even train their men to aim their muskets. Speed rather than marksmanship was the key to victory in this kind of warfare. Seasoned Redcoats could get off three or four volleys in a minute.

Volleys were exchanged at close range, and so there were numerous opportunities for hand-to-hand combat. At such times, a compact formation proved an advantage. Officers who kept their men massed together stood a better chance of repelling a bayonet charge or of driving one home. Before Steuben reached America, the Continentals and their militia auxiliaries had had to learn these lessons the hard way, and they did not always live long enough to profit from their dearly purchased knowledge.

Yet, the Continental Army would have introduced certain refinements to the practice of linear warfare, even had Steuben not appeared on the scene. Continental regiments went into battle in two ranks, which enabled them to cover more ground. Unlike their opponents, Continentals always aimed their muskets, a habit that improved their kill ratio. Washington directed his men to give their cartridges more sting by loading a few buckshot with the standard musket ball. Firing 'buck and ball' at close quarters allowed a Continental to bring down several men with one round. Following the Trenton-Princeton Campaign, Washington always attached an artillery company of two to four light guns to each of his infantry brigades. Schooled to move rapidly and fire their fieldpieces without delay at enemy infantry formations, these direct-support companies greatly augmented the Continental Line's firepower.

As mentioned earlier, a significant percentage of Continentals were armed with the American long rifle, a weapon whose accuracy and increased range intimidated many Redcoats. Experienced riflemen could achieve hits at distances of 300 to 400 yards. Yet the rifle of the day was not free of drawbacks. It took much longer to load than a common musket—the rifling within the bore

resisted the passage of the charge. Furthermore, rifles were not made to carry bayonets, so riflemen alone could not hold a fixed position—they had to be supported by musketmen. During the Revolution, the rifle proved most valuable for skirmishing and sharpshooting.

On 27 May 1778, a month before Monmouth, Congress approved a third reorganization plan for the Continental Army. The number of foot regiments was reduced to eighty, and five states received smaller quotas.

Table 2. Reduced State Quotas for Continental Infantry Regiments, 1778

New Jersey	3 regiments	Virginia	11 regiments
Pennsylvania	11 regiments	North Carolina	6 regiments
		Georgia	1 regiment

The men from eliminated units were absorbed by those remaining. The structure of the Continental infantry regiment was modified too. A light infantry company was added to each battalion, bringing the total up to nine. Regimental strength was decreased to a more realistic figure of 585 officers and men. A company now embraced a captain, a lieutenant, an ensign, three sergeants, three corporals, a drummer, a fifer, and fifty-three privates. Regimental field officers also functioned as company commanders, and their companies had no captains. As Congress forbade the appointment of any more colonels, many regiments ended up commanded by lieutenant colonels. A surgeon, a surgeon's mate, a

PLATE 4: THE REGULATIONS OF 1779: IDEAL AND REALITY, 1779–82

12. Private, Kirkwood's Delaware Battalion, 1780: *This crack outfit served in 1777 in cocked hats with yellow tape and blue coats faced and lined in red. In October 1780, North Carolina issued the ragged veterans new shoes, linen hunting shirts, and ticking overalls with blue stripes. The tin canister on the right hip contained forty extra rounds. This man holds a trophy of the Battle of Guilford Court House (15 March 1781), a grenadier's cap taken off a dead Coldstream Guardsman.* **13. Fifer, 2nd New Hampshire Regiment, 1781:** *Following the practice in European armies, Continental company musicians wore coats with reversed colors. This elegant uniform was reconstructed from an order, dated 26 March 1781, in the regiment's orderly book. When not in use, the fife rode in a tin container worn on the right hip.* **14. Private, 4th Massachusetts Regiment, 1779:** *A report on deserters in the* Independent Chronicle, *10 June 1779, revealed that the enlisted men of this regiment possessed blue coats faced white and breeches or overalls of white, brown, and green cloth. Partaking too freely of a bottle of rum, this jolly soldier has jammed his bayonet backwards into its scabbard. An estimated 5,000 blacks joined the Continental Army or found other ways actively to aid the Patriot cause.*

13. Fifer, 2nd New Hampshire Regiment,
1781

12. Private, Kirkwood's Delaware
Battalion, 1780

14. Private, 4th Massachusetts Regiment,
1779

Sub-Lieutenant Jean-Baptiste de Verger of the French Army's Royal Deux-Ponts Regiment, a participant in the Yorktown Campaign, painted this watercolor of Continental foot soldiers in 1781. Left to right: a black private of the Rhode Island Regiment in a black leather cap with blue and white feathers, a white fringed hunting frock with red cuffs, and white small clothes; a private from an unidentified regiment in a black cocked hat, a brown coat with red facings, a white waistcoat, red overalls, a brass plate on his white cartridge box strap, and a brass-hilted hanger; a rifleman in a black flat-brimmed hat with blue, black, red, and white feathers, a white hunting shirt, and brown overalls; and a Continental artilleryman with a black cocked hat and a blue coat with red facings.

sergeant major, a drum major, and a fife major remained on the regiment's staff, but one captain and two lieutenants detailed from the line pulled double duty as paymaster, quartermaster, and adjutant.

The Monmouth Campaign was already under way when Congress decreed these changes. More than a year elapsed before they were fully effected.

The new light infantry companies became the pride of Washington's army. Regimental commanders were instructed to keep their light companies at full strength by choosing for service in them the best men from the line companies. In 1779, a staff officer described the Main Army's light troops as 'proper sized men from five feet seven to five feet nine inches high, who have been in Actual Service two, three, and Some almost four years, a very few excepted, who are natives.' Writing in 1781, a Continental surgeon characterized the light infantry as a 'select corps consisting of the most active and soldierly young men and officers.' Light infantrymen needed special qualities. As Joseph Plumb Martin, a member of the 8th Connecticut's light company in 1778, related:
'The duty of the Light Infantry is the hardest, while in the field of any troops in the army. . . . During the time the army keeps the field they are always on the lines near the enemy, and consequently always on the alert, constantly on the watch. Marching and guard-keeping, with all the other duties of troops in the field, fall plentifully to their share. There is never any great danger of Light Infantry dying of the scurvy.'

During the campaign season, light companies were detached from their parent regiments and brigaded together in a separate Corps of Light Infantry. The corps furnished scouts and skirmishers for the Main Army. Washington also employed its members as shock troops. The courageous bayonet assaults the Corps of Light Infantry launched against British fortifications at Stony Point (15 July 1779) and Yorktown (14 October 1781)

definitively proved that Continentals could wield cold steel as well as their adversaries.

While the Continental Army was reordering itself to comply with the 1778 guidelines, a succession of mishaps in the South imposed a drain on its manpower. Between December 1778 and May 1780, the British overran Georgia and South Carolina. In the process, they captured or destroyed the Continental lines of Georgia, South Carolina, North Carolina, and Virginia (save for the 9th Virginia Regiment at Fort Pitt). British operations rendered Continental recruiting south of Virginia all but impossible. Washington dispatched the splendid Maryland Line and the Delaware Regiment to redeem the Carolinas, but those troops were decimated at the Battle of Camden (16 August 1780). By September 1780, the infantry element of the Continental Army was 13,000 men below its legal level.

In yet another effort to fit the number of regiments to the number of men willing to serve, Congress subjected the 'regular army of the United States' to a new re-organization scheme, effective as of 1 January 1781. Congress limited the Continental infantry to 18,000 men distributed among fifty regiments, and state quotas were adjusted proportionately (see Table 3). Though there were fewer of them, infantry regiments were now stronger. Field officers no longer doubled as company commanders, so every company normally had a captain once more. A company's enlisted contingent was increased to one first sergeant, four sergeants, four corporals, one drummer, one fifer, and sixty-four privates. Three new lieutenants joined the staff as adjutant, paymaster, and quartermaster. In addition, each regiment received a lieutenant, a fifer, and a drummer who were detached for recruiting duty in the unit's home state. The total paper strength of a re-modeled Continental infantry regiment was 711 of all ranks.

Philadelphia belles called Colonel Walter Stewart of the 2nd Pennsylvania Regiment the 'Irish beauty.' He certainly looked the part when he struck this swaggering pose for Charles Willson Peale in 1781. The red facings on Stewart's exquisite blue coat are edged in silver. The silver buttons on the coat and waistcoat are set in pairs, and the buttonholes are bound with silver lace. Note Stewart's silver epaulettes, the profusion of lace on his cuffs, the cocked hat with the black-and-red plume and black-and-white cockade, and the sword with the silver hilt and knot. White breeches and black riding boots with spurs complete his dashing ensemble.

Whatever benefits greater consolidation might have brought the Main Army were spoiled by the need to channel more Continentals to the South. In the spring of 1781, Washington sent two-thirds of the Corps of Light Infantry and the whole Pennsylvania Line to oppose British thrusts into Virginia. As of July 1781, the Commander-in-Chief had a scant 5,077 Continentals and 406 Connecticut state troops spread on a wide arc to keep 17,000 British, Hessian, and Tory troops penned up in New York City. It was therefore an act of supreme daring when Washington pulled 2,000 Continentals out of their New York lines in the latter half of August for his celebrated march to Yorktown.

Table 3. State Quotas for Continental Infantry Regiments, 1781*

New Hampshire	2 regiments	*Delaware*	1 regiment
Massachusetts	10 regiments	*Maryland*	5 regiments
Rhode Island	1 regiment	*Virginia*	8 regiments
Connecticut	5 regiments	*North Carolina*	4 regiments
New York	2 regiments	*South Carolina*	2 regiments
New Jersey	2 regiments	*Georgia*	1 regiment
Pennsylvania	6 regiments		

*Hazen's Canadian Regiment was not placed on any state's quota. It absorbed the remnants of the 1st Canadian Regiment and all foreign foot soldiers in the Continental Army.

After Yorktown, it soon became apparent that the British would mount no further efforts to subdue America. Congress, weary of heavy military expenditures and fearful that its unpaid soldiery might turn on the civil government, grew anxious to disband the Continental Army. In August 1782, Congress authorized a wholesale amalgamation of Rebel forces, instructing the states to reform their lines into 500-man battalions. This measure eliminated many weak units. On 23 April 1783, Washington received a congressional mandate to furlough as many troops as he thought fit. The men were to go home and await their discharge pending ratification of the final peace treaty. By late June 1783, Washington had released all his Continentals except four Massachusetts regiments, one Connecticut regiment, five New Hampshire companies, two companies from Hazen's Canadian Regiment, two Rhode Island companies, and five companies of artillery. On 18 October, Congress furloughed most of these men, leaving only 500 infantry and 100 artillery in a formation called Colonel Henry Jackson's Continental Regiment. By ratifying the Treaty of Paris on 14 January 1784, Congress formally ended the Revolutionary War. On 2 June it dissolved Jackson's command. A mere eighty soldiers—fifty-five at West Point and twenty-five at Fort Pitt—were retained in service to guard military stores.

The Continental Army was no more.

3 An Unhappy Childhood
1784–1815

When Congress disbanded the Continental Army, it defended its action by asserting that 'standing armies in time of peace are inconsistent with the principles of republican governments, dangerous to the liberties of a free people, and generally converted into destructive engines for establishing despotism.' This was a classic example of the guiding philosophy of the American Revolution. It was also an expression of incredible naïveté. Events soon proved that even a peace-loving republic needed a regular army large enough to defend its borders. Events soon proved that even a peace-loving republic needed a regular army large enough to defend its borders, but the American people were reluctant to acknowledge that fact. Their stubborn refusal to face the realities of military preparedness was an invitation to humiliation and disaster.

By the Treaty of Paris, the United States received title to all the territory west of the Appalachian Mountains bounded by the Great Lakes, the Mississippi River, and the 31st Parallel. This vast region, known today as the Old West, represented a fortune in furs, timber, farmland, and other natural resources. Congress eagerly hoped to exploit the riches of the area north of the Ohio River, the Old Northwest, whose fertility operated like a magnet on pioneer farmers. Denied the power to levy taxes by the Articles of Confederation (the new nation's frame of government until 1789), Congress hoped to pay off its crushing Revolutionary War debt by selling land in the Old Northwest.

However, in the world of international relations, title to territory means nothing without actual possession, and the trans-Appalachian country of the 1780s was swarming with enemies bent on preventing the young republic from exercising full sovereignty over the Old West. The Spanish, anxious about their outposts in the Floridas and Louisiana, hatched numerous schemes to block American expansion. The Old West's Indian population was approximately 76,000 in 1783, including 19,000 braves. Many tribesmen had been British allies during the Revolution, and the peace treaty did not diminish their determination to keep Americans off their hunting grounds. The 5,000 warriors of the Old Northwest exerted every effort to discourage whites from settling north of the Ohio. They also raided across the river into Kentucky, killing 1,500 people by 1790. The Indians were egged on by the British in Canada. Incensed by their country's defeat in the War of

Independence, royal officials did all they could to contain the growth of Britain's former colonies. In violation of the Treaty of Paris, British troops continued to man forts within the northern fringes of American territory until 1796. From these posts the British dominated the frontier fur trade, armed the natives, and incited them against the Americans. Without a strong regular army, the United States would never rule the Old Northwest.

Under the mistaken impression that the Old Northwest could be tamed with a modest show of force, the American government decided to send a small, temporary army to the frontier. On 3 June 1784, the day after it abolished the Continental Army, Congress asked Pennsylvania, Connecticut, New Jersey, and New York to field a regiment of eight infantry and two artillery companies, comprising 700 non-commissioned officers and privates. Pennsylvania's quota was 260 men; Connecticut's, 165; New York's, 165; and New Jersey's, 110. The men were to be detached from their state militias for a maximum of one year's service. As the provider of the largest contingent, Pennsylvania was entitled to name thirty-one-year-old Josiah Harmar, a former Continental officer, as the unit's lieutenant-colonel commandant. The corps also had two majors

PLATE 5: A FEEBLE FRONTIER GUARDIAN, 1784–91
Josiah Harmar and his troops at Fort Finney, a post built in 1786 at present day Louisville, Kentucky.
15. Sergeant Major, 1st American Regiment, 1787: *Originally dressed in Continental Army surplus clothing, the 1st American Regiment graduated to coats with new-fangled 'standing' collars by 1787. A sergeant major was entitled to two epaulettes made of silver bullion and white silk. The red chevron on the left arm, a distinction reserved for 'old soldiers,' was awarded for 'every 3 years of service.'* **16. Lieutenant Colonel (Josiah Harmar), 1st American Regiment, 1787:** *Field officers in the infantry battalion wore a pair of silver epaulettes. Captains rated one epaulette on the right shoulder; lieutenants, one on the left. Harmar's multi-colored silk cockade is housed in the William L. Clements Library, University of Michigan.* **17. Private, 1st American Regiment, Fatigue Dress, 1786:** *Harmar's enlisted men donned sleeved waistcoats for fatigue duty and blue woolen overalls in the winter, switching to white linen overalls for warmer weather. The regiment's round cockade was leather (silk had been the favored cockade material in the Revolution). The Short British Land Pattern musket was Continental surplus.* **18. Drummer, 1st American Regiment, 1787:** *The newborn U.S. Army continued the tradition of dressing musicians in coats with reversed colors.*

15. Sergeant Major, 1st American Regiment, 1787

16. Lieutenant Colonel, 1st American Regiment, 1787

17. Private, 1st American Regiment, Fatigue Dress, 1786

18. Drummer, 1st American Regiment, 1787

(one from New York and one from Connecticut), eight captains, ten lieutenants, ten ensigns, one chaplain, one surgeon, and four surgeon's mates.

Only Pennsylvania displayed any promptness in filling its quota of three seventy-man infantry companies and fifty artillerymen. New Jersey furnished just one company. Connecticut did not start recruiting until the spring of 1785, and New York raised no men at all. In the fall of 1784, Harmar assembled his 250-odd Pennsylvanians into what he called the 'First American Regiment' and set out for the upper Ohio. Sixty men deserted before the year's end, which kept the arrival of reinforcements from boosting the regiment's actual strength above the 250-mark.

Though the 1st American Regiment was too small to intimidate the British or the Indians, the need for a continuing American military presence in the Old Northwest was obvious. Between 1783 and 1790, at least 50,000 squatters crossed the Ohio to settle on Indian land without permission or on government land without paying for it. These hardy souls and their Kentucky neighbors repaid Indian depredations with raids of their own, which intensified and widened the cycle of frontier violence.

On 12 April 1785, Congress extended enlistments in the 1st American Regiment to three years, but the semblance of permanence did little to fill the ranks. Service in the new regular corps was unattractive. A private's pay was $4 a month, and in 1790 that was reduced to $3, with $1 deducted for medicine and clothing. For such a paltry reward, 700 men were expected to police the 248,000 wild square miles of the Northwest Territory. Between December 1784 and August 1789, the little United States Army built or refurbished nine forts along the Ohio and Wabash rivers, establishing a thin defensive line linking the Great Lakes to the Mississippi. But the posts were too far apart and their garrisons too small to bring peace to the frontier. And, as though the difficulties were not daunting enough, the weak Confederation Congress failed repeatedly to equip, clothe, pay, and even feed its small band of soldiers.

Harmar's recruiting officers were instructed to accept only healthy 'men of the best character' aged eighteen to forty-five and no shorter than 'five feet six inches.' Blacks, mulattoes, and Indians were excluded, but, as in the Revolution, the most numerous candidates for the misery and peril of a soldier's life were the poor and homeless. Many recruits were urban tramps, along with large numbers of Irish immigrants. Despite its reliance on human driftwood, the 1st American Regiment counted a mere 518 men on duty by July 1786.

On 20 October 1786, Congress decided to expand the 1st American Regiment into a legionary corps of 2,040

enlisted men by raising 1,340 extra infantry, artillery, and dragoons. But cutback legislation, approved on 9 April 1787, meant that only two new artillery companies were in fact added to the regular army. This modest augmentation left the 1st American Regiment with an authorized total of 840 rank and file. On 3 October 1787, Congress officially fixed the size of the infantry contingent at '1 lieutenant colonel commandant, 2 majors, 7 captains, 7 lieutenants, 8 ensigns, 1 surgeon, 4 mates. Eight companies, each of which to consist of four sergeants, four corporals, two musicians, and sixty privates.' By the following July, Harmar's corps mustered 666 enlisted men, but 250 were new recruits awaiting transportation west, and 174 of the troops on the frontier were due for discharge in 1789.

Around this time, the United States exchanged the ineffective Articles of Confederation for a much stronger central government. George Washington, the first President elected under the Constitution, hoped to win the friendship of the Indians of the Northwest. When his peace overtures were spurned, his administration resolved to 'extirpate, utterly, if possible,' the hostile tribes. On 30 April 1790, the enlisted strength of the U.S. Army was increased to 1,216. Nine hundred and twelve non-commissioned officers and privates were assigned to the 1st Regiment of Infantry, a twelve-company organization divided into three battalions. The remaining 304 troops went into the Battalion of Artillery. Each battalion had a major, an adjutant, a quartermaster, and a surgeon or surgeon's mate.

Late in September 1790, Harmar, now a brigadier general, set out from Fort Washington (present day Cincinnati) at the head of 353 regulars (two weak infantry battalions and one artillery company, and 1,133 militia (four battalions of infantry and one of cavalry). Harmar's motley array did not always move quickly, but it maintained good march discipline and enemy tribesmen fled at its approach. Between 18 and 21 October, his troops burned five abandoned Indian towns along the Maumee River. Craving more than a mere moral victory, Harmar rashly sent out two unsupported detachments to hunt for Indians lurking beyond the reach of the main American column. Both parties found Indians—or rather, the Indians found them—and each time the militia bolted at the first exchange of fire. A total of seventy-five regulars fought and died virtually unaided, while 108 militia, not as fleet as their fellows, were also cut down. Returning to Fort Washington by 3 November, Harmar claimed success for his punitive expedition, but his bungling only inflamed the natives and filled them with contempt for American troops.

Realizing the situation in the Northwest required stiffer measures, Congress nearly doubled the regular army by adding a second infantry regiment of 912 men

Dressed in a cocked hat, a blue coat with buff facings and lining, and buff smallclothes, Major General Anthony Wayne watches as his Legion of the United States engages hostile Indians at Fallen Timbers, 20 August 1794. An infantry lieutenant with a spyglass reports on the battle. In the background, an infantry captain brandishing a spontoon leads his company toward the enemy. Aside from Wayne, the troops pictured here have red facings and white smallclothes. As a general, Wayne was entitled to gold epaulettes and buttons. Officers of lesser rank had such items made of silver.

on 3 March 1791. It also empowered President Washington to raise a Corps of Levies, 2,000 six-month volunteers formed into five infantry battalions and one rifle battalion. Governor Arthur St Clair of the Northwest Territory was elevated to major general and put in charge of this impressive paper army. Unfortunately, recruiting did not progress quickly. Only 718 new regulars and 1,574 levies were enlisted in time for the campaign, and their quality was disappointing. According to St Clair's adjutant general: 'Picked up and recruited from the offscourings of large towns and cities; enervated by idleness, debaucheries, and every species of vice, it was impossible they could have been made competent to the arduous duties of Indian warfare.' Another contemporary commented: 'These men who are to be purchased . . . at two dollars per month will never answer our purpose for fighting Indians.'

St Clair could not open his campaign until 17 September 1791, two months behind schedule. With the addition of 418 Kentucky militia, his army was 2,400 strong. Most of the men were green and untrained. Many of the levies were near the end of their enlistments by this time, and they were not eager to defy death in the wilderness. With winter approaching, speed was imperative, but St Clair squandered ten precious October days building a fort to guard his supply line. Poor weather, scanty provisions, low morale, and heavy desertions soon beset the expedition. On 31 October, sixty to seventy militia deserted in a body. St Clair unthinkingly dispatched 262 of Harmar's veterans in the

1st Regiment, his only seasoned corps, to fetch back the runaways. He would have reason to rue that decision within four days.

On 3 November, the 1,400 men still under St Clair's personal command pitched their tents at a point on the upper Wabash 100 miles north of Fort Washington. Despite numerous signs that Indians were all about them, the Americans did not fortify their cramped campsite. A thousand warriors surrounded and attacked St Clair's camp the next day. The majority of the Americans promptly panicked, huddling together in the open where they became easy marks for hostile bullets and arrows. The 2nd U.S. Regiment and some of the levies fought back bravely for a while, but, as the enemy picked off the officers, the leaderless troops milled about in confusion. After two hours of one-sided slaughter, St Clair ordered a charge to the rear, and those men still on their feet clawed their way out of the Indians' ring of death. But 657 men, nearly half the army, died, and 271 of the survivors suffered wounds. St Clair's debacle was the bloodiest Indian defeat ever sustained by the U.S. Army.

Eager to redeem the country's honor, on 5 March 1792 Congress created three new regular infantry regiments and four troops of light dragoons, authorizing the President to restructure the entire U.S. Army in any way he deemed 'expedient.' To improve its chances in the woodlands, Washington and Secretary of War Henry Knox formed their new force into four self-contained mini-armies known collectively as the 'Legion of the United States.' The Legion boasted a paper strength of 5,120 rank and file divided into four 1,280-man sub-legions. A brigadier general commanded a sub-legion, assisted by a surgeon and three staff officers. They oversaw eight infantry companies, four rifle companies, one light dragoon company, and one artillery company. An infantry company's make-up was one captain, one lieutenant, one ensign, six sergeants, six corporals, two musicians, and eighty-one privates. A rifle company followed a similar configuration, except it had just one musician—a bugler—and eighty-two privates. Infantry and rifle companies were grouped by fours in separate battalions, each run by a major, an adjutant, a quartermaster, a surgeon's mate, a sergeant major, a

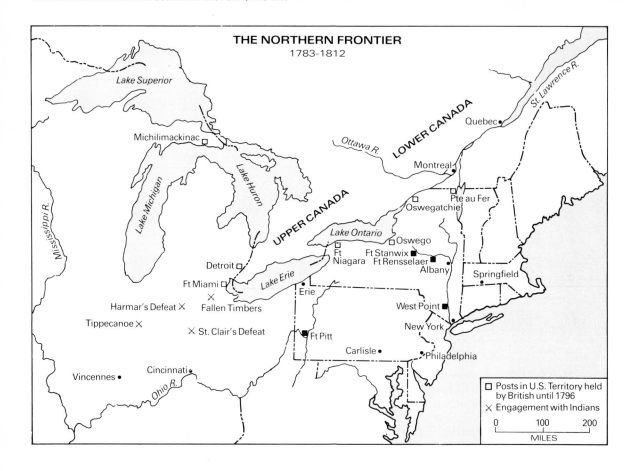

THE NORTHERN FRONTIER
1783-1812

☐ Posts in U.S. Territory held by British until 1796
✕ Engagement with Indians

0   100   200
MILES

quartermaster sergeant, and a senior musician. Because only 3,578 men were enlisted in the Legion by 5 June 1794, the rifle battalions of the 3rd and 4th Sub-Legions were not activated. The Legion offset this loss by training one company in each infantry battalion to function as light infantry.

Major General Anthony Wayne, a vain, hot-tempered martinet who had displayed a flair for tackling tough assignments during the Revolution, obtained command of the Legion and inherited the task of subduing the tribes of the Northwest. Though renowned for his impetuosity, Wayne devoted more than a year to training his army. Recruiters were admonished to enlist only 'brave, robust, faithful soldiers,' but the men they sent Wayne were little better than those who had followed St Clair. Wayne employed steel discipline to pound his rabble into shape. During fourteen months spanning the years 1792 and 1793, the Legion witnessed 190 courts-martial. A tenth of these cases resulted in death sentences; most other offenders were flogged. Wayne also introduced positive methods to promote confidence and *esprit de corps*, such as frequent drills and target practice, and passwords like 'Soldierly Appear-

ance' and 'Always Ready.' Each officer received a copy of Steuben's 'Blue Book' and was expected to know it inside out. Common soldiers were thoroughly schooled in the evolutions of linear warfare and also trained to fire individually at marks. The process was not always pleasant, but in the end Wayne molded his Legion into a superb offensive machine.

PLATE 6: THE LEGION OF THE UNITED STATES, 1792–6
19. Corporal, Light Infantry Company, 3rd Sub-Legion, Legion of the United States, 1794: The Legion's light troops *wore coatees and leather caps. A soldier's sub-legion was indicated by the color of the plume, turban, and binding on his headgear. The 1st Sub-Legion wore white; the 2nd, red; the 3rd, yellow; and the 4th, green. The Legion infantry carried .69-caliber French Charleville muskets into the Battle of Fallen Timbers.* **20. Captain, Battalion Company, 1st Sub-Legion, Legion of the United States, 1794:** When in garrison, battalion officers wore large cocked hats of stiffened black felt. **21. Lieutenant, Battalion Company, 2nd Sub-Legion, Legion of the United States, Field Dress, 1794:** In the field, battalion officers sported round hats with bearskin crests. They also carried short spears called spontoons.

19. Corporal, Light Infantry Company, 3rd
Sub-Legion, Legion of the United States,
1794

20. Captain, Battalion Company, 1st Sub-
Legion, Legion of the United States, 1794

21. Lieutenant, Battalion Company, 2nd
Sub-Legion, Legion of the United States,
Field Dress, 1794

1. The color of the 3rd Battalion, 1st Sub-Legion, Legion of the United States, 1793. This white silk flag measures fifty-six by forty inches and bears a painted device consisting of a brown shield under a blue knot. Both the shield and the scroll are edged with gold paint and all lettering is gold.

2. Captain Samuel White served in the 11th U.S. Infantry, a regiment in the temporary New Army, from 8 January 1799 until his discharge on 15 June 1800. This engraved portrait by Charles Balthazar Julien Févret de Saint-Mémin features White's blue coat, red facings, and silver buttons. His rank is indicated by a silver epaulette on the right shoulder.

3. Captain Henry B. Brevoort, 2nd U.S. Infantry, won fame as the commander of a detachment of soldiers acting as marines aboard the Niagara, a brig that helped Oliver Hazard Perry win the Battle of Lake Erie, 10 September 1813. Bass Otis painted Brevoort in a blue single-breasted coat with a red collar and silver buttons and lace—standard wear for U.S. Infantry officers at the start of the War of 1812.

4. Captain Moses Hook, 1st U.S. Infantry, circa 1807–8. U.S. Army fashions changed markedly during the first decade of the 19th century. Infantry officers still wore blue coats with red facings and silver metallic trim, but collars and lapels were wider and tails were cut narrower. The Army abolished the queue in 1801. Miniature portrait on ivory.

5. Edmund Pendleton Gaines had been a 2nd U.S. Infantry captain for a year when Saint-Mémin captured his likeness in 1808. Gaines wears a blue coat with red facings, silver buttons, and a silver epaulette on his right shoulder. His buttonholes and lapels are bound with silver lace. Rising to the rank of brigadier general in the War of 1812, Gaines died on 6 June 1848, after more than fifty years in the regular army.

6. Jean T. David joined the 15th U.S. Infantry as an ensign on 7 May 1812, and he was made regimental paymaster on 24 July. In this fine Thomas Sully portrait, completed 3 March 1813, David wears the all-blue coat authorized for infantry officers by the Rules and Regulations of the Army for 1813. David asserted his individuality by having his collar adorned with silver embroidery arranged in a floral design. The cut of his cuffs is also unorthodox.

△1

△4

△2 ▽3

△5 ▽6

In October 1793, Wayne advanced seventy-five miles north of Fort Washington and erected a large camp called Fort Greenville. He rightly judged that a winter in Indian country would complete the Legion's training. Wayne also telegraphed an ominous message to the enemy when on 24 December he marched eight companies to the site of the St Clair Massacre and threw up the works of Fort Recovery.

There followed more than six months of scouting, conditioning, and repelling Indian raids. Then the Legion finally stood ready for its ultimate test. On 28 July 1794, Wayne led 3,500 troops—2,000 regulars and 1,500 volunteer mounted riflemen just arrived from Kentucky—out of Fort Greenville, plunging north into the forbidding forests in search of a fight.

Some 500 to 1,000 Indians, supported by a company of Canadian militia, tried to halt Wayne at Fallen Timbers, an area on the northwest bank of the Maumee which had been turned into a natural fort by a tree-toppling tornado. At 10:00 a.m. on 20 August, a telling fusillade from hidden Indian marksmen peeled away the battalion of Kentuckians screening Wayne's advance. Unruffled, Wayne deployed his regular infantry in two lines and had them charge with the bayonet. Unnerved by the Americans' steady courage, the Indians gave ground. 'We drove the Enemy for about one mile directly out,' exulted a Legion officer. 'The Troops were . . . in full Speed pressing the Enemey [sic].' The Indians' withdrawal became a rout when Wayne turned their flanks with the Legion cavalry and his mounted Kentuckians. The battlefield's rough terrain allowed the scurrying braves to outdistance their pursuers. They also inflicted 133 casualties on the Americans at a loss of no more than twenty to forty dead. But the victory was Wayne's. By besting the Indians in open battle, Wayne convinced them that his Legion was irresistible. A year later, the hostile tribes made peace with the United States in the Treaty of Greenville, opening two-thirds of Ohio and a corner of eastern Indiana to white settlement.

Once peace came to the Northwest, however, Congress discarded vigilance for frugality and scrapped the legionary system. On 30 May 1796, the U.S. Army was ordered to cut back to four eight-company infantry regiments, a corps of artillerists and engineers, and two light dragoon companies. Wayne did not long outlive his beloved Legion. He died on 15 December 1796, a month-and-a-half after the May reductions went into effect.

International tensions soon precipitated an augmentation of the Army. In 1792, Great Britain and France began a series of bitter wars which would not end until Napoleon's final defeat at Waterloo in June 1815. As the possessor of the world's largest neutral merchant marine, the United States was deeply affected when the two belligerents resorted to economic warfare. For a variety of reasons, republican France made herself particularly obnoxious, not merely preying on American ships, but also insulting American diplomats.

At length, President John Adams, Washington's successor, decided to teach the French to respect his country's maritime rights. Armed American merchantmen and the fledgling U.S. Navy sallied forth to chastise French corsairs. Meanwhile, the President's Federalist supporters in Congress moved on their own initiative to construct an army capable of repulsing a direct French attack on American soil. On 27 April 1798, Congress created a second regiment of artillerists and engineers, and a month later, it authorized a three-year 'Provisional Army' of 10,000 men to be raised if the United States was menaced with war or invasion. On 16 July, Congress added two companies and three supernumerary staff officers to each infantry regiment, raising the regimental aggregate from 535 to 743 officers and men. Recruits were awarded a $12 bounty in return for a five-year enlistment, and a private's pay climbed to $5 a month. That same day, the regular establishment was fattened further by the creation of the 'New Army,' twelve infantry regiments and six light dragoon companies intended to serve during 'the existing difficulties between the United States and the French Republic.' Finally, on 2 March 1799, Congress empowered the President to call out a 30,000-man 'Eventual Army,' including twenty-four infantry regiments and a regiment and a battalion of riflemen, should the nation face the threat of war or invasion.

Bravely resisting pressure from within his own party to make an open break with France, Adams refused to activate the Provisional and Eventual Armies, preferring diplomacy and naval retaliation to wring decent

PLATE 7: THE WAR OF 1812 BEGINS

Three regulars guard the entrance to Fort Niagara, New York.
22. Private, 4th U.S. Infantry, 1812: *An Ohio volunteer who saw this unit in the summer of 1812 declared: 'I never saw a finer Regiment of men than the 4th. . . . The Colonel was permitted to uniform them to suit himself, and it was the first time I ever saw the bucket cap, with cord and tasse[l]s and the cartridge box worn around the waste [sic], instead of over the shoulder of the coatee.'*
23. Captain (John E. Wool), 13th U.S. Infantry, 1812: *Wool's coatee, typical of those worn by American regular infantry officers at the war's start, is in the possession of the Rennselaer County Historical Society.* **24. Drummer, 22nd U.S. Infantry, 1812–13:** *A shortage of blue cloth, cap plates, and other uniform items affected the infantry regiments added to the regular army in 1812. At the year's end, the 22nd received overalls of 'Blue and white speckled' wool and drab coats with green collars and cuffs. Buttonholes were laced with black tape rather than regulation white. Musicians wore coats with reversed colors.*

22. Private, 4th U.S. Infantry, 1812

24. Drummer, 22nd U.S. Infantry, 1812–13

23. Captain, 13th U.S. Infantry, 1812

26. Private, Ohio Volunteer Militia, 1812

25. Corporal, 17th U.S. Infantry, 1813

27. Private, 17th U.S. Infantry, Summer
Field Dress, 1812

treatment from the French. Early in 1800, Adams attained his goals, and by 15 June, the 3,399 infantrymen recruited for the New Army were discharged.

As of 23 December 1801, the U.S. Army numbered 4,051 out of a sanctioned 5,438 officers and men. They were distributed among four infantry regiments, two regiments of artillerists and engineers, and two dismounted companies of light dragoons. Over 2,300 of these troops were infantrymen. It was not a formidable array, and it was destined to become even smaller.

In the fall of 1800, Thomas Jefferson defeated John Adams for the presidency. Jefferson and his fellow Democratic-Republicans harbored little love for standing armies. On 16 March 1802, the new government translated its ideals into legislation. Congress pruned the Army down to twenty companies of infantry, twenty companies of artillery, and a diminutive corps of engineers. The badly mutilated regular establishment now comprised 3,212 men of all ranks. By 4 February 1805, the Army had dwindled to 2,579 officers and men, including 1,295 in the 1st and 2nd Infantry Regiments.

Jefferson's reductions occurred during a lull in the fighting in Europe, but, in May 1803, England and France resumed their struggle. Hurling his magnificent Grand Army at the allied powers of Europe, Napoleon soon placed the Continent under his heel, but England remained supreme on the high seas. The Anglophobic Jefferson and his Democratic-Republicans were increasingly offended as the Royal Navy took to seizing American merchantmen bound for French-controlled

PLATE 8: DISASTER AND RECOVERY IN THE NORTHWEST, 1812–13

Wary Americans stand watch on the ramparts of Fort Meigs, Ohio.
25. Corporal, 17th U.S. Infantry, 1813: *Raised in the summer of 1812, the 17th took the field in the autumn in light summer uniforms of white linen. Early in 1813, the men received black coatees with red facings. These were probably issued before company tailors could attach their white trim or all their buttons. At the same time, the Army of the Northwest received overalls made of gray, drab, brown, and speckled wool. A corporal wore his rank on his right shoulder in the form of a white epaulette.* **26. Private, Ohio Volunteer Militia, 1812:** *A British participant in the Detroit Campaign (July–August 1812) wrote: 'The . . . levies of men taken from the forests of Ohio [are] scarcely inferior as riflemen to the Indians. Dressed in woollen [sic] frocks of a gray color, [they are] trained to cover their bodies behind the trees from which they fired, without exposing more of their persons than was absolutely necessary for their aim.'* **27. Private, 17th U.S. Infantry, Summer Field Dress, 1812:** *In January 1813, with many of his men still in the remnants of their summer uniforms, Major General William Henry Harrison complained: 'A fine body of regular troops belonging to the 19th and 17th . . . Rgts . . . has been nearly destroyed for want of Clothing.' Figures 25 and 27 are both armed with Model 1812 contract muskets.*

ports and impressing Yankee seamen to serve aboard British men-of-war.

In the summer of 1807, blind fury overcame the American people's prudence, and war fever swept the land. Congress voted on 12 April 1808 to swell the U.S. Army with 6,000 regulars recruited for five years. This 'Additional Military Force' was composed of five infantry regiments, one rifle regiment, one light artillery regiment, and one light dragoon regiment. An infantry or a rifle regiment consisted of one colonel, one lieutenant colonel, one major, one adjutant, one quartermaster, one paymaster, one surgeon, one surgeon's mate, one sergeant major, one quartermaster sergeant, two principal musicians, and ten companies, each containing one captain, two lieutenants, one ensign, four sergeants, four corporals, four musicians, and sixty-eight privates. Within eleven months, the Army's old 'Peace Establishment' held just over 3,000 men, and the Additional Military Force amounted to 3,700 troops. Thankfully, war with Britain was postponed for three more years. During that period, the Army's strength fluctuated between 5,500 and 7,000 effectives. A War Department report of January 1810 revealed that the seven infantry regiments ranged in size from 362 to 680 officers and men, while the new Regiment of Riflemen numbered 597.

One infantry regiment of the Additional Military Force saw combat in 1811, but it won its first battle honor fighting Indians, not Redcoats. Alarmed by the multitudes of white settlers encroaching on the remaining tribal lands in the Old Northwest, a Shawnee war chief named Tecumseh realized that Indian unity was the only effective means of curbing American expansion. Tecumseh began to spread this message in 1805, and he was greatly aided by the mystical pronouncements of his brother, a soothsayer known as the 'Prophet.' By 1810, 1,000 braves loyal to Tecumseh were living at the juncture of Tippecanoe Creek and the upper Wabash in a village known as Prophet's Town. In the summer of 1811, Tecumseh journeyed south to entice other tribes into his confederation.

Noting the growth of Tecumseh's power with rising apprehension, Governor William Henry Harrison of Indiana Territory seized his chance to strike at the Indian confederation while its mercurial founder was far from home. In August, Harrison called out local militiamen for extra drill and organization into a field army. The War Department had already dispatched the 4th U.S. Infantry on a 1,500-mile junket from Philadelphia to help defend the Indiana frontier, but the canny governor had something more offensive in mind for the approaching regulars.

On 26 September 1811, Harrison set out for Prophet's Town with a force variously estimated at 970 to 1,290 men (including 350 to 400 regulars)—nine companies of the 4th Infantry, six companies of ordinary Indiana militia, one company of Indiana riflemen, seven companies of mounted riflemen or dragoons from Indiana and Kentucky, and a platoon of scouts. Harrison later claimed he was simply out to awe the Indians with a 'demonstration of force,' but, on 6 November 1811, he encamped within 150 yards of Prophet's Town. It certainly looked as though Harrison was goading the Indians into a fight, and they gladly obliged him.

At 4:00 a.m. on 7 November, 550 to 700 painted warriors crept silently toward the sleeping Americans. A shot fired by a vigilant sentry roused the camp just in time. A surrounding chorus of war cries and gunshots greeted Harrison's men as they tumbled from their tents to find the waning darkness flickering with musket flashes. Stiffened by the 4th Infantry, the Americans manned a rectangular perimeter and beat off several furious assaults. As day dawned, Harrison hurled his 270 horsemen at his now visible adversaries, throwing the Indians into a precipitate retreat.

The Battle of Tippecanoe cost Harrison sixty-two dead and 126 wounded, more than a fifth of his ragtag army. The bodies of thirty-six warriors were left on the battlefield, and Prophet's Town lay abandoned to the Americans' firebrands. Harrison returned to his capital at Vincennes to claim a great victory. Tippecanoe did damage Tecumseh's confederation, but it also filled many Indians with a thirst for revenge. Their opportunity was soon at hand.

Westerners generally blamed the British for Tecumseh and other Indian troubles. Western representatives in Congress shrilly advocated the conquest of Canada as the surest way to safeguard the American frontier. By the summer of 1811, President James Madison, Jefferson's successor, was convinced that only war would persuade the British to stop flouting his country's rights in the Old West and on the high seas. Cut off from trade with Europe by Napoleon's Continental System, England depended on Canada for naval stores and other raw resources. If the United States occupied Canada, Madison reasoned, the British would have to grant the Americans concessions or surrender to Napoleon.

Called into special session to gird the nation for war, Congress moved first to raise the U.S. Army from its existing strength of 5,447 officers and men to its full complement of 10,000. Legislation passed on 24 December 1811 offered a $16 bounty to any man who enlisted, or re-enlisted, for five years. Faithful soldiers could expect a bonus of three months' pay and 160 acres of land upon honorable discharge. The day after New Year's, Congress approved funding for six companies of rangers—mounted, one-year volunteers—to patrol the

Old Northwest. Warming to its task, the national legislature inflated its military establishment to an unprecedented level on 11 January 1812 by giving life to an 'Additional Army' with billets for 25,000 regulars. The Additional Army encompassed ten regiments of infantry, two of artillery, and one of light dragoons. Congress set the size of each new infantry regiment at eighty-four officers, 150 non-commissioned officers, thirty-six musicians, and 1,800 privates, over twice the number of men allocated to similar units in the Peace Establishment and the Additional Military Force. Furthermore, the 8th through 17th Infantry boasted eighteen companies apiece, which were grouped into two nine-company battalions for easier handling. Realizing that a five-year enlistment was unattractive to most Americans, on 8 April Congress allowed the Army to accept 15,000 men recruited for eighteen months.

During the remaining months of peace, Congress also strove to provide the regular army with numerous auxiliaries for the projected thrust into Canada. On 6 February, the President was empowered to summon 30,000 one-year volunteers from the state militias. As of 10 April, Madison could require state governors to hold 80,000 militia in readiness for immediate federal service.

Having taken the seemingly appropriate precautions, Congress declared war on Great Britain on 18 June 1812.

When the War of 1812 started, most Americans assumed total victory would come quickly and without much sacrifice. True, England was one of the world's mightiest powers but almost all her 250,000 regular troops and 600 warships were committed to the defeat of Napoleon in Europe, leaving just about 6,000 Redcoats—plus 2,100 local volunteers and 71,000 poorly armed militia—to defend Canada. Not counting the 35,592 regulars approved by Congress, the United States had 695,000 males aged eighteen to forty-five in its state and territorial militias, 662,000 of them infantry. Reviewing the odds, ex-President Jefferson wrote blithely: 'The acquisition of Canada this year as far as the neighborhood of Quebec will be a mere matter of marching.'

Rarely has the American propensity for self-delusion exposed the republic to disaster on so grand a scale. Deprived of the actual impetus of war, recruiting lagged far behind expectations for the first half of 1812. By the outbreak of hostilities, only 6,744 officers and men belonged to the Army's older regiments, and the Additional Army contained barely 5,000. Even with the new bounty and land grant, military service was no bargain for the poor. A private's pay in 1812 was still what it had been in 1799—$5 a month. The average laborer could earn $9 in the same amount of time.

The week after the declaration of war, Congress standardized the table of organization for all infantry regiments on the three regular establishments, boosting their total number to twenty-five. Henceforth, a regiment had ten companies, and each company was complete if it had one captain, two lieutenants, one ensign, four sergeants, six corporals, two musicians, and ninety privates.

Needed as it was, such streamlining did not solve the Army's manpower dilemma. The War Department lured a scanty 9,823 men into the Additional Army by November 1812, and the grand total of regulars enlisted by the year's end was a disappointing 15,000 to 19,000. The infantry regiments formed in the summer and fall of 1812 went off to war at one- or two-thirds strength.

Aside from the discipline and low pay, other factors accounted for the paralysis in Army recruiting. The war was unpopular in many quarters, especially New England, where elected officials openly discouraged participation. In some communities, judges snatched enlistees from recruiting officers with writs of *habeas corpus*. Those citizens willing to fight usually opted for briefer stints outside of the regulars. Of the 527,654 Americans who saw some service in the conflict, 458,463 were militiamen or volunteers. A number of prospective regulars sat out the duration vainly awaiting a general draft so they could sell themselves as substitutes to the highest bidders.

Supply shortages also hampered the recruiters' efforts. Because of trade stoppages occasioned by the Napoleonic Wars, there was not enough blue wool on hand to clothe immediately all the troops. Infantrymen in the newer regiments were first issued summer uniforms of white linen. Woolen winter uniforms were not delivered until the late fall of 1812 or the early spring of 1813. In the meantime, the men went about in rags and worn-out shoes, not a very inspiring sight to other lads who contemplated answering their country's call. Insufficient clothing, rancid food, and inattention to sanitation also bred diseases which incapacitated large portions of the half-filled regiments.

The feeble state of its regular forces compelled the Madison Administration to rely on citizen soldiers to advance its Canadian strategy. Although the Federalist governors of Connecticut, Massachusetts, and Rhode Island ignored the central government's appeals for militiamen, the governors of Kentucky, Tennessee, Ohio, and New York spared no pains in meeting their quotas. Likewise, Pennsylvania, Virginia, Maryland, Louisiana, Mississippi Territory, and the District of Columbia furnished significant numbers of short-term troops at crucial moments of the war. However, most militiamen shunned service in volunteer units, preferring to campaign for no longer than a couple of months in the company of their friends and neighbors. Governor Jonathan R. Meigs, the level-headed chief

executive of Ohio, drafted militia to fill volunteer units, and other governors tried to render volunteer service more palatable by cutting enlistments to six months instead of a year.

Frequently untrained and indifferently officered, American militiamen and volunteers compiled a mixed record in the War of 1812. Prone to flight when attacked, citizen soldiers were also of little use for offensive purposes. The Constitution granted Congress the power to call 'forth the Militia to execute the Laws of the Union, suppress Insurrections and repel Invasions.' Militiamen conveniently interpreted this clause to mean they had a 'constitutional' right to decline service outside of the United States. Volunteers, who considered themselves militia first, also claimed the same exemption. The Madison Administration never sponsored legislation to settle this issue, an omission attended by shameful consequences.

Able leaders might have sorted through the confusion and welded respectable field armies out of the materials available in the summer of 1812, but good American commanders did not make an impact on the war until well into its second year. In the interim, the United States paid the penalty for neglecting to nurture a strong military tradition. The fitful rounds of expansion and contraction that had governed the Army's development since 1784 convinced many officers there was no future in a military career. The more enterprising returned to civilian life, while the majority who remained with the

PLATE 9: 'THOSE ARE REGULARS, BY GOD,' 1814–15

28. Pioneer, 25th U.S. Infantry, 1814: The infantry regiments in Brigadier General Winfield Scott's brigade campaigned on the Niagara Front in 1814 in gray jackets (garments usually issued to militiamen) and trousers of unbleached linen. In 1813, the U.S. Army followed Britain's lead by replacing its felt cap with the 'Belgic' shako, which was made of polished black leather. Pioneers carried saws, axes, spades, or picks. They wore linen aprons to protect their uniforms from flying debris and kept their cartridges in 'belly' boxes attached to their waistbelts. **29. Color Sergeant, 22nd U.S. Infantry, 1814:** *A sergeant was marked by two white worsted epaulettes, a crimson sash, and a short sword. The regimental color of the 22nd Infantry is preserved at the West Point Museum. The shako plate shown here is the large type made for the old felt cap.* **30. Lieutenant Colonel (Samuel Boyer Davis), 44th U.S. Infantry, 1815:** *Based on a portrait by Thomas Sully. Davis and his regiment fought bravely at New Orleans (8 January 1815). The U.S. Army's Dress Regulations of 1813 stripped the officer's coat and enlisted man's coatee of their red facings and most of their lace. A field officer rated a chapeau bras and a pair of silver epaulettes.* **31. Corporal, 7th U.S. Infantry, Dress Uniform, 1815:** *White breeches and long gaiters (leggings) were put on for reviews, parades, and other formal occasions. The corporal's weapon is the Model 1812 contract musket.*

29. Color Sergeant, 22nd U.S. Infantry, 1814

31. Corporal, 7th U.S. Infantry, Dress Uniform, 1815

28. Pioneer, 25th U.S. Infantry, 1814

30. Lieutenant Colonel, 44th U.S. Infantry, 1815

colors simply marked time. Under Jefferson, the chief criterion for awarding commissions was political loyalty. Winfield Scott, one of the few alumni of the Additional Military Force of 1808 to enhance his reputation in the War of 1812, characterized his brother officers as 'swaggerers, dependents and others fit for nothing else,' which 'made them totally unfit for any purpose whatever.' Isolated in small, frontier garrisons until 1812, these ill-prepared leaders had no idea of what it took to command more than a few hundred men.

The outbreak of hostilities brought no reforms to upgrade officer procurement. An early graduate from the ten-year-old Military Academy at West Point commented on his colleagues: 'The officers were utterly ignorant of their duty, or to use the words of a worthy young officer . . . "many of them [were] incapable of learning it." Peter Porter, a New York militia general, described the regular officers he knew as 'men fresh from lawyers' shops and counting rooms, who knew little of the physical force of man or of the proper mode of its application. With them the whole of the military art consists in knowing how to manoeuvre a regiment, how to form and display a column, and the scientific shape in which the troops are to be presented to meet a given movement or position of the enemy.' Such commanders could hardly inspire confidence or turn green recruits into real soldiers. An American sergeant condemned his officers as 'ignorant, willful, ugly, ill-natured puppies,' a commonly shared opinion in the ranks.

Training was unnecessarily complicated by the retirement of Steuben's 'Blue Book' in 1812. During the war, the Army experimented with two manuals written by armchair generals. The authors tried to incorporate innovations in the art of war originated by Napoleon's Grand Army, but their lack of actual combat experience rendered their works decidedly inferior to the Steuben system.

Early in the conflict, the Madison Administration distributed generals' appointments mostly to Revolutionary War veterans. The regular officer corps was so devoid of distinction that some top command slots went to men who had not donned a uniform in thirty years. In their late fifties or early sixties, these relics of an earlier era had grown too fat or brittle for active campaigning. As junior officers in the War of Independence, they had received no experience in managing entire armies. Lacking forcefulness, charisma, or acuity of mind, they were invariably overwhelmed by the responsibilities of high command.

Thus the United States entered her second war with England with an army of amateurs led by befuddled old men. The weaknesses in the American military machine manifested themselves from the outset. On 16 August 1812, Brigadier General William Hull timidly surrendered 450 to 580 regulars (including the whole 4th U.S. Infantry), 1,450 Ohio volunteers, and 200 Michigan militia to an inferior British force at Detroit. During the Battle of Queenston Heights, 13 October 1812, 1,300 New York militia refused to cross the Niagara River into Canada. They stood by and watched while roughly 450 regulars (drawn largely from the 13th U.S. Infantry) and 850 to 1,000 braver militiamen were cut to pieces or captured as they strove to maintain a precarious foothold on the enemy side of the river. An effort to invade Canada via Lake Champlain fizzled out a month later when 2,000 citizen soldiers balked rather than leave American soil.

Disappointed by the performance of the militia, Congress contrived a string of gimmicks to beef up the regular forces. A private's pay jumped to $8 per month on 12 December 1812, and finally to $10 before the war's end. On 20 January 1813, the enlistment bounty was more than doubled to $40. Under the same legislation, each infantry regiment received a second major, and each foot company received a third lieutenant and a fifth sergeant. Nine days later, Congress gave the go-ahead for twenty new infantry regiments composed of short-term regulars enlisted for one year. This curious measure raised regular troop levels to 57,351 on paper, but with unskilled laborers earning $16 to $20 a month during the growing season, no more than 24,000 soldiers were gotten into uniform by January 1814. And contrary to the will of Congress, only forty-four infantry regiments took an active part in the war.

The good news of 1813 was the emergence of two generals who could squeeze the best out of American troops. In the Northwest, William Henry Harrison mobilized an army of 2,500 regulars (mainly in the 17th, 19th, 24th, 26th, 27th, and 28th Infantry) and 3,500 Kentucky volunteers. He then proceeded to liberate Detroit and occupy a chunk of Upper Canada. To the south, Andrew Jackson hunted down marauding Creek Indians. Early in 1814, Jackson smashed Creek power for all time with the help of the 39th U.S. Infantry and more than 4,000 Tennessee volunteers. Less than a year later, Jackson decimated a crack British army during his celebrated defense of New Orleans.

On 27 January 1814, Congress threw off fiscal restraint and offered a $124 bounty to any man joining the regulars for five years or the duration. Enlistments in the twenty newest infantry regiments were lengthened to five years. Congress next pumped the authorized troop levels up to 62,773 officers and men on 10 February by creating the 2nd, 3rd, and 4th Regiments of Riflemen. Tempted by the lavish bounty, 20,300 new names were inscribed in the Register of Enlistments by October, but the departure of the eighteen-month men of 1812 and the twelve-month men of 1813 meant that the Army mustered scarcely more than 30,000 men throughout most of the year. Regular strength peaked at 38,186 in September, but then quickly ebbed. Hoping to reverse the downward flow, Congress doubled the discharge land grant to 320 acres on 10 December.

During the summer of 1814, the regular army produced a national hero in the person of Winfield Scott, a twenty-eight-year-old brigadier general from Virginia. Scott began his long and illustrious military career in 1808 as a captain in the U.S. Regiment of Light Artillery. Though educated as a lawyer, Scott delighted in and excelled at soldiering. A man of action with a taste for professional reading, he invariably included a compact library featuring the latest European military treatises as part of his campaign baggage. Elevated to lieutenant colonel in the 2nd Artillery in 1812, Scott distinguished himself leading American regulars in their doomed stand at Queenston Heights. Receiving his brigadier's star in March 1814, Scott was assigned to oversee the training of six regular regiments on the Niagara front, the 9th, 11th, 21st, 22nd, 23rd, and 25th Infantry.

Armed with a worn copy of Napoleon's regulations for the French Army, Scott established a camp of instruction near Buffalo, New York. Like Steuben at Valley Forge, the tall Virginian was his own drill sergeant. He started his lessons with the officers. Once they mastered their trade, they passed on their knowledge to the troops. For three months, Scott drilled his soldiers ten hours a day, teaching them to maneuver and fight by squad, company, battalion, and brigade. The men responded well to the intensive schooling. On 6 May Scott wrote a friend: 'If, of such materials, I do not make the best army now in service, by the 1st of June, I will agree to be dismissed from the service.'

Scott's chance to prove that boast arrived two months later. On 2 July 1814, Major General Jacob Brown crossed the Niagara River with an American army of 2,738 regulars, 753 volunteers, and 600 Indians. Scott commanded the 9th, 11th, 22nd, and 25th Infantry in Brown's largest brigade. Late on the afternoon of 5 July, a British army of 1,400 Redcoats, 100 dragoons, 300 Canadian militia and Indians, and six fieldpieces was spotted approaching Scott's camp a mile below the Chippewa River. Scott instantly sallied forth to confront the enemy with his 1,384 infantry and eighty-nine 2nd Artillerymen manning three guns. On account of the prevailing scarcity of blue cloth, Scott's foot soldiers wore plain gray coatees, items normally issued to the militia.

As Scott's column lumbered into view, the British commander, Major General Phineas Riall, whooped with relief: 'Why, those are but Buffalo militia.' But as Scott's troops, oblivious to enemy cannon fire, wheeled into line and came ahead with flawless precision, Riall altered his opinion: 'Those are regulars, by God!'

Riall tried to break Scott's line by sending his Redcoats forward in two dense columns. Scott countered by holding his center back and allowing his two flanks to bow ahead slightly—so as to catch his opponents in a crossfire. Raked by heavy American musketry and canister, which took a high toll of their officers, the Redcoats faltered and came to a standstill. At that dramatic moment, Scott spurred his horse to the front of the 11th Infantry and shouted: 'They say the Americans

Mounted at left, Brigadier General Winfield Scott leads his crack brigade into the Battle of Chippewa, 5 July 1814. Though dressed in the gray coatees normally issued to militiamen, Scott's regulars fought with the impassive steadiness of blooded veterans, winning the respect of their British opponents.

Major Thomas Harrison, 42nd U.S. Infantry, a primitive portrait, circa 1815. Harrison's plain blue coat, with its silver eagle buttons and epaulettes, is a faithful reflection of the Army's 1813 uniform regulations. A Boston native, Harrison entered the 21st Infantry as a second lieutenant on 15 May 1812. Transferring to the 9th Infantry ten months later, he was promoted to captain on 15 August 1813, and he lost a leg at the Battle of Chippewa. The crippled patriot was promoted to major in the 42nd Infantry, but he resigned his commission in June 1815 with the reduction of the regular army.

The national color of the 11th U.S. Infantry, reputedly carried at the Battle of Chippewa, 5 July 1814. This blue silk flag displays a bald eagle painted in natural colors (brown and white feathers with a gold beak and talons). The shield on the eagle's chest is red, white, and blue with a gold border. The scroll below the eagle is red with gold edging. All the stars and lettering are gold.

are good at long shot but cannot stand the cold iron! I call on you instantly to give the lie to that slander! Charge!' As Scott's cheering troops swept forward behind a row of glittering bayonets, their battered adversaries retreated.

Riall lost 500 men at the Battle of Chippewa. Scott's casualties were 328. Yet the real significance of the engagement lay not in its statistics. For the first time in the War of 1812, American regulars had met and defeated a comparable number of British regulars in open battle. Winfield Scott had shown that, with the right training and leadership, Americans could match any troops on earth. The U.S. Infantry had grown out of its unhappy childhood.

A belated taste of glory was the only prize the U.S. Army earned during 'Mr. Madison's War.' Incredibly, the 'Yankees' fought even better when Napoleon's first abdication in April 1814 temporarily released thousands of the Duke of Wellington's veterans for duty in North America. Nevertheless, strong American showings at Lundy's Lane, Baltimore, Fort Erie, Plattsburg, and New Orleans could not obscure the fact that the war was a terrible mistake. Luckily for the United States, Britain remained too preoccupied with the unsettled state of European affairs to throw her full weight into the struggle. On 24 December 1814, British and American ministers signed a peace treaty at Ghent, Belgium, which ended the War of 1812 as a draw.

As for glory, the American people and the U.S. Army found it an acceptable substitute for Canada. In Winfield Scott and other exemplary officers who won their laurels in the struggle, the U.S. Infantry now had what it had always needed—a generation of leaders capable of molding a few thousand regulars into the nation's sword and shield.

PLATE 10: THE REGIMENTS OF RIFLEMEN, 1812–14

32. Sergeant, 1st U.S. Regiment of Riflemen, Winter Uniform, 1812: *Riflemen wore green coats with black facings, yellow collar lace, and yellow metal buttons. This regiment's non-commissioned officers sported yellow worsted epaulettes. A rifleman carried his ammunition in a 'belly' box, a shot pouch, and a powder horn. Sergeants had brass-mounted swords, and all enlisted men received scalping knives. Riflemen donned green woolen overalls in the winter and white linen legwear in the summer. This man is priming a Model 1803 rifle.* **33. Private, 4th U.S. Regiment of Riflemen, 1814:** *A shortage of green wool forced the Army to order gray uniforms for the three rifle regiments created in 1814. Before these garments were delivered, the new riflemen dressed in hunting smocks of green linen. These units also received 1813 leather shakos with round brass plates and Model 1814 rifles.* **34. Captain, 1st Regiment of Riflemen, 1812:** *Rifle officers wore gold lace, epaulettes, hatcords, and tassels. They used whistles to relay orders to troops fighting in open order. White pantaloons served as summer wear.*

32. Sergeant, 1st U.S. Regiment of Riflemen, Winter Uniform, 1812   **33.** Private, 4th U.S. Regiment of Riflemen, 1814   **34.** Captain, 1st U.S. Regiment of Riflemen, 1812

4 A Handful of Regulars and a Host of Troubles

1815–44

With the ratification of the Treaty of Ghent on 14 February 1815, the United States no longer wanted a large military establishment. Most of the 33,424 officers and men on the Army's rolls at the close of the War of 1812 were soon seeking other employment.

On 3 March 1815, just two weeks after the proclamation of peace, Congress fixed the size of the regular army at 10,000 enlisted men, exclusive of a corps of engineers. An alteration in the Army's structure accompanied the decrease in numbers. While the Corps of Artillery (formed in 1814) and the older Regiment of Light Artillery were retained, the Army lost all its dragoons. The 1st, 2nd, 3rd, and 4th Regiments of Riflemen were merged into a single Rifle Regiment. A more intricate series of contractions metamorphosed the Army's forty-four regiments of line infantry into eight.

The new Peace Establishment was three times larger than the one sanctioned by the Jefferson Administration, but lamentable clumsiness marred the reductions of 1815. The reorganization of the U.S. Infantry was conducted without any sensitivity to regimental identity, lineage, or tradition. Units were fused together arbitrarily with no effort to preserve the seniority of even the most distinguished corps. The old 1st Infantry, originally Harmar's 1st American Regiment, joined the 5th, 17th, 19th, and 28th Infantry in a new 3rd Regiment of Infantry. The 2nd, 3rd, 7th, and 44th Infantry were amalgamated as the new 1st U.S. Infantry. And so it went, down to the new 8th Infantry, which came to life with the melding of the old 10th and 12th.

On paper, the Army's revamped infantry arm was allowed a total of 6,584 officers and men, not counting the Rifle Regiment. The new tables of organization provided every infantry regiment with a colonel, a lieutenant colonel, a major, an adjutant, a quartermaster, a paymaster, a surgeon, two surgeon's mates, a sergeant major, a quartermaster sergeant, and a pair of principal musicians. As before, there were ten companies per regiment, with one captain, two lieutenants, four sergeants, four corporals, two musicians, and sixty-eight privates apiece. The Rifle Regiment was similarly arranged, except it had billets for only 660 privates.

Two captains of the 5th U.S. Infantry flanked by a pair of privates in a watercolor by Charles Hamilton Smith, a British Army officer and a spy who operated in the United States in 1816 and 1817. The officers sport black chapeau bras with white plumes, blue coats with silver epaulettes and buttons, crimson sashes, white breeches, and black boots. The privates are in their dress uniforms, complete with black gaiters and white breeches. Their coatees conform to the regulations governing Army dress from 1813 to 1821, except that the collars, cuffs, turnbacks, shoulder straps, and pocket flaps are bordered with white lace. One officer holds the 5th's regimental color, a white silk flag with a blue scroll edged in yellow.

The changes ordered by Congress were carried out by 17 May. More than 20,000 infantrymen were expelled from the service, and nearly 1,700 officers from all branches of the Army lost their commissions. Vacancies in the officer corps were filled from the list of disbanded officers until May 1816. After that, preference was given to graduates of the Military Academy at West Point.

Though not large enough properly to serve the interests of the bustling republic, the Peace Establishment of 1815 was a respectable force. Furthermore, the Army had little difficulty maintaining itself at nearly full strength over the next two years. On 14 January 1817, the Acting Secretary of War reported there were 10,024 officers and men in uniform, including 5,249 in the eight infantry regiments and 795 in the Rifle Regiment. However, this happy state of affairs deteriorated during the next eleven months as the veterans who had enlisted in 1812 completed their five-year hitches. By 22 December, the Army's ranks were noticeably thinner. Only 3,935 infantrymen were still with the colors. The officers missed the departing veterans. In a letter dated 20 April 1820, Lieutenant Colonel Zachary Taylor complained that his regiment, the 8th Infantry, was 'composed entirely of recruits without organization, subordination, or discipline.'

Nevertheless, Congress eventually decided that even this understrength Army was excessive. After six years, the traditional American mistrust of standing armies and a yearning for frugal government combined to produce drastic military cuts.

In legislation passed on 2 March 1821, Congress pruned the maximum size of the Army to 6,000 rank and file. The law halved the number of generals with the elimination of one major general and two brigadiers. The Corps of Artillery, the Regiment of Light Artillery, and the Ordnance Department were compressed into four artillery regiments totaling 2,180 officers and men. The congressional ax fell with particular heaviness upon the infantry, slashing the official complement to 3,829 of all ranks. Each company suffered the loss of one sergeant and twenty-six privates. In addition, the Rifle Regiment and the 8th Infantry were dissolved altogether, their enlisted men absorbed respectively by the 6th and 7th Infantry.

Throughout the decade following the reductions of 1821, the Army never quite atttained its legal strength of 6,184 officers and men. Figures compiled for Congress on 9 November 1825 revealed a force of 5,719 regulars, among them 3,237 infantry, 1,921 artillery, and 430 fresh recruits. The Army's actual size fluctuated between 5,500 and 5,700 until the end of the 1820s.

In the most recently published official history of the U.S. Army, the three decades separating the War of 1812 from the Mexican War are characterized as 'The Thirty Years' Peace,' but this is a misrepresentation. True, the United States avoided formal hostilities with foreign powers, but the period was hardly a tranquil one for the young republic's thin blue line. More than once, the Army was alerted for possible clashes with Spanish, Mexican, and British forces. On at least five occasions between 1816 and 1836, U.S. regulars, acting without prior approval from Washington, sortied onto foreign soil to protect American lives and property. And throughout these 'interwar years,' the Army was continuously occupied and severely tested by a succession of Indian troubles.

The War of 1812 broke the power of the tribes of the Old West, but Indian affairs were still marked by spates of violence. As a consequence of their recent defeats, the woodland tribes were pressured into signing treaties ceding millions of acres of their ancestral lands. From time to time, small bands of resentful warriors salved their injured pride by attacking the hardy souls who settled on America's newly enlarged public domain, not to mention squatters who trespassed upon tracts still reserved to the native population. Land frenzy also tempted a growing number of pioneer farmers to cross the Mississippi River and take possession of the eastern fringes of the gigantic Louisiana Territory, which Thomas Jefferson had purchased from France in 1803. All these people had to be defended from the Indians they had come to displace.

Immediately following the reorganization of 3 March 1815, the U.S. Army was deployed as a border police force, its chief occupation for the next thirty years. In short order, chains of forts—each post usually housing fewer than 100 troops—were constructed to shield the Old Northwest, the Old Southwest, and the trans-Mississippi frontier. By 1818, the Army was manning seventy-three posts, their puny, isolated garrisons struggling to impose law and order over thousands of square miles of untamed country. A hard-pressed handful of regulars repeatedly heard the call to chase and punish Indian marauders, evict squatters from Indian lands, and apprehend white renegades selling liquor to the tribesmen. The Army performed another valuable service by preventing British traders from doing further business with the Indians of the United States. The interruption of this historic commerce deprived the tribes of the weapons and goading that had accounted for so much of their previous resistance to American expansion.

From 1815 to 1832, the federal government, handicapped by its habitual stinginess, viewed duty on the far-flung frontier as the exclusive province of the hapless foot soldier. Cavalry was written off as an unjustifiable extravagance, a rationalization which placed a tremendous burden on America's infantrymen.

Second Lieutenant Charles Holt, 1st U.S. Infantry, circa 1823–4. The 'General Regulations for the Army' adopted by Congress on 2 March 1821 directed 'company officers of infantry' to wear blue, single-breasted coatees with wings 'of silver bullion' instead of epaulettes. Collars were four inches high and virtually covered with silver lace.

PLATE 11: 'TAR BUCKETS' AND PIPECLAY: THE REGULATIONS OF 1821 AND 1825

On the parade ground at Fort Snelling, Minnesota Territory.
35. Captain, Grenadier Company, 5th U.S. Infantry, Parade Order, 1827: *The Regulations of 1821 substituted a pair of silver wings for the company officer's single epaulette. A captain sported a silver chevron on each arm above the elbow; subalterns wore chevrons on their lower sleeves. Officers donned white cassimere pantaloons for parade. During the 1820s, the color of the pompon on the 1821-pattern, bell-crowned leather cap (familiarly known as a 'tar bucket') identified an infantryman's company. A regiment's eight battalion companies received white pompons; the grenadier company, red; and the light infantry company, yellow.* **36. Lieutenant, Battalion Company, 5th U.S. Infantry, Winter Service Dress, 1827:** *Company officers and their men put on gray kersey pantaloons 'for winter service.'* **37. First Sergeant, Light Infantry Company, 5th U.S. Infantry, Winter Service Dress, 1827:** *Under the Regulations of 1821, a sergeant wore a worsted chevron on each arm below the elbow. A corporal sported only one chevron—sewn to his right upper sleeve. In 1825, the sergeant's chevrons were moved to the upper sleeves, and corporals were ordered to wear a chevron on each arm below the elbow. Pictured here are a Model 1822 musket and a Model 1818 non-commissioned officer's sword.* **38. Drummer, Grenadier Company, 5th U.S. Infantry, Parade Order, 1827:** *The musician's red coat, with white lace on the breast and cuffs, is based on an extant specimen owned by the Ohio Historical Society. Enlisted men were issued pantaloons of white wool or cotton drilling for parade. A sheepskin leg protector prolonged the life of a drummer's pantaloons.*

36. Lieutenant, Battalion Company, 5th
U.S. Infantry, Winter Service Dress, 1827

38. Drummer, Grenadier Company, 5th
U.S. Infantry, Parade Order, 1827

35. Captain, Grenadier Company, 5th U.S.
Infantry, Parade Order, 1827

37. First Sergeant, Light Infantry
Company, 5th U.S. Infantry, Winter
Service Dress, 1827

And the U.S. Infantry was not the only branch of the Army to suffer because of this congressional narrow-mindedness. Because Indian wars almost never involved formal siege operations or the use of massed batteries, most artillerymen were armed and employed as infantry during the 1820s and 1830s. Indeed, some companies were more expert in the handling of muskets and musketoons than cannon.

The exploits of America's frontier regulars of 1815-44 are not as well-commemorated as those of the Indian-fighting Army of 1865-90, but that earlier generation of 'Bluecoats' faced similar privations and perils with a fortitude that defies rational explanation. The following episodes are representative of the alarms and excursions which enlivened an infantryman's days in the years leading up to the Mexican War.

The War of 1812 brought no peace to Georgia's southern frontier. Unimpressed by American victories over their Creek neighbors, Seminole Indians and runaway black slaves living in Spanish Florida frequently entered American territory to raid white farms and plantations, carrying off cattle and Negroes. Diverted by creole revolutions elsewhere in her American empire, Spain could not garrison Florida with enough troops to seal the border. Spanish impotence quickly exhausted the patience of Brigadier General Edmund P. Gaines, the American commander on the Florida frontier. In the summer of 1816, Gaines thrust a punitive expedition built around the 4th U.S. Infantry into Florida to clean out the 'Negro Fort,' a sturdy stronghold for black bandits overlooking the Apalachicola River. A lucky shot from an American gunboat exploded a powder magazine within the fort on 27 July, flattening its walls and killing 270 to 330 of its defenders. Angered by the slaughter of their allies, the Seminoles increased their depredations. Under orders from Gaines, Major David E. Twiggs, 7th U.S. Infantry, and 250 soldiers attacked Fowltown, a Seminole village just within American territory, on 21 November 1817. The Indians retaliated nine days later by massacring a boatload of soldiers and camp followers on the Apalachicola near Fort Scott.

Disturbed by the mounting violence, the War Department dispatched Major General Andrew Jackson to take charge in southern Georgia. No respecter of diplomatic niceties, the fiery Jackson threw together an army of 500 regulars, 1,000 white militia, and 1,600 to 2,000 friendly Creek braves, and, at the end of March 1818, he launched the First Seminole War by invading Florida. As the Seminoles fled before the American horde, Jackson conducted a rapid, two-month campaign highlighted by the capture of Spanish posts at St. Marks and Pensacola. In between marches, skirmishes, and pursuits, Jackson executed two Seminole chiefs and two British subjects accused of inciting the natives. Though

Madrid strenuously protested Jackson's temporary violation of Spanish sovereignty, the incident demonstrated that the Americans could seize Florida whenever the fancy struck them. Bowing to the inevitable and ridding themselves of a profitless headache, the Spanish ceded Florida to the United States in February 1821. The Seminoles, momentarily awed by Jackson's ruthless foray, were now entirely Washington's problem.

The Army, however, devoted its attention to more than shielding the existing line of white settlements. Occasionally, troops supported the activities of frontier entrepreneurs who ventured out onto the trackless expanses of the Great Plains and Rocky Mountains. In fact, Army men were largely responsible for calling the attention of their acquisitive fellow citizens to the economic potential of the trans-Mississippi West. As soon as the Louisiana Purchase was finalized, President Jefferson sent small parties of regulars to uncover and map the riches of America's mammoth annexation. Legendary figures like Captain Meriwether Lewis of the 1st U.S. Infantry, Lieutenant Zebulon Pike of the same regiment, and William Clark (a former artillery officer) earned a niche in history leading these expeditions. Following the War of 1812, other Bluecoats tramped across the plains to assert American authority over a region destined to become the breadbasket of much of the world.

In the beginning, it was furs and not food which drew Americans to the lands beyond the Mississippi Valley. Generally, the fur traders tried to win the Indians as friends and trading partners, but they met with checkered success. On 2 June 1823, Arikara braves fell on a party of Americans on the Missouri River in Dakota, killing thirteen whites and wounding ten. Learning of the attack, Colonel Henry Leavenworth left Fort Atkinson on 18 June with six companies of the 6th U.S. Infantry and two 6-pound cannon, and headed up the Missouri toward the Arikara villages. Ninety vengeful traders with a howitzer and over 800 Yankton and Teton Sioux joined Leavenworth's 220 regulars. Dubbing his motley army the 'Missouri Legion,' Leavenworth pressed on, covering the 640 miles from his starting point to the heart of Arikara country by 9 August. As it turned out, the colonel had little stomach for killing Indians, but his expedition was one of the largest displays of white force yet seen on the northern Great Plains.

Early in the 1820s, Missouri merchants blazed an overland trade route to Santa Fe, the capital of the remote Mexican province of New Mexico. The profits to be garnered at the end of the Santa Fe Trail were considerable. Forty thousand goods-poor New Mexicans willingly paid inflated prices for American manufactures. In 1824, a modest expedition of eighty men from

While a sergeant makes notations in a ledger, two privates of the 5th U.S. Infantry pick up their company's bread ration at the Fort Snelling bakery. The baker is attired in a two-button fatigue frock of white linen. The sergeant and privates wear the service dress prescribed by the Regulations of 1821, gray kersey jackets trimmed with white tape. Each man sports a blue 'chakos,' a fatigue cap adopted by the Army in 1825. The cap was decorated with white braid and had a white metal company letter sewn on the front.

A member of the interpretive staff at Historic Fort Snelling, St Paul, Minnesota, models the winter service uniform of a private from Company A, 5th U.S. Infantry, circa 1826. The overcoat was made of gray wool kersey, as were the trousers. The crossbelt plate was made of plated brass with the initials 'U.S.' cast in low relief.

Independence, Missouri, delivered merchandise valued at $25,000 to $30,000 in exchange for over $190,000 worth of New Mexican silver and furs.

Whatever the payoff, the road to Santa Fe was fraught with danger and hardship. The wagon trains plying the 800 miles between western Missouri and New Mexico became the targets of Comanche and Kiowa raiders. In 1828, Indians hounded two caravans on the Santa Fe Trail, killing three traders and running off all of one train's livestock.

Responding to pressure from Missouri's business community and political representatives, Washington directed the Army to provide an escort for the next trading expedition to Santa Fe. The novel assignment fell to Brevet★ Major Bennet Riley and four companies of the 6th Infantry. On 11 June 1829, Riley's detachment rendezvoused with a caravan of sixty men and thirty-six wagons under the guidance of Charles Bent, a famous frontiersman. Riley accompanied the caravan to a point on the Arkansas River where the stream formed a section of the Mexican-American border. There he pitched camp on the north bank to await the traders' return from Santa Fe.

★A brevet was an honorary or temporary rank awarded in wartime.

Once the caravan had gone on its way, Riley and his 170 regulars were besieged by the Comanches. Unlike the woodland Indians the Army was accustomed to fighting, the Comanches were mounted, and they rode as if they had been born on horseback. The Indians would swoop down on Riley's pickets and other tempting targets, unloose a salvo of arrows, and then gallop out of musket range before the flustered soldiers had time to react. The Comanches killed four unwary infantrymen and absconded with Riley's livestock. Under the circumstances, pursuit was impossible. 'Think of what our feelings must have been to see them going off with our cattle and horses,' Riley later wrote, 'when if we had been mounted, we could have beaten them to pieces; but we were obliged to content ourselves with whipping them from our camp.'

Bent's caravan did not rejoin its beleaguered escort until mid-October. After Riley returned to Fort Leavenworth on 8 November, he filed a graphic report

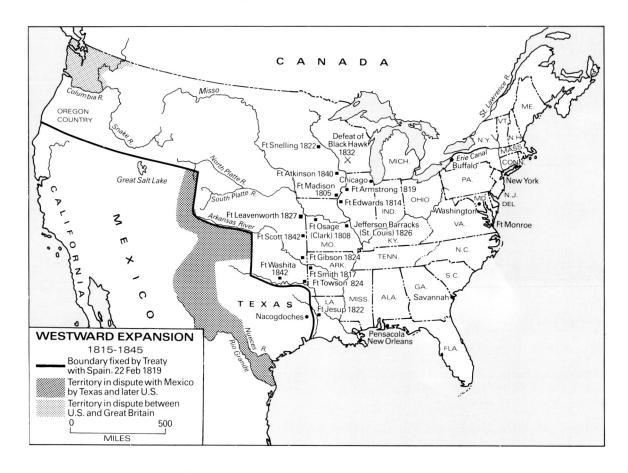

WESTWARD EXPANSION
1815-1845
Boundary fixed by Treaty with Spain, 22 Feb 1819
Territory in dispute with Mexico by Texas and later U.S.
Territory in dispute between U.S. and Great Britain
0   500
MILES

which furnished ample proof that the U.S. Army could not hope to tame the Plains Indians with foot soldiers alone. Eventually, even Congress acknowledged this fact. Experimenting first for one year with a quasi-regular battalion of mounted rangers, Congress finally created the 749-man U.S. Regiment of Dragoons, the Army's first permanent cavalry unit, on 2 March 1833.

Despite his military background, when Andrew Jackson became President of the United States in 1829, he contemplated no increases for the regular army. But 'Old Hickory' vastly widened the scope of the military's duties by his aggressive Indian policy.

Appropriating an idea originated by Thomas Jefferson, Jackson believed that separation of the races was the best way to end the centuries of conflict that began with the meeting of white men and red. Jackson's notion of Indian removal entailed the deportation of the Eastern tribes to a new 'Indian Territory' that would be established on the huge, arid grasslands lying west of the Mississippi Valley. This flat, forbidding region, dubbed the 'Great American Desert' by Army explorers, was

PLATE 12: CHANGES IN THE DRESS UNIFORM, 1832–51
Regulars on the parade ground at Fort Gibson, Indian Territory.
39. First Sergeant, 2nd U.S. Infantry, Full Dress, 1841: *The enlisted man's version of the 1831 dress shako was made of black felt with a patent leather top, chinstrap, and visor. Sergeants warranted two worsted epaulettes, three buttons and lace loops on each coat cuff, and white stripes half-an-inch wide down the outer seams of their 'blue-mixture' trousers. A company's first sergeant wore a red worsted sash. This man has a Model 1822 musket, a Model 1840 non-commissioned officer's sword, and a new eagle plate on his sword belt.* ***40. Bandsman, 7th U.S. Infantry, Full Dress, 1834:*** *During this period, an infantry regiment was allowed ten bandsmen. These musicians usually received fancy, non-regulation uniforms to signify their special status. From 1 May to 30 September of each year, regulars were entitled to wear trousers of plain white cotton or linen.* ***41. Drummer, 3rd. U.S. Infantry, Full Dress, 1834:*** *Company musicians continued to wear red coats when the uniform was changed in 1832. Note the handsome pair of wings on the drummer's shoulders.* ***42. Private, 4th U.S. Infantry, Full Dress, 1846:*** *Privates wore two lace loops on each cuff. Waistbelts and round eagle shoulder belt plates made their appearance between 1839 and 1841. Figure 42 holds a Model 1835 musket.*

39. First Sergeant, 2nd U.S. Infantry, Full
Dress, 1841

41. Drummer, 3rd U.S. Infantry, Full
Dress, 1834

40. Bandsman, 7th U.S. Infantry, Full
Dress, 1834

42. Private, 4th U.S. Infantry, Full Dress,
1846

considered uninhabitable for white farmers—an impression later dispelled by advances in agricultural science and technology. Ironically, proponents of the removal plan gave little thought to how woodland Indians, many of them farmers, could survive on the Great Plains.

On 28 May 1830, Congress passed the Indian Removal Act, legislation granting the federal government the authority to compel Eastern tribes to sign treaties surrendering their ancestral lands in exchange for new homes in the trans-Mississippi West. Land-hungry whites eagerly enforced the new law. The Army was detailed to help transport the uprooted tribes west, shield the red emigrants from indigenous Plains Indians, and man a line of forts confining all the nation's red men to a permanent Indian frontier.

In the Old Northwest, where the Indian population had been whittled down to 14,000, the removal process encountered few noteworthy snags. The tribes were too weak to fight back. The only major altercation occurred when some dispossessed natives tried to visit their former haunts.

On 6 April 1832, an obdurate Sac chief named Black Hawk led 1,500 of his people (500 of them warriors) across the Mississippi into northwestern Illinois. Homesickness, not bloodlust, motivated the Indians, but their appearance on the 'white' side of the Mississippi threw a scare into nearby settlers. Between 12 April and 8 May 1832, Brevet Brigadier General Henry Atkinson concentrated six companies of his own 6th Infantry and four companies of the 1st at Fort Armstrong, a post on the Mississippi just above the site of Black Hawk's crossing. The 340 regulars were joined by Governor John Reynolds and 1,600 Illinois militia, men burning with zeal to repel the red intruders. After eighty Sacs routed 275 militia cavalry on 14 May, most of the citizen soldiers were so disheartened they had to be discharged. However, the energetic Reynolds raised another field force of 2,000 militia by the end of June.

Faced with such odds, Black Hawk's only choice was a hasty retreat. On 1 August 1832, the red fugitives, their numbers reduced to 500 by hunger, exhaustion, and white attacks, reached the east bank of the Mississippi two miles below the mouth of the Bad Axe River. Unfortunately, the cannon of the steamboat *Warrior* prevented the Indians from escaping to the west. At dawn the next day, General Atkinson overtook Black Hawk with 400 regulars from the 1st, 2nd, and 6th U.S. Infantry and 1,300 mounted volunteers.

The resulting Battle of Bad Axe was nothing less than a massacre. Forming a line with his regular infantry in the center and most of his citizen soldiers on the flanks, Atkinson charged the Indians head on. At the same time, 300 dismounted Illinois cavalry struck Black Hawk's

First Lieutenant Pierce Mason Butler, 7th U.S. Infantry, circa 1821. Under the Regulations of 1821, the exact rank of a company officer of infantry was indicated by the position of a silver chevron on each arm of his coatee. Captains wore their chevrons above the elbow, and lieutenants, as in Butler's case, below.

Louis T. Jamison, an 1824 graduate of West Point, reached the rank of captain in the 5th U.S. Infantry on 31 October 1836. This portrait depicts him in the winter dress uniform adopted for the regular army in 1832. The buttons, lace, and epaulettes on his dark blue, double-breasted coat are silver. An officer's grade was revealed by the design of his epaulettes and the number of small buttons and lace loops on each of the coat's slashed cuffs. Field officers rated four loops; captains, three; and lieutenants, two. The regulations decreed sky blue trousers with white kerseymere stripes down the outer seams. However, Jamison's trousers seem almost as dark as his coat.

rear. About 150 Indians, many of them noncombatants, were slain, and perhaps another 150 drowned in a desperate bid to swim to safety. White casualties amounted to twenty-four killed and wounded.

The 60,000 to 79,000 Indians of the Old Southwest posed a much greater challenge to the removal policy. Some tribes accepted exile with comparatively little fuss. Others had to be prodded onto the 'Trail of Tears' at bayonet point.

In the spring of 1836, the War Department mobilized 1,103 regulars and 9,055 militia under Brevet Major General Winfield Scott to eject restive Creek Indians from Georgia and Alabama. Between July and September 1836, Scott's command shipped 14,609 Creeks west, including 2,495 who put up some resistance.

Scott mounted a similar operation in 1838, when the Cherokees refused to leave their domains within the states of North Carolina, Georgia, and Alabama. Inaugurating his removal campaign on 26 May 1838, Scott relied primarily upon two regiments of Georgia volunteer infantry and other smaller militia units until the 4th U.S. Infantry, the 4th U.S. Artillery, and six companies of the 2nd U.S. Dragoons reached Cherokee country. By 17 June, Scott had enough regulars on hand to discharge the volunteers. The general thought professional soldiers would behave with more humanity toward the Indians, but it was impossible to turn the expulsion of a people from their homeland into a pleasant experience. A highlight of the campaign was Scott's October decision to mount Company A of the 4th Infantry on horses. These improvised dragoons functioned as a special strike force, rounding up Cherokee hold-outs who took to the hills to evade the soldiers.

The fiercest stand against Indian removal was made by the 5,000 Seminoles of Florida. Anticipating trouble with these chronic malcontents, the War Department and local authorities deployed 536 regulars (two infantry and nine artillery companies) and 500 mounted volunteers throughout the territory by 9 December 1835. The Seminoles were unimpressed. On 28 December, along a lonely stretch of road between Fort King and Fort Brooke, 180 Indians ambushed Francis L. Dade, a

brevet major in the 4th Infantry, seven other officers, and 100 artillerymen armed with muskets and one 6-pounder. All but three of the soldiers were shot or hacked to death.

The Dade Massacre was an appropriate opening to the Second Seminole War, one of the longest and dirtiest conflicts in American history. It lasted seven years, required the expenditure of $30,000,000 to $40,000,000 in government funds, and cost the lives of 1,466 regulars, including 328 killed in action. The U.S. Infantry contributed thirty-five officers and 770 men to that death toll (see Table 4). Thirty-five citizen soldiers fell in battle with the Seminoles, and many more succumbed to the diseases endemic to a torrid climate.

Altogether, 10,169 regulars served in Florida, though the maximum present in the territory at any one time was 5,076. For most of the struggle, the number of regulars engaged varied from 1,900 to 4,600. Nevertheless, these figures represented a substantial drain on the Army's manpower resources. Garrisons all over the United States were stripped to the bone to provide trained soldiers for the Florida campaigns. Contingents of short-term volunteers, some 30,000 in all, augmented the regular cadres. However, the largest number of citizen soldiers gathered in Florida for a specific operation was about 4,000.

Pitted against the teeming white hosts were a mere 500 to 1,400 Seminole warriors. Yet these fearless, ingenious fighters baffled and eluded the U.S. Army and its auxiliaries for seven long years, and, despite steadily shrinking numbers, they remained dangerous foes until the struggle's bitter end.

A major factor in the Seminoles' prolonged resistance was the nature of Florida itself. Most of the territory's 58,560 square miles were still unknown to whites. Much of the land was overlaid with swamps, creeks, and rivers —obstacles which shielded the Seminoles from their antagonists. Captain George A. McCall of the 4th Infantry pulled two tours of duty against the Seminoles. He described the theater of war in December 1841: 'You cannot form the most remote idea of the region we passed through, and which the Indians doubtless thought would prove an impassable barrier. The bottom was boggy, and the water was filled with old logs, snags,

Table 4. Regular Infantry Losses in the Second Seminole War

Regiment	Term of Service in the War	Dead
1st Infantry	November 1837–August 1841	6 officers, 135 men
2nd Infantry	June 1837–May 1842	2 officers, 131 men
3rd Infantry	October 1840–August 1842	3 officers, 65 men
4th Infantry	December 1835–September 1842	6 officers, 128 men
6th Infantry	September 1837–February 1842	10 officers, 129 men
7th Infantry	May 1839–July 1842	4 officers, 116 men
8th Infantry	November 1840–August 1842	4 officers, 66 men

cypress knees, and vines innumerable.' McCall once told of 'forty days constant marching through mud and water, exposure to the heavy dew, without tents, and at times a scarcity of food,' adding: 'We have to follow the flying savage into fastness in which the wolf would starve.' Florida summers were so scorching that white officers regularly suspended field operations rather than see their commands decimated by fever and heat prostration.

In truth, the U.S. Army was poorly prepared for the Second Seminole War. Regular infantry and artillerymen still carried smoothbore muskets, while the Seminoles had rifles—weapons better adapted to Florida's tangled terrain. The infantry manuals the Army developed after 1814, all of them bearing the unmistakable stamp of Winfield Scott, trained American soldiers to fight according to French modes in European-style wars. But the Seminoles employed hit-and-run guerrilla tactics against the large, unwieldy columns the Army sent thrashing about the Florida wilds, frustrating a succession of the Army's best officers—Duncan L. Clinch, Winfield Scott, Edmund P. Gaines, Thomas S. Jesup, and Zachary Taylor— in their efforts to bring the war to a swift conclusion. Sometimes the dogged soldiers brought the hostiles to bay, but the engagements that resulted were indecisive. As Captain McCall explained: 'For in the battles . . . with these Indians, the most that is accomplished is a few killed and the rest dispersed. And when once a tribe scatters, the pursuit by troops is worse than useless.'

Twice during the hostilities, Congress tried to ease the Army's task by infusions of additional manpower. On 23 May 1836, Congress created the 2nd Regiment of U. S. Dragoons (749 officers and men). That same day, the legislators authorized the enlistment of 10,000 volunteers for terms of six to twelve months, instead of the standard three. However, regular officers had little liking for citizen soldiers, who lacked discipline, stamina, and a tolerance for the less glamorous aspects of soldiering. On 5 July 1838, therefore, President Martin Van Buren, Jackson's successor, signed a bill raising the paper strength of the regular army from 7,958 to 12,539 officers and men. A sergeant and thirty-eight privates were added to each infantry company, and sixteen privates were added to each artillery company. The U.S. Infantry received a new regiment, the 8th, and every artillery regiment received a new company. These increases were certainly a boon for the military, but, as in the past, it was impossible to keep the newly expanded ranks filled to capacity. As of 12 April 1839, the Army contained 8,497 enlisted men instead of the sanctioned 11,510. The eight infantry regiments averaged 552 rank and file apiece.

It was not just reinforcements, but also a change in tactics, that ultimately quelled the Seminoles. As the years passed, American soldiers developed a better understanding of their foe and of Florida. Discarding conventional methods, officers refashioned their battalions and companies into compact, fast-moving partisan detachments. Instead of attempting to force the Seminoles into set-piece battles, invariably an exercise in futility, the troops concentrated on harassment. They combed the swamp country over and over again, destroying the Indians' villages and crops. In 1840 and 1841, the soldiers even campaigned during the summer, denying their prey a moment's rest. The Army's new approach was well expressed in a June 1841 order from Colonel William J. Worth of the 8th Infantry, then the senior officer in Florida: 'Scorn the exposed points in every direction,—keep the men in constant motion—tax their strength to the utmost.' Threatened by starvation as well as white bullets and bayonets, hundreds of the most hardened hostiles eventually surrendered. The Army also made use of treachery, inviting the Seminoles to parleys where tribesmen were seized for shipment westward. By 14 August 1842, with only an estimated 300 Indians yet at large in the Florida swamps, Colonel Worth declared an end to this sordid, miserable contest.

No sooner had the emergency subsided, than the U.S. Army was shorn of much of its newly acquired muscle. On 23 August 1842, the military establishment was cut back to 8,613 officers and men. This time, however, no regiments were disbanded. Certain positions were eliminated from the Army staff and companies were restricted to forty-two privates. The 2nd Dragoons was also dismounted and converted into a rifle regiment, a short-lived experiment which was thankfully reversed in March 1844.

PLATE 13: HUNTING THE SEMINOLES, 1835–42

43. Private, 6th U.S. Infantry, Undress, 1837: *By the start of the Second Seminole War, American infantrymen were wearing an undress uniform of sky blue wool. The collapsible leather forage cap was in vogue from 1832 to 1839. In the 1830s, chevrons indicated length of service instead of rank. The 1832 regulations stated that soldiers who served 'faithfully for the term of five years, shall be permitted . . . to wear a chevron on the sleeves of their coats, above the elbow, points up; and an additional chevron on each arm for every additional five years of faithful service.'* **44. Captain, 4th U.S. Infantry, Campaign Dress, 1842:** *Following a sweep through the Big Cypress Swamp, Captain George A. McCall of the 4th Infantry wrote on 27 February 1842: 'On all these marches, I carried my seven days' rations in a bag rolled in my blanket and strapped across my shoulders, together with an extra flannel shirt (the only wear on such tramps) and pair of socks, besides my double gun—swords being worse than useless.' The cloth forage cap was introduced in 1839.* **45. Private, 6th U.S. Infantry, Summer Undress, 1838:** *During warm weather, infantrymen campaigned in jackets and trousers of plain white cotton. Figures 42 and 44 carry Model 1835 muskets.*

44. Captain, 4th U.S. Infantry, Campaign
Dress, 1842

43. Private, 6th U.S. Infantry, Undress,
1837

45. Private, 6th U.S. Infantry, Summer
Undress, 1838

Whenever regular troops were not chasing Indians or white desperadoes, they were given plenty of other work to do. Because of the congressional mania for minimizing military expenses, soldiers ordinarily erected the stockades, barracks, and other structures composing the Army's frontier forts. They also maintained military buildings, cut the wood required to heat them, and built the roads that linked the posts to a rudimentary defense network and opened much of America to white settlement.

For all their undeniable utility, such activities were not relished by the soldiers. Writing in March 1829, 4th Infantryman George McCall, then a lieutenant, observed: 'No soldier likes *"fatigue duty!"* It stands on the *Roster* below *"Duty under Arms;"* and every good soldier's pride leads him to rejoice when detailed on the latter, while he dislikes or even detests the former. I never knew but one instance of a soldier volunteering for fatigue.' What galled the troops most was the knowledge that some civilians could earn as much as $1 a day for the same labor, while the pittance paid to a private until early 1833 was a measly $5 a month.

Of more concern to line officers was the effect the constant construction details had on their men's morale and military bearing. 'The ax, pick, saw & trowel,' complained Lieutenant Colonel Zachary Taylor in a letter dated 18 September 1820, 'has become more the implement of the American soldier, than the cannon, musket or sword.' In the same document, Taylor asserted that his regiment, the 8th Infantry, had so little time for drill that it 'cannot even go through its facings correctly, much less through its fireings [*sic*] & battalion evolutions.'

Low pay, stern discipline, indifferent food, rude living conditions, and the prospect of danger caused most Americans to shun a soldier's life. The Army's *General Regulations* of 1820 defined acceptable recruits as 'all free white male persons, above eighteen and under thirty-five years, who are able bodied, active, and free from disease,' but such high standards were not always observed. In the summer of 1829, following a transfer to the 1st Infantry, Lieutenant Colonel Taylor raged about 'the drunken materials the rank, & file of our army are now composed of.' After his promotion to captain, George McCall ran a recruiting 'rendezvous' in Philadelphia in 1837, a duty he found 'irksome and disagreeable . . . in the extreme,' because:

'The recruits I made were almost without exception of the unsophisticated, untutored, and intractable sons of Erin. . . . It had become too plain that the ranks of our army could not be filled with men whose intelligence and industry enabled them to fill higher places in the walks of life. It was therefore imperative not only to accept foreigners, but to reduce the standard of height.'

The Model 1832 dress cap for infantry officers was made of black beaver with a black leather band around the base, a chinstrap of the same material, and a black patent leather visor. The plume consisted of white cock feathers drooping from an eight-inch stem anchored in a gilt socket. The front of the cap was decorated with a gilt eagle, a silver bugle horn, and a regimental number (not pictured) placed within the curve of the bugle horn.

Outsiders were equally uncharitable in their assessments of the American soldier. 'The most worthless characters enter the army,' commented a British traveler in 1833, 'which consists of a melange of English deserters [from the royal regiments in Canada], Dutch, French, Americans, &c. . . . There is no great inducement to belong to an army which is held in no great estimation by the citizens generally.' In an 1835 book, Charles J. Latrobe sneered at 'the rag-tag-and-bob-tail herd drafted into the ranks of the regular army. . . . The ordinary recruits consist either of the scum of the population of the older states, or of the worthless German, English, or Irish emigrants.'

The *General Regulations* of 1825 forbade the further enlistment of foreigners, but that produced such a sharp dip in recruiting that the policy was amended in 1828 to permit the enrollment of naturalized citizens. In practice, however, most recruiting officers accepted any fit men willing to be 'sworn in.' By the 1840s, nearly half of the Army's enlistees were immigrants, with Irishmen and Germans predominant among them. The presence of so many foreigners in the ranks, especially those reared in countries where English was not spoken, further complicated the Army's training problems. 'It is no pleasant task to instruct raw recruits,' Inspector General George Croghan noted in 1830, 'but when those recruits are ignorant of your language, the task becomes ten times more tedious and disagreeable.'

Keeping the common soldiers in the service proved almost as difficult as enticing them into uniform in the first place. While 16,437 men joined the Army between 1823 and 1830, 6,932 deserted. Of the 2,451 deserters who ran off from 1 October 1822 until 30 September 1825, 945 were infantrymen. With a bureaucrat's gift for self-justification, the Army's Adjutant General reported on 11 January 1826: 'Within the first twelve months after enlistment desertions are more numerous from any given military force than during the remaining four years of the term of enlistment. . . . The class from whence a majority of private soldiers are drawn scarcely regard . . . desertion as an act of turpitude.'

Eventually, some politicians realized that armies do not exist on patriotism alone. In March 1833, Congress passed an act calculated 'to improve the condition of the non-commissioned officers and privates of the army and marine corps . . . and to prevent desertion,' raising a private's pay to $6 per month. There was one catch. One dollar a month was to be withheld for two years. At the end of that time, the soldier would receive the outstanding $24, provided that he had served faithfully. Veterans were offered a re-enlistment bounty of two months' pay, and privates who signed on for a second hitch received their full monthly salary without having to undergo another probation period. The Army's term of enlistment was also shortened to three years.

In the summer of 1838, Congress restored the traditional five-year enlistment and increased a private's pay to $7 a month. However, now the military kept back $1 each month until the end of the soldier's hitch to ensure his loyalty and good behavior. Congress also enlarged the re-enlistment bounty to three months' pay.

Congress felt the legislation of 1833 and 1838 was generous, but, in reality, the new inducements were still too miserly to affect the Army's growth and retention rates.

Though the Army's lower echelons were burdened with some of the sorriest materials imaginable, the officer corps came to be increasingly dominated by products of the United States Military Academy, a development which promoted a definite rise in quality. The soldierly attributes of the era's average West Pointer were proudly described by Cadmus M. Wilcox, who joined the 4th U.S. Infantry upon his graduation in 1846: 'Being well posted in the tactics of the three arms of service, he is at once competent and efficient in drilling enlisted men, either as cavalry, artillery, or infantry, and in charge of details to construct batteries or field fortifications he directs with intelligence, due to his

familiarity with the text books in use at the Academy. Subordination, deference, and respect for superior officers have been thoroughly inculcated during his four years' instruction and training at West Point, and to the usages of the service he readily adapts himself.'

Even crusty Zachary Taylor, who entered the service in 1808 directly from civilian life, admired the learning and professionalism of the West Pointers assigned to his 8th Infantry, calling them men 'that would do honor to any army.' Reflecting on the Army's most frequent duties, the practical lieutenant colonel quipped on 18 September 1820: 'Such unfortunately is the passion in our country for making roads, fortifications, and building barracks . . . with soldiers . . . that a man who would make a good overseer, or negro driver, is better qualified for our service than one who had received a first rate military education.'

To be sure, the officer corps had its critics too. One was Ethan Allen Hitchcock, an 1817 graduate of West Point. After four years with the Corps of Artillery, Lieutenant Hitchcock was transferred to the 1st Infantry. Hitchcock disparaged his colleagues in the 1st as 'thirty idle officers . . . a majority of them dissipated men without education,' whose speech smacked of 'profanity, ribaldry, and blustering braggadocio.'

Allowing for a measure of truth in Hitchcock's cynical appraisal, there were still enough able officers in the Army to turn a good many of the immigrants, outcasts, and ne'er-do-wells they led into dependable soldiers. An incident from the Second Seminole War testifies to the caliber of the Army's officers—particularly those of the U.S. Infantry.

During the Battle of Lake Okeechobee, 25 December 1838, 175 officers and men from five companies of the 6th U.S. Infantry advanced through mud and water nearly waist deep while under heavy rifle fire from 380 to 480 Seminoles hidden behind a hummock. Within a few minutes, all but one of the 6th's officers were hit. The battalion commander, Lieutenant Colonel Alexander Ramsey Thompson, was pierced by three bullets. The unit's sergeant major, four sergeants, four corporals, and forty-five privates sank into the muck killed or wounded. Propped up against a tree, Thompson fought off death long enough to shout: 'Keep steady, men! Charge the hummock! Remember the regiment to which you belong!' Rallying, the 6th's unwounded stalwarts renewed the attack, joining 173 men of the 1st Infantry, 160 from the 4th Infantry, and seventy-one mounted infantrymen in driving the Indians from the field.

Heroics like Thompson's embued the U.S. Infantry with a tradition and an élan that would stand its members in good stead as they entered America's second major war of the 19th century.

5 A Headlong Rush for Glory
1845–8

When the United States annexed Texas in 1845, she placed herself on a collision course with Mexico. The ill-feelings aroused by that inconsiderate transaction culminated in America's third major war with a foreign power. But unlike the Revolution and the War of 1812—arguably cases of Americans defending their liberty—the Mexican War was a clear-cut instance of American aggression.

Historians may debate the morality of America's war against Mexico, but one thing is indisputable. The conflict proved that thirty years of frontier experience had shaped the U.S. Infantry into the toughest compact fighting force in the Western Hemisphere. Writing to a friend about one of the war's first engagements, the ordinarily phlegmatic Ulysses S. Grant, then a second lieutenant in the 4th U.S. Infantry, warmly praised the conduct of American regulars: 'Our troops rushed forward with shouts of victory and would kill and drive away the Mexicans from evry [sic] piece of Artillery they could get their eyes upon.' In a like vein, Captain Philip N. Barbour, 3rd U.S. Infantry, told his wife about a Mexican general captured at the same battle who could not get over the reckless abandon of his opponents. The general declared 'that he had fought Texans, Mexicans, Spaniards and Indians, but had never before seen troops that would charge into the mouth of a battery, under a storm of grapeshot. It was this that disheartened the Mexicans and put them to flight. . . . They thought we were devils incarnate.'

Nearly every other battle of the Mexican War inspired similar comments concerning the valor and staying power of American infantrymen—teasingly known in those days as 'doughboys.' For the U.S. Infantry, the contest was a headlong rush for glory. In view of the many brave feats that quest entailed, it is amazing that the price paid in American lives ran so low.

Texas, the root cause of the Mexican War, was set up by Spain in 1716 as a buffer to shield the riches of Mexico from the French and Anglo-Americans. Understandably

enough, few Spaniards wanted to settle in the garrison province. As of 1821, the year Mexico threw off Spanish rule and took possession of Texas, the region's non-Indian population was a meager 4,000 souls.

Eager to cement its hold over Texas by peopling it with industrious farm folk, the Mexican government threw open the area to foreign emigration, offering generous tracts of land at nominal fees to anyone who would become a Roman Catholic and a Mexican citizen. Such blandishments proved irresistible to certain denizens of the Mississippi Valley, which was mired in an agricultural depression in the 1820s. By 1835, 35,000 Americans called Texas home.

Ironically, Mexico's success at colonization cost her what she sought to save. The new Texans were mostly staunch Protestants who also had no intention of

American regulars storm the Convent of San Mateo at Churubusco, Mexico, 20 August 1847, in this lithograph by Carl Nebel, a German artist. Nebel portrayed several officers in trousers of white cotton or linen, which the Army allowed for summer wear. Some officers also sport straw hats for extra sun protection and shell jackets instead of heavier and hotter frock coats.

switching national allegiance. Late in 1835, the American settlers staged an uprising, and they won their freedom at the Battle of San Jacinto, 21 April 1836. Mexico lacked sufficient might to subdue the rebels, but she refused to acknowledge Texan independence, and she let the United States know that any attempt to annex the 'Lone Star Republic' would be regarded as an act of war.

Mexico's threats bluffed Washington into leaving Texas alone for seven years, but there was no extinguishing the American hunger for new territory. In 1843, the administration of President John Tyler started maneuvering to add Texas to the Union. As its plans matured, the federal government decided to deploy troops near Texas to deter the Mexicans from interfering. However, with the bulk of its regulars strung out among more than 100 coastal and frontier forts, the U.S. Army's only strategic reserve consisted of eight companies of the 3rd Infantry and eight companies of the 4th Infantry at Jefferson Barracks, Missouri. In April 1844, these units were ordered down the Mississippi to a position on the Louisiana/Texas border near Fort Jesup. There they joined seven companies of the 2nd Dragoons. The commander of this hastily assembled 'Corps of

Observation' was Brevet Brigadier General Zachary Taylor, the rough-hewn, well-liked colonel of the 6th Infantry and hero of the Battle of Lake Okeechobee. Taylor's instructions were to keep his 1,200 troops ready to march 'at short notice to any point in the United States or Texas.'

Washington politics immobilized Taylor's regulars for over a year, delaying congressional acceptance of annexation until 1 March 1845. Three months later, Taylor received permission to enter Texas and protect it from possible Mexican reprisals. Dispatching the 2nd Dragoons southward by an overland route, Taylor shipped his infantry from New Orleans by steamer. The American forces, now known as the 'Army of Occupation,' rendezvoused at Corpus Christi on the Nueces River in August.

Over the next two months, reinforcements drawn from garrisons across the United States tripled the size of the Army of Occupation. By mid-October, Taylor's camp contained the 3rd, 4th, 5th, 7th, and 8th U.S. Infantry, a twelve-company battalion of 'red-legged infantry' (artillerymen armed with muskets), three light batteries, seven companies of the 2nd U.S. Dragoons,

Second Lieutenant Parmenas Taylor Turnley, 1st U.S. Infantry, 1847. The Model 1839 forage cap and single-breasted frock coat constituted the standard field dress for infantry officers in the Mexican War. Turnley's buttons and the embroidered borders of his shoulder straps are silver.

Captain Henry Lewis Little, 7th U.S. Infantry, in his 1832-regulation full dress coat, circa 1847–8. Little behaved bravely as a lieutenant of the 5th Infantry during Zachary Taylor's assault upon Monterrey in September 1846. Sixteen years later, he was slain while serving as a Confederate brigadier general at Iuka, Mississippi.

and a company of Texas Rangers. These 3,922 officers and men included more than half of the actual strength of the U.S. Army and represented the largest concentration of American regulars in a single body since the War of 1812. To assemble this minor spectacle, the Army had to withdraw all but four regiments from the Canadian border and the 1,500-mile Indian frontier.

Despite their proximity to the Mexicans and the likelihood of war, Taylor's soldiers were surprisingly merry. For men accustomed to serving in puny details, the sight of enough whole regiments to make up three brigades was exhilarating. 'I consider myself very fortunate in being sent here, for it is probable that I may not see so many regulars together in twenty years,' Second Lieutenant John P. Hale of the 3rd Infantry wrote his sister from Corpus Christi. 'Many old officers have never seen so many troops at one time.'

Nevertheless, the sudden mobilization of American power revealed embarrassing problems peculiar to the U.S. Army. Snatched from their far-flung posts, companies from the same regiment had a hard time learning to work together. For all his enthusiasm, Lieutenant Hale recognized the problem:

'The different parts of the Army vary much in the state of discipline. Some of them have not been together for many years. The Fifth [Infantry], for instance, . . . is all together for the first time in nine years; this of course has

prevented them learning the battalion drill, and as the officers had no occasion to practice they had forgotten all their tactics.'

Likewise, the Army's long frontier dispersion had deprived senior officers of experience in dealing with large bodies of men. Lieutenant Colonel Ethan A. Hitchcock, the acting commander of the 3rd Infantry, was flabbergasted by the practical and theoretical ignorance of his colleagues. 'What a pretty figure we cut,' he fumed. 'Neither General Taylor nor Colonel [William] Whistler [commander of Taylor's 3rd Brigade] . . . could form . . . [the army] into line! . . . As for manoeuvring, not one of them can move a step in it. Egotism or no egotism, I am the only field officer who could change a single position . . . according to any but a militia mode.' Hitchcock's edge stemmed from his West Point education. But Taylor and most of the Army's other senior officers had never received formal military schooling.

The American high command was further handi-capped by age. Until 1861, the U.S. Army had no retirement list, and career officers without promising prospects in the civilian world often clung to their commissions until they were decrepit, burned-out wrecks. Taylor himself turned sixty-one in 1845. His brigade commanders and other leading subordinates ranged in years from fifty-five to sixty-six. Not only was

Sergeant Jacques M. Lasselle, 1st Indiana Infantry Regiment, 1846. According to a contemporary newspaper, the rank and file of this outfit were issued 'blue cloth tight bodied coats trimmed with silver lace . . . on the breast' and 'pants of blue satinet, also trimmed with silver lace.'

Captain Stanislaus Lasselle, 1st Indiana Infantry Regiment, 1846. Like the enlisted men, officers of the 1st Indiana wore blue coats with silver lace and buttons, but their uniforms were less ostentatious.

it difficult for these old dogs to learn new tricks, but active service in a southern climate severely taxed their health. Lieutenant Grant related what happened to his elderly colonel, Josiah Vose, when the latter attempted to put the 4th Infantry through the manual of arms at New Orleans on 15 July 1845, prior to the unit's voyage to Corpus Christi:

'On the evening of the 15th . . . Col Vose, for the first time since I have been in the Army, undertook to drill his Regiment. He was . . . probably some what embarrassed and gave his commands in a loud tone of voise [*sic*]; before the drill was over I discovered that he put his hand to his breast when ever he commenced to give any command, and before he was through with the parade he was compelled to leave the field and start for his qarters [*sic*], which were hardly fifty paces off, and just upon . . . arriving there he fell dead upon the poarch [*sic*].'

At least the pathetic Vose tried to do his duty. According to Captain William S. Henry, another articulate 3rd Infantryman, not all of Taylor's senior infantry officers were so dedicated:

'One regiment had all its field officers absent; its colonel for years laid upon the shelf; its lieutenant-colonel . . . cut down by disease; its major, a gallant soldier, but broken in constitution; this regiment was commanded by a captain! Another had its colonel absent, its lieutenant-colonel enjoying a brigadier's command, its major bed-ridden for years! This regiment was commanded by a brevet major. Another regiment, its colonel and lieutenant-colonel absent, its major enjoying a brigadier's command; this regiment was commanded by a captain, and only one captain led his company.'

Henry's observations highlighted a second sore point. Because of its small size, the Army relied on officers detached from the line for staff work, recruiting, and other special assignments. This meant that regular outfits suffered chronic officer shortages. When the 4th Infantry first joined the Corps of Observation, six of its officers were absent on staff assignments.

Yet if the Army's head was not totally sound, its body possessed a strength out of all proportion to its limited physical size. By 1845, there were about 500 graduates of the U.S. Military Academy serving in the officer corps, mostly as captains and lieutenants. With their background in the classroom and as Indian fighters, the West Pointers made ideal company and regimental commanders. Under their tutelage, Taylor's reunited regiments quickly attained a respectable proficiency at drill and a resilient *esprit de corps*. 'My regiment is one of the best in the service, if not the very best and there is a great deal of regimental pride in it,' penned Lieutenant Hale of the 3rd Infantry. That opinion was seconded from the ranks by Private Barna Upton: 'The Third Regiment is acknowledged to be the best disciplined regiment in the United States and [I] have nothing to say to the contrary. Every finger and toe and joint must be placed exactly according to custom.' With disarming candor, Ulysses S. Grant later described Taylor's rank and file as 'inferior . . . material out of which to make an army, . . . principally foreigners [from] our large cities, . . . men who had enlisted in time of peace, to serve for seven dollars a month.' Nevertheless, 'They were brave men, and . . . drill and discipline brought out all that was in them. A better army, man for man, probably never faced an enemy than the one commanded by General Taylor.'

Despite the annexation of Texas, Washington might have averted war had it dealt delicately with Mexico. Fate decreed otherwise. On 4 March 1845, James K. Polk succeeded John Tyler as President of the United States. Polk, an avid and inflexible expansionist, craved additional Mexican territory. He believed that the true boundary of Texas lay not along the Nueces River, as the Mexicans insisted, but much further south along the Rio Grande. Polk also coveted New Mexico and Upper California. The steel-eyed Democrat tried to purchase what he wanted, but the Mexicans, smarting from the loss of Texas, refused to deal with what they considered a nation of thieves. Furious, Polk abandoned diplomacy and applied military pressure.

On 3 February 1846, Taylor received directions from the War Department to advance the Army of Occupation to 'positions on or near' the Rio Grande. Consuming more than a month with preparations, Taylor did not get his troops to the north bank of the Rio Grande until 28 March. To the Mexicans, the American occupation of the Nueces-Rio Grande strip was the last straw, and in April they assembled an army of 5,000 men under Major General Mariano Arista at Matamoros, just across the river from Taylor's camp. The Americans were not impressed by the show of force. 'The Mexican Officers I have seen are . . . fine looking fellows,' sniffed Captain Barbour of the 3rd Infantry. 'But their soldiers are half-starved looking devils and excite in us only feelings of contempt.'

Arista soon taught the 'Yanquis' the danger of smugness. On 25 April 1846, 1,600 Mexican cavalry and light troops annihilated a patrol of sixty-three American dragoons. Learning of the debacle the next day, Taylor sent President Polk an urgent dispatch: 'Hostilities may now be considered as commenced.' Taylor also appealed to the governors of Texas and Louisiana for 5,000 emergency volunteers. But the Army of Occupation would have to take on Arista before reinforcements arrived.

Leaving the 7th Infantry and two artillery companies to hold an earthwork fort opposite Matamoros, Taylor hastened northeast to ensure the security of his supply base on the Gulf of Mexico. These detachments reduced Taylor's effective field force to 2,200 officers and men, but he moved boldly to grapple with Arista, who was now north of the Rio Grande leading a column of 3,709 troops. Scorning the odds, Taylor's officers welcomed the coming clash of arms. 'In numbers they [the Mexicans] are far above us,' wrote Captain George A. McCall of the 4th Infantry, 'but we have confidence in our troops, and the men are eager for a contest with them.' Taylor struck the same note in orders issued on 7 May:

'The commanding general has every confidence in his officers and men. If his order and instructions are carried out, he has no doubt of the result, let the enemy meet him in what numbers they may. He wishes to enjoin the battalions of Infantry that their main dependence must be in the bayonet.'

The following day, 8 May 1846, the opposing armies met in the Battle of Palo Alto. Since Arista's superiority in numbers forced Taylor's infantry to assume a defensive posture, the American side of the fight was largely borne by three superbly served batteries. The

PLATE 14: WAR WITH MEXICO: THE REGULARS, 1846–8

46. Corporal, 3rd U.S. Infantry, Undress, 1846: *Sky blue kersey jackets and trousers served as the U.S. Infantry's combat uniform in the Mexican War. Pictorial evidence suggests that by 1846 infantry non-commissioned officers were wearing downward-pointing rank chevrons in emulation of the privilege enjoyed by the U.S. Dragoons since 1833. The upward-pointing chevrons on the lower sleeves stand for a successfully completed hitch in the regular army, and the red borders indicate wartime service.* **47. Second Lieutenant (Ulysses S. Grant), 4th U.S. Infantry, Undress, 1847:** *Based on an 1845 photograph in the U.S. Military Academy Archives. With the Regulations of 1832, infantry officers received single-breasted frock coats for wear on most non-dress occasions. Grant insisted on closing his cuffs with four small silver buttons— instead of the regulation two. On 3 May 1847, Grant wrote a friend: 'I have a beard more than four inches long and it [is] red.'* **48. Lieutenant Colonel (John H. Savage), 11th U.S. Infantry, Undress, 1847:** *Based on a photograph in the Michael F. Bremer Collection. The Regulations of 1847 authorized double-breasted frock coats for field officers. Savage's rank is denoted by silver leaves on the ends of his shoulder straps. (The insignia for an infantry colonel was a silver eagle; for a major, a gold leaf; for a captain, two silver bars; and for a first lieutenant, one silver bar. A second lieutenant's shoulder straps were plain with silver borders.)* **49. First Sergeant, 8th U.S. Infantry, Undress, 1847:** *The Regulations of 1847 introduced upward-pointing rank chevrons. Regulars in Mexico with Winfield Scott whitened their russet leather musket slings and black knapsack straps. Although the U.S. Army adopted the percussion system in 1842, resistance from General Scott meant that most regular infantrymen began the war with flintlocks, such as the Model 1835 muskets illustrated here.*

46. Corporal, 3rd U.S. Infantry, Undress,
1846

48. Lieutenant Colonel, 11th U.S. Infantry,
Undress, 1847

47. Second Lieutenant, 4th U.S. Infantry,
Undress, 1847

49. First Sergeant, 8th U.S. Infantry,
Undress, 1847

gunners pounded the Mexican line and broke up several attacks with their rapid and accurate fire. Only one American infantry regiment played a conspicuous part in the battle. When a Mexican cavalry brigade endeavored to turn Taylor's right flank, the 5th Infantry formed square and checked the charging lancers with two sharp volleys. Arrayed within range of the enemy's cannon, other doughboys exhibited impressive sang-froid. Captain Barbour proudly testified:

'There was no wavering in my regiment; the men and officers all stood, drawn up in line, and received the enemy's fire with a coolness and steadiness almost incredible, cracking jokes the whole time and sending up, whenever one of our guns made a big gap in the Mexican lines, a shout that must have struck terror to their hearts.'

After losing 257 men to Taylor's fifty-five, the Mexican army disintegrated and withdrew as dusk fell. Regrouping his disheartened troops, Arista continued the retreat to a dried out river-course known as Resaca de la Palma. Taking advantage of the natural trench, he deployed his men there for another stand.

Following at a respectful distance, Taylor eventually opened the Battle of Resaca de la Palma at 3:00 p.m., 9 May 1846. Once he located the foe, Taylor unleashed his glory-hungry infantry. Owing to the thick chaparral masking Arista's position, Taylor's regiments could not maintain their alignment as they pushed forward. Companies lost contact with each other and then splintered even further. 'I was for half an hour trying to work my way through the thicket in which our regiment was deployed,' recalled Captain Barbour, 'and finally getting out with only 12 men of my company went ahead on my own hook.'

Such adverse conditions did not daunt the *Yanquis*. It was just like fighting the Florida Seminoles all over again. Groping toward the smoke and the sound of the guns in clusters of tens and twenties, the doughboys burst from the chaparral and sprang on the Mexicans. A lieutenant of the 8th Infantry, rushing to the aid of a brother officer, cut down two enemy soldiers with his sword. 'Our men expected no quarter,' wrote Brevet Second Lieutenant Edmund Kirby Smith, 5th U.S. Infantry, 'and fought with perfect desperation—it was hand to hand conflict—a trial of personal strength in many instances, where the bayonet failed, the fist even was used—but in moral courage as well as personal strength—we were far their superiors and have given

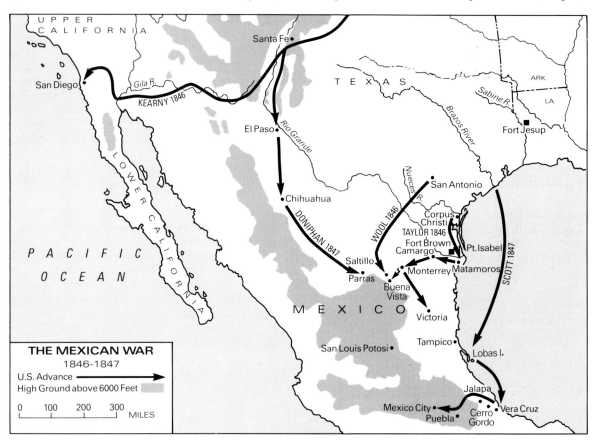

THE MEXICAN WAR
1846-1847
U.S. Advance ———▶
High Ground above 6000 Feet ▨

0   100   200   300
MILES

Lieutenant John M. Hollingsworth of the 7th New York Volunteers drew this self-portrait in his journal. His uniform consisted of a blue hat with yellow trim, a blue frock coat with gold buttons and epaulettes and red facings, white summer trousers, and a crimson sash. Mustered into service on 1 August 1846 for the duration of the Mexican War, the 7th was formed to provide a garrison for California, and many of its members remained there as settlers.

Captain James Miller of Company K, 2nd Regiment, Pennsylvania Volunteer Infantry, 1846. Miller's frock coat is identical to those worn by regular infantry officers, but the captain has violated regulations by unfastening his collar and rolling it down. The 2nd Pennsylvania followed Winfield Scott from Vera Cruz to Mexico City in 1847. Miller later died in the Civil War while leading the 81st Pennsylvania Volunteer Infantry at Fair Oaks, Virginia, 1 June 1862.

them a lesson, which ages cannot remove.' At length, the Mexican troops—unable to match the Americans in tenacity—turned their backs for a second time on the Army of Occupation, leading Taylor to exult, 'Bayonet to bayonet, & sword to sword, we completely routed them.'

In addition to killing, wounding, or capturing 515 Mexicans, the Americans seized eight of Arista's guns. Taylor's losses were thirty-three killed and eighty-nine wounded. Looking beyond the statistics, Second Lieutenant George Gordon Meade, an engineer on Taylor's staff, summed up the deeper meaning of his chief's two victories:

'The affair of today [Resaca de la Palma] . . . proved the superiority of our infantry, as that of yesterday did of our artillery. We have whipped them in the open plain, and we have done so in the bushes, and I now believe the war will soon be ended. . . . No troops could have behaved better than ours both yesterday and to-day.'

Meade was wrong on one important point. The war would last nearly two more years. More troops were needed to prostrate Mexico and expand America's borders to the limits desired by President Polk.

On 11 May 1846, two days after he learned that Arista was over the Rio Grande, Polk asked Congress for a declaration of war against Mexico. Congress complied in two days and then turned its attention to raising an army of sufficient size for the struggle. At the outbreak of hostilities, the U.S. Army was composed of 637 officers and 5,925 enlisted men, 2,057 below the authorized complement. The Mexican Army was four times as large.

Between 13 and 19 May, Congress approved legislation boosting regular troop levels to 17,812. Every company was granted a wartime strength of 100 privates. The legislators also created two new units, the U.S. Regiment of Mounted Rifles and the Company of Sappers, Miners and Pontoniers.

As in the War of 1812, recruiters failed to fill all the slots in the new establishment. As late as November 1846, no more than 10,690 officers and men were with the colors in regular commands. However much they favored the war, aspiring soldiers balked at leaving home for a five-year hitch. Young American males also were loath to risk life and limb for $7 a month. In desperation, the government relaxed physical requirements and paid $2 a head to anyone who brought in acceptable cannon fodder. Eventually, enlistees were offered a $12 bounty. None of these expedients worked exceptionally well.

Congress offered a solution to the problem on 11 February 1847 by passing the 'Ten Regiment Bill.' The law authorized ten new regiments—the 3rd U.S. Dragoons, the 9th, 10th, 11th, 12th, 13th, 14th, 15th, and 16th U.S. Infantry, and a regiment of 'voltigeurs and foot riflemen . . . provided with a rocket and mountain howitzer battery.' Service in the new regiments would be for only the length of the war. Furthermore, an honorably discharged soldier from any of America's forces was assured a land bonus of 160 acres for twelve months' service, and forty acres if he served less than a year. To compensate for the shortage of field officers, each regular regiment—old and new—was allowed a second major.

At its inception, the U.S. Regiment of Voltigeurs and Foot Riflemen was envisioned as a combined command containing dragoons, infantry, and artillery. Half of the men were supposed to be mounted on horses. For rapid movement, each foot rifleman would climb up behind the saddle of a voltigeur. The unit's table of organization also featured a company of mountain howitzers and rockets. In actual practice, however, the Voltigeur Regiment functioned as infantry, and its men gave a good account of themselves with the famous Model 1841 ('Mississippi') rifle, the Army's first general-issue percussion shoulder arm.

Congress made another effort to entice recruits into the regular army on 3 March 1847. Every soldier in Mexico who re-enlisted for the duration was now eligible for the $12 bounty. A private who earned a certificate of merit for bravery would have his pay augmented by an extra $2 a month. Non-commissioned officers who distinguished themselves were promised special honors. The law also added two more companies to each regular artillery regiment.

Congress had acted wisely. Five thousand two hundred fresh regulars were enlisted, organized into battalions, and sped on their way to Mexico during the first sixty days after the opening of recruiting stations for the ten new regiments. Altogether, 1,016 officers and 35,009 men were accepted into the regular army between 13 May 1846 and 5 July 1848, making a total of 42,587 for the war. Of these, 30,954 actually did some fighting.

Initially, members of the old regular army despised the fellows who entered the service under the provisions of the Ten Regiment Act. Professional officers were upset because so many commissions were awarded to appointees from civil life, including West Point washouts and former officers who had resigned from the Army to pursue lucrative civilian careers. The new officers were ridiculed as 'very young men, and men of very little general information.' A Navy lieutenant called them 'hard-looking citizens, who . . . required much drilling and "breaking-in," to be rendered serviceable.' As for the other ranks, they were dismissed as 'raw levies.' But observers not blinded by professional

jealousy admitted that the short-term regulars were 'generally good looking men.' Given the opportunity, the newcomers would prove their mettle on the battlefield.

Despite his administration's success in bolstering the regular army, President Polk harbored little love for professional soldiers. He hoped to place his primary reliance on citizen soldiers, and since the militia had decayed so badly since 1815, his administration bent every effort to field an imposing army of volunteers.

On 13 May 1846, the same day it declared war, Congress authorized the President to summon 50,000 volunteers from the states to serve 'for twelve months, or during the war.' Volunteers were to furnish their own uniforms, but they would be reimbursed by the federal government. Those who joined cavalry units had to provide their own horses and riding equipment in exchange for 40¢ a day for 'use and risk.' On top of all that, citizen soldiers could expect the same pay as regulars. At the regimental level, volunteer officers would be selected according to state militia laws, which often meant election by the rank and file. Generals and staff officers would be federal appointees. Finally, Congress empowered the President to call out the militia for six months, instead of three.

On 19 May 1846, the War Department issued a circular inviting ten states to furnish 13,208 volunteer infantrymen (in seventeen regiments) and 3,945 cavalrymen (five regiments). The public's response, especially in the South and those states watered by the Mississippi or Ohio Rivers, exceeded government expectations. A Mississippi politician wrote on 22 May: 'Our people are in a state of the highest excitement. Old and young, rich and poor, democrats and whigs, are ready to volunteer.' Indeed, many Mississippians were angry because their state had been asked for only one infantry regiment. In

PLATE 15: WAR WITH MEXICO: THE VOLUNTEERS, 1846–8

50. Corporal, Company A, 2nd Illinois Infantry, 1846: Based on a primitive painting and the following written description by Samuel E. Chamberlain: 'We were uniformed as each company selected and strange grotesque costumes now filled the Camp. Ours, Co. A, 2nd Regiment, made choice of jacket and pants of blue mixed Kentucky jeans with yellow stripes across the breast like a Dragoon bugler.' **51. Captain, 1st Regiment of Ohio Volunteers, 1846:** *Ohio officers had ornate silver badges embroidered on the front of their forage caps. Plain white trousers of 'white linen or cotton without stripe' were authorized for wear 'from 1st May to the 30th of September.'* **52. Sergeant, South Carolina Regiment ('Palmetto Regiment'), 1847:** *South Carolina volunteers wore jackets with wing-style shoulder straps and white cuff lace. Caps and belt plates bore the regiment's palmetto symbol. Red flannel shirts were popular with the men of this regiment. Note the Model 1835 musket and Model 1840 non-commissioned officer's sword.*

50. Corporal, Company A, 2nd Illinois
Infantry, 1846

51. Captain, 1st Regiment of Ohio
Volunteers, 1846

52. Sergeant, South Carolina ('Palmetto')
Regiment, 1847

Ohio, 3,000 men stepped forward in two weeks, 900 from Cincinnati alone. Before the war's end, Illinois raised fourteen regiments, ten more than its quota, and Tennessee offered 30,000 men when the Polk Administration requested 3,000. Bowing grudgingly to the popular clamor, by July 1846 the federal government had accepted eighteen regiments, four battalions, and eight companies of volunteer infantry, plus six regiments of cavalry.

Washington tried to organize volunteer outfits in much the same way as the regular forces. Infantry regiments were supposed to have ten companies with a flexible strength of sixty-four to 100 privates per company. Each company was also permitted two second lieutenants. But the volunteers had minds of their own, and they disregarded federal guidelines as often as not. The Baltimore-Washington Volunteers took the field with only six companies. The 1st Mississippi Rifles went to war with 926 men in ten companies. A regiment later raised in Virginia turned out with fourteen companies and 1,182 men.

Opinions of the volunteers' soldierly qualities were mixed. As might be expected, regular officers, speaking with the professional's haughty disdain for amateurs, were harsh judges. Lack of discipline, slovenliness in dress and drill, inattention to sanitation, and mistreatment of government property ranked among the most frequent complaints. 'Every regiment of volunteers costs equal to three of regulars, plus loss of arms, accoutrements and equipage,' fumed a brigade commander in the Army of Occupation. 'Thirty-three percent are sick, and the remaining 66 not worth a straw.' An Army surgeon called the volunteers 'sickly boys, and invalid men (many of whom came into the service with a view to improve their impaired health).' George Meade characterized them as 'a most disorderly mass.' 'Their own officers have no command or control over them,' Meade confided to his wife, 'and the General [Taylor] has given up in despair.' 'Some of the volunteers . . . don't know the butt from the muzzle of a musket,' sneered a subaltern of the 4th Artillery. 'They want everything that constitutes the soldier.'

A number of citizen soldiers blackened their reputation further by committing atrocities against Mexican civilians. Looting, rape, murder, and the desecration of churches were common offenses. Much of this reprehensible behavior was attributable to religious hatred. Beginning in the 1830s, many native-born American Protestants, alarmed by the mounting tide of immigrants from Ireland and Germany, succumbed to anti-Catholic hysteria. This prejudice made it easier for certain volunteers to brutalize or butcher Catholic Mexicans. Regular outfits, with a high percentage of Catholic immigrants in their ranks, were much gentler in their treatment of enemy civilians.

For all their faults, the vast majority of volunteers were not as worthless as their critics charged. In fact, some units exuded an elite aura. 'They were the culled men of the country,' claimed one of Taylor's surgeons, 'and were mostly young men,—the majority of them from the best ranks of society—men of education and refinements. Gentlemen were as often found in the ranks . . . as amongst the officers.'

The volunteers had their rough edges, but these were ground away by training and regimentation. An outfit's conduct invariably depended on the quality of its officers. Some of these were hopeless incompetents, but many were intelligent and dutiful patriots, who studied their drill manuals, kept their men in line, and picked up the tricks of the soldier's trade by carefully watching their regular comrades. The volunteer officer corps also benefited from a sprinkling of West Point alumni, men like Colonel Jefferson Davis, who made the 1st Mississippi Rifles as fine a regiment as any that fought beneath the Stars and Stripes. Indeed, all but a few volunteer units bore up well in battle.

The most exasperating fault ascribed to the volunteers of 1846 was their tendency to go home at critical junctures in the war. When the first calls for citizen soldiers were issued, Polk committed the blunder of allowing them the option of serving one year or the length of the war. Most volunteers chose the shorter hitch. Thus, when the spring of 1847 rolled around, thousands of volunteers demanded their discharge—even though the war's end was nowhere in sight.

Recognizing the flaws in its original volunteer mobilization plan by the autumn of 1846, the Polk Administration resolved to enlist all additional citizen soldiers for the duration. In November, the War Department released a series of calls for 6,750 long-term volunteers in eight infantry regiments, a separate foot company, and a cavalry regiment. On 19 April 1847, the Secretary of War requested three more regiments, five battalions, and several unattached companies.

Unfortunately, by the time the government adopted its new enlistment policy, popular support for the war was waning. 'No sir-ee!' exclaimed a Massachusetts man. 'As long as I can work, beg, or go to the poor house, I won't go to Mexico, to be lodged on the damp ground, half starved, half roasted, bitten by mosquetoes [sic] and centipedes, stung by scorpions and tarantulas—marched, drilled, and flogged, and then stuck up to be shot at, for eight dollars a month and putrid rations.' Even staunch patriots were reluctant to sign up for so indefinite a period as 'during the War with Mexico.'

To encourage enlistments, Congress offered volunteers the same land bonuses made available to regulars by the Ten Regiment Act. Veteran volunteers already in

Mexico were tempted to re-enlist for the war with a $12 bounty. Broadsides for Colonel Caleb Cushing's Massachusetts Volunteer Regiment advertised a $24 bounty and a $21 advance in pay to each man who joined. Other units proffered similar fringe benefits, but none of these enticements met with more than partial success.

Swallowing their scruples, recruiters snared the gullible and the desperate by stooping to underhanded tricks. A member of the 1st New York Regiment ruefully recalled: 'The privates . . . were all promised "roast beef and two dollars a day," "plenty of whiskey," "golden Jesuses," "pretty Mexican gals," "safe investments, quick returns," and everything pictured to the fancy.' Lies like these lured 800 men into the 1st New York, but only 300 were white, native-born Americans. The rest were European immigrants, with a handful of Chinamen and American Indians. The regiment was also reduced to accepting jailbirds, tramps, paupers, and men previously rejected as unfit. 'A more rascally, *lousy* set was never thrown among decent men,' wrote one of their brothers-in-arms.

The United States fielded 71,776 to 73,260 volunteers during the Mexican War. Twenty-seven thousand were one-year men, and 33,500 served the duration. The remaining 12,500 or so were classified as statutory militia, who soldiered three to six months. Volunteers constituted 58 per cent of America's combat force, and all but 2,000 saw some sort of active duty.

European observers, mindful of the U.S. Army's dismal showing in the War in 1812, expected the Mexicans to thrash their opponents. Instead, the Mexican War became a sequence of American triumphs.

Striding across the Great Plains in staggered batches, the Army of the West, a conglomeration of American regulars and volunteers, overran New Mexico with surprising ease, and then dispatched a detachment to help American settlers and naval units take control of California. During these operations, two foot formations displayed admirable fortitude and endurance. Departing Fort Leavenworth in June 1846, a two-company battalion of 'long-legged infantry' from Missouri tramped 600 miles in twenty-nine days. The five-company Mormon Battalion, drawn from refugees fleeing religious persecution in Illinois, covered the 1,125 tortuous miles between Santa Fe and San Diego in 102 days, the troops marching themselves ragged and nearly shoeless to drag the first wagon train over the Rocky Mountains.

While the Army of the West was accomplishing so much with very little, Washington funneled most of its military resources to Zachary Taylor for a campaign in northern Mexico. In September 1846, Taylor hurled his army of 6,220 at the city of Monterrey, which he took from a garrison of 7,303 in three days of savage combat. The 3rd, 4th, 5th, 7th, and 8th U.S. Infantry, the 1st Tennessee and 1st Ohio Regiments, and the 1st Mississippi Rifles won recognition for their valor, but at a frightful cost. Losing a quarter of its men to carry a fort, the 1st Tennessee earned the nickname the 'Bloody First.' In stubborn street fighting on 23 September, the 3rd Infantry saw five out of twelve officers present slain.

As Taylor's army licked its wounds and consolidated its gains, the Polk Administration abruptly changed its military strategy. The President and his advisers decided that the swiftest way to end the war was to land an army at Vera Cruz and march it inland to capture Mexico City, the enemy capital. Having developed an intense dislike for Taylor, Polk entrusted the undertaking to Major General Winfield Scott.

Scott stripped Taylor's army of almost all its regulars and seasoned volunteers to assemble enough men for the Vera Cruz expedition. By February 1847, a disgusted Taylor commanded only 4,759 troops, including 4,242 volunteers—all but 368 of the latter uninitiated to the sting of battle. Hurrying northward before Scott could invest Vera Cruz, Mexico's leading general, Antonio Lopez de Santa Anna, struck Taylor with an army of 15,142 at Buena Vista on 22 February 1847. Outnumbered three-to-one, the Americans held their ground for two days, inflicting 3,439 casualties on their assailants. Taylor's artillery saved the day for the *Yanquis,* ably supported by such volunteer organizations as the 1st Illinois, 2nd Illinois, 2nd Kentucky, and 3rd Indiana Infantry. Perhaps the outstanding heroes of the battle were Jefferson Davis and his Mississippi Rifles, who counter-attacked repeatedly against superior numbers and halted two major Mexican drives. Taylor lost 14 per cent of his men before the fighting closed, but he beat Santa Anna. Buena Vista was the shining hour of the American volunteer in the Mexican War.

A few days later, General Scott disembarked 8,600 troops near Vera Cruz, which surrendered on 29 March after a short siege. Pushing west from the coast, Scott found Santa Anna and 12,000 Mexicans blocking the road to Mexico City in the mountain pass at Cerro Gordo. Slipping a column around the enemy's left, Scott neatly extricated Santa Anna from the pass on 17-18 April, capturing over 3,000 Mexican troops at a tenth of the cost.

Shortly thereafter, Scott was forced to suspend his offensive when 3,000 of his short-term volunteers refused to extend their enlistments. Their departure crippled Scott's army. But reinforcements were on the way—elements of the ten new regular regiments and long-term volunteers. On 7 August 1847, Scott renewed his march on Mexico City with over 10,000 effectives at his beck and call.

The blue silk regimental color of the 8th U.S. Infantry, carried through eight engagements in the Mexican War. The flag was planted on the Mexican battlements at Churubusco by the 8th's adjutant, First Lieutenant James Longstreet. Second Lieutenant George E. Pickett bore the banner in the assault on Chapultepec. Both officers were destined to become famous Confederate generals. The bald eagle was painted with brown and white feathers, clutching a green olive branch with red berries in one talon, and a bunch of arrows with gold heads, brown shafts, and white feathers in the other. The flag's fringe, the lettering, the stars, and all edging around the red scrolls and the eagle's shield are gold.

Scott's Mexico City Campaign was one of the most brilliant in the military annals of America. Cutting loose from his supply line in the face of 30,000 Mexican soldiers, Scott advanced relentlessly over rough, semi-mountainous terrain, preserving the lives of his own troops whenever possible by substituting skillful flanking movements for frontal assaults. Yet for all Scott's finesse, he had to fight some desperate battles. The Mexicans made things doubly difficult by emplacing their infantry and artillery behind earthworks, stone buildings, and other fortifications, but at every encounter, American generalship and American bravery proved unbeatable.

Scott's victories were emblazoned upon the colors of the regiments which followed him—Contreras and Churubusco (19–20 August 1847), Molino del Rey (8 September), Chapultepec, the Belen Gate, and the San Cosme Gate (13 September)—culminating in the fall of Mexico City on 14 September. In the process, Scott's splendid little army killed or wounded 7,000 Mexican troops, took 3,700 prisoners, and captured seventy-five cannon. A nonplussed Santa Anna commented: 'I believe if we were to plant our batteries in Hell the damned Yankees would take them from us.'

Throughout the campaign, the hardest work usually fell to Scott's regular infantrymen, and they never flagged. This account of the advance of Bennet Riley's brigade at Contreras by Second Lieutenant William M. Gardner, 2nd U.S. Infantry, typifies the behavior of all the doughboys who had a hand in the seizure of Mexico City:

'We [the 2nd Infantry, 7th Infantry, and 4th Artillery—the latter acting as 'red-legged infantry'] marched towards them . . . under heavy fire of musketry, . . . then halted, and deployed column. During all this time we had not fired a shot and men were dropping in our ranks at every moment. I admire the coolness of our men during this trying time even more than their headlong impetuosity after the word *charge* was given. When we had deployed in line of battle, we gave them a volley and then made a head long rush, the enemy could not stand this more than twenty minutes. They then broke.'

With Vera Cruz and their capital in American hands, the Mexicans had no hope of winning the war, but months passed before this proud people admitted defeat. A peace treaty was finally signed at Guadalupe Hidalgo on 2 February 1848. Under its terms, Mexico renounced ownership of Texas, Upper California, and New Mexico. In return, the United States paid Mexico $15,000,000 and agreed to assume up to $3,250,000 in damage claims held against Mexico by American citizens.

The United States paid another price for her new western empire in a medium more precious than gold—lives. The regular army lost 930 dead as a result of combat, and 4,899 more carried off by accident or disease. Another 2,745 American regulars suffered non-fatal wounds, and 2,554 were invalided out of the service. Seven hundred and eleven volunteers were killed or mortally wounded, 6,256 died of sickness or accidents, and 7,200 were discharged for sickness. American forces also suffered 9,207 desertions—5,331 from the regulars and 3,876 from the volunteers. Only 1.5 per cent of the American troops engaged in the Mexican War died of battlefield causes, but more than 25 per cent were maimed, crippled, or killed by some ailment or mishap.

6 A Skeleton Grappling with a Giant

1848–61

The U.S. Army emerged from the Mexican War with an improved image, heightened morale, and heavier responsibilities. Between 1845 and 1848, the United States pushed her boundaries across North America to the Pacific, snapping up 1,200,000 square miles of territory. While using force to secure the safety of Texas and wrest an additional 592,201 square miles from Mexico, the Polk Administration acquired most of the Oregon Country south of the 49th parallel in an 1846 treaty with Great Britain.

America's expansionist spree saddled the Army with tremendous challenges. In 1848, there were 400,000 non-Indians—Americans, Europeans, former Mexican nationals, and Negro slaves—living west of the first tier of trans-Mississippi states. The lush Pacific Northwest attracted American farmers like a magnet. California grew even more alluring when gold was discovered

there in 1848, sparking a rush of fortune hunters that blossomed into one of history's great mass migrations. Subsequent gold and silver strikes over the next decade spread the mining frontier across the Sierra Nevada and Rocky Mountains. The same period witnessed the first significant lodgment of American farmers on the Great Plains, with the opening of Kansas and Nebraska in the mid-1850s. By 1860, the number of settlers in the Far West had tripled, and all those people were clamoring for protection against their Indian neighbors. Bounding beyond the picket line of forts overlooking the

When Frank B. Mayer sketched these regular infantrymen at Fort Snelling, Minnesota Territory, in 1851, they were still wearing the Model 1839 forage caps and the sky blue jackets and trousers of the Mexican War era.

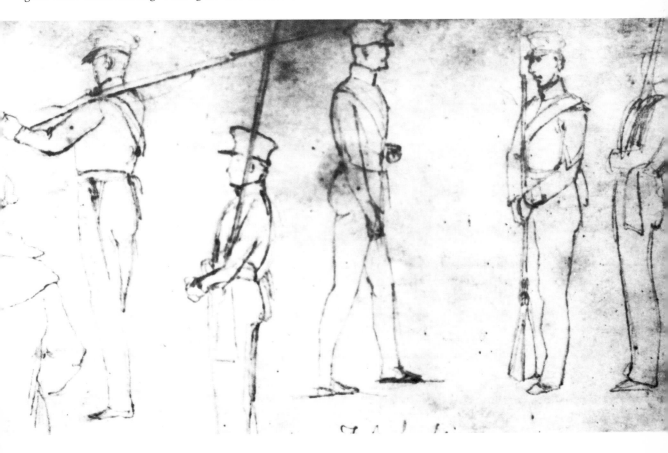

Captain Julius Hayden, 2nd U.S. Infantry, was still wearing an 1847-regulation frock coat when he sat for this photograph in 1852 or 1853. But he did have a pair of the new light blue shoulder straps with gold borders and bars. The Regulations of 1851 also permitted officers to have white vests with small regimental buttons as pictured here.

approaches to the Great Plains, Americans rendered the notion of a permanent Indian frontier obsolete. Now soldiers would have to enter Indian country and take up permanent residence there.

The vast realm the United States obtained in the 1840s was home to 200,000 Indians. In addition, the Army had to worry about the 75,000 nomadic tribesmen still roaming wild and free on the unorganized stretches of the Louisiana Purchase, plus the 84,000 civilized Indians dumped on the eastern fringes of the Great Plains. At first, many tribes were favorably disposed towards Americans, but the teeming waves of emigrants surging across the plains and deserts after the Mexican War altered native attitudes. The pale-skinned intruders disturbed the migratory habits of the buffalo and other game on which the red man depended. They spread

virulent diseases and liquor among the tribes. They stole Indian land, and they murdered natives who got in the way. Proud peoples like the Sioux, Cheyenne, Apache, Navajo, Kiowa, Comanche, Yakima, and Spokane reacted to the mounting white pressure by striking back. As a result, the Army was compelled to engage the tribes of the Far West in more than 200 battles and skirmishes during the years 1848 to 1861.

The need for a large regular force to police the country's enlarged western holdings was obvious, but the American people and their elected officials, ignoring inconvenient realities, saw things differently. On 6 July 1848, President Polk assured Congress that 'the old army, as it existed before the war with Mexico,' was more than ample for any contingency. Before the summer was out, the 3rd Dragoons, the Voltigeur Regiment, the 9th through 16th Infantry, and all the volunteers were disbanded. Of the units formed during the Mexican War, only the Regiment of Mounted Riflemen, eight companies of regular artillery, and the Company of Sappers, Miners and Pontoniers were incorporated into the standing army. Congress also limited the military establishment to 10,000 officers and men. The number of privates declined to forty-two per infantry and artillery company, fifty per dragoon company, and sixty-four per Mounted Rifle company. Each regiment was also allowed to keep the second major approved on 11 February 1847.

The reductions of 1848 diminished the Army's morale as much as its size. The idea of 10,000 soldiers defending a country with a land area of 3,000,000 square miles was not a cheering thought to the men in blue. A smaller Army meant a logjam in officers' promotions and more work for all hands. Once again, regiments splintered into company-sized bits, which were then scattered over some of the most godforsaken terrain ever seen by the American soldier. With only three cavalry regiments in its order of battle, the Army's composition clashed with the nature of its frontier mission. Roughly four-fifths of the regulars were foot soldiers—infantry and artillery— and yet the government expected them to contend with superbly mounted tribesmen. An irritated Texas congressman characterized the Plains Indians as 'the most expert riders in the world, not excepting the Arabs. You can neither fight nor pursue them with infantry or artillery. . . . These corps might as well be a thousand miles distant. They never can come up with the enemy.'

Nonetheless, the Army tried hard with what it had. In the twelve years following the Mexican War, a few thousand overworked regulars erected dozens of forts in Texas, the Mexican Cession (California and New Mexico), the Oregon Country, and the Great Plains, giving some substance to America's claims over her new possessions.

First Lieutenant Winfield Scott Hancock, the adjutant of the 6th U.S. Infantry, posed proudly with his three-year-old son, Russell, in 1853. Hancock is garbed in the 'plain dark blue body coat' authorized in 1851 strictly for off-duty wear.

In the days before transcontinental railroads, supplying the Army's western garrisons was a nightmare. Many new posts were situated far from navigable rivers in desert or hill country. The cost of transporting men and matériel to such locations was high, and the process was time consuming. In the interests of speed, the War Department sometimes shipped units to the Pacific Coast via Panama. Sailing from an Atlantic port, the troops would disembark on the isthmus, march to the Pacific shore, and then board steamers for the second leg of the voyage. While it was certainly quicker than an overland trek across the Great Plains and the Rockies, the Panamanian passage could be deadly. Crossing the isthmus in the summer of 1852, the 4th U.S. Infantry lost over 100 soldiers, camp followers, and children (one-seventh of the regimental party) to yellow fever and other diseases. Even after it cleared Panama, First

Lieutenant Ulysses S. Grant knew that the 4th's trials had only just begun. 'How we will be situated is as yet all in the dark,' he wrote his wife on 16 August. 'It may be that we will have to tramp over the country looking after Indians for months, or it may be that we will be quiet, but in tents, without a single comfort.'

Whenever western tribes took to the warpath, doughboys and red-legged infantry—either on their own or in concert with dragoons and Mounted Riflemen—took the field to chastise the red marauders. That usually meant tortuous forced marches for the foot soldiers. In March 1856, the 3rd U.S. Infantry hiked 500 miles up and down New Mexico Territory in search of hostile Gila and Mogollon Apaches. Later that year, Company K of the 4th Infantry hotfooted it forty miles a day for several days to head off an Indian uprising in the Pacific Northwest. Between 1855 and 1859, Company E of the 6th Infantry, a regiment that saw extensive service on the Great Plains, traversed 7,500 miles—6,000 on foot and 1,500 by water. Of that distance, 2,400 miles were marched in a single year!

The toll such campaigning took of the men in the ranks was described by Eugene Bandel, a Prussian immigrant and a sergeant in the 6th Infantry's Company E. On 6 September 1857, he scribbled in his diary: 'Our sufferings have been severe, sometimes because of scarcity of water and sometimes on account of too much moisture. . . . Our shoes are absolutely worn out, and the best of mending will do no good. Some of the men are barefoot, which is no pleasure where rattlesnakes are numerous, and scorpions and tarantulas abound, and where the cactus and Spanish bayonet often grow ranker than the grass, and where we often have to march for miles over solid rock.'

A determined pursuit did not always guarantee the foot soldiers success—especially when the Indians were vigilant. Enterprising infantry officers occasionally improved unit mobility by mounting their companies on horses or mules for field operations. The practice was common among the 1st, 3rd, and 8th Infantry while they were stationed in Texas. Congress sanctioned the idea in June 1850, and it caught on throughout the Army. Company I of the 4th Infantry functioned mounted in the Pacific Northwest late in the summer of 1854. Company E, 10th Infantry, fought mounted on 3 September 1855 at the Battle of Ash Hollow, a resounding white victory over the Brule and Oglala Sioux. Early in 1861, a company of the 7th Infantry rode mules from Fort Buchanan to Apache Pass for a confrontation with the famed Chiricahua chief, Cochise.

Not everyone was impressed by the performance of mounted infantrymen. Foot soldiers made indifferent riders, and they found it awkward to load and fire their weapons from horse or muleback. At the very best, these ersatz dragoons were a stopgap measure. What the Army urgently needed was more men.

Congress could not ignore the facts forever. On 17 June 1850, it authorized the President to raise the number of privates in every regular company assigned to the frontier to seventy-four. In effect, the legislation expanded the Army's statutory strength to about 14,000. However, the Army's actual size failed to stretch much above the 10,000-mark until a second troop increase in 1855.

As soon as the Mexican War became history, the American public lost its new-found respect for the regular army. Yesterday's heroes were now just another irksome government expense. 'A soldier at that period was but little respected,' recalled Augustus Meyers, who enlisted in the 2nd Infantry as a drummer in 1854. With so many opportunities for economic success in the civilian world, most Americans suspected that a soldier was, as Meyers phrased it, 'an individual too lazy to work for a living.'

Recruiting regulars in peacetime remained as difficult as ever, and the Army continued to draw on its traditional sources of manpower—the destitute, the dissolute, the disoriented, and the naïve. During the 1850s, twice as many immigrants enlisted as native Americans, a trend that did nothing to endear the Army to the xenophobic nation it served. Half of the foreigners hailed from Ireland and a fifth from Germany. By and large, they made good soldiers. Fewer of them deserted or were dishonorably discharged than soldiers born in the United States. But many foreign enlistees were recent arrivals who had not yet adjusted to American life. Army recruiters also disregarded age and physical standards with alarming regularity. After touring the Department of New Mexico in the second half of 1853, Colonel Joseph K. F. Mansfield of the Inspector General's Department warned against 'enlisting near sighted men and men that cannot understand English.'

Whatever their national origins, America's common soldiers were mainly of the rough and tumble variety. 'The greater part of the army consists of men who either do not care to work, or who, because of being addicted to drink, cannot find employment,' asserted Sergeant Bandel. 'There are some exceptions to this. . . . These get on very well. . . . The others have nothing to do with me, nor I with them, except so far as my duty brings me in contact with them.'

The Army was accustomed to turning society's rejects into solid soldiers, but desertion emptied the ranks almost as fast as they were filled. The scourge was particularly prevalent on the West Coast, where hundreds of troops slipped away after succumbing to gold fever. Elsewhere, the causes of desertion were the same as they had been since the Army's inception. Even an outstanding non-commissioned officer like Sergeant Bandel admitted that soldiering was rarely fun: 'It is either a very lazy, tedious sort of life, or else one that demands the last ounce of physical strength and such as only an iron constitution can stand.' Toward the end of his enlistment in 1859, Bandel wrote: 'The hardships in the United States army are greater than any other. . . . Moreover, a soldier here is always in places where civilization has not yet arrived, and everything is therefore very expensive.'

During the 1850s, the U.S. Army suffered an annual attrition rate of 28 per cent due to desertion, discharge, and death from combat, accident, or disease. Consequently, western garrisons were woefully short-handed. While in New Mexico in August 1853, Colonel Mansfield counted the names of 798 captains, lieutenants, and enlisted men on the company rolls of the 3rd Infantry. That averaged out to nearly eighty soldiers per company, just six short of the total approved for frontier service. But upon closer examination, Mansfield ascertained that only seventeen officers and 629 other ranks were present for duty with their respective commands, and forty-three of them were too sick to stand in line. That whittled down the average to approximately sixty-one per company.

Conditions were worse in the Pacific Northwest, with its proximity to the California gold fields. Take as a

PLATE 16: THE REGULATIONS OF 1851—AND VARIATIONS
On the parade ground before the officers' quarters at Fort Scott, Kansas.
53. Drummer, 3rd U.S. Infantry, Recruiting Service, 1853: With the Regulations of 1851, uniform styles inspired by the French Army superseded the marked British influence that had flavored American military dress since the colonial era. At the same time, 'light or Saxony blue' became the U.S. Infantry's facing color. A company musician sported a light blue plastron on the breast of his newly authorized frock coat. Each half-chevron on the lower sleeve stood for five years of service; a red border signified wartime service. *54. Private, 9th U.S. Infantry, Dress Uniform, 1857:* In 1854, the light blue band on the infantryman's dress cap was reduced to a narrow welt. The coat's facings suffered a similar fate, and brass scales replaced the worsted epaulettes. Upon their organization in 1855, the 9th and 10th Infantry received chasseur-à-pied frock coats, Model 1855 rifles, saber bayonets, and chasseur waistbelts, which held Model 1855 cartridge boxes and brass attachments for knapsack straps. *55. First Sergeant, 3rd U.S. Infantry, Recruiting Service, 1853:* The Regulations of 1851 restored downward-pointing rank chevrons. Aside from recruiting parties, infantry units did not receive their frock coats until 1854. All enlisted men wore dark blue welts down the outer seams of their trousers. Sergeant majors, quartermaster sergeants, chief musicians, chief buglers, and first sergeants were to wear a red worsted sash. Figure 55 is armed with a .69-caliber Model 1842 percussion musket and a Model 1840 non-commissioned officer's sword.

53. Drummer, 3rd U.S. Infantry, Recruiting
Service, 1853

54. Private, 9th U.S. Infantry, Dress
Uniform, 1857

55. First Sergeant, 3rd U.S. Infantry,
Recruiting Service, 1853

typical example Company B, 4th U.S. Infantry, part of the garrison at Fort Humbolt in northern California. In July 1854, Company B's first lieutenant was absent on recruiting duty, and its second lieutenant was detached for service in New Mexico. Out of an aggregate of thirty-eight enlisted men, just two sergeants, two corporals, one musician, and seventeen privates were present for duty, and one man was in the guardhouse, two were sick, and eleven were assigned extra daily duty. That left one captain and eight rank and file to carry on with the everyday work of the post.

Another major deficiency in the Army of the 1850s was lack of thorough training. Recruits were shipped west with little or no schooling in any military skills. It was expected they would pick up what they needed to know once they joined their companies. 'Here it is proper to remark,' noted Colonel Mansfield in 1853, 'that there has been too few officers at their companies to secure instruction to the rank and file.' Whatever

Colonel George Wright of the newly formed 9th U.S. Infantry, circa 1855. Wright's double-breasted 1851-regulation frock coat has gilt buttons and a pair of large gold epaulettes. Accompanying his regiment to the Pacific Northwest in 1856, Wright soon earned a reputation as one of the Army's best Indian fighters.

training a soldier received came at those rare intervals in the frontier Army's grinding routine of post-building, post maintenance, road construction, escort duty, and campaigning. In the same report quoted above, Mansfield particularly criticized the failure of frontier commanders to encourage marksmanship:

'My impressions are that the practice of firing at the target with ball and buck is not sufficient. The mere discharge of the guard of the previous day at the target to get rid of the load [in each sentry's musket] is not sufficient practice, and there is not interest enough taken in it by the men to produce any real improvement. It requires great use of the ball cartridge to make the soldier confident in what he can do with his musket. It requires a good sized cartridge to throw a ball to produce effect at long range, and light as the musket now is the soldier frequently flinches at the recoil, which practice alone can correct.'

As Mansfield sweated over his inspection reports, someone in Washington was working just as hard to remedy the Army's ills. That champion was Jefferson Davis, the Mississippi politician and Mexican War hero who served as Secretary of War from 1853 to 1857, during the presidency of Franklin Pierce. A West Point graduate with seven years of regular service to his credit (five with the 1st Infantry and two with the 1st Dragoons), Davis came to his cabinet post with a keen appreciation of the Army's problems. Throughout his tenure at the War Department, he lobbied unceasingly to provide the military with the manpower and the tools it needed to accomplish its mission.

Wielding all the patronage and pressure the Pierce Administration could muster, Davis prevailed on Congress to accept a substantial pay raise for the Army on 4 August 1854. Each enlisted man received $4 more a month. An infantry private's salary shot from $7 to $11; a corporal's to $13; and a sergeant's to $17. The legislation contained other good news for the common soldier. For the first time in its history, the regular army was permitted to offer veteran troops longevity pay. Any man who stayed in the service was pledged an extra $2 a month for his first re-enlistment, and $1 more a month for each hitch after that. Davis did not forget the commissioned ranks either. On 21 February 1857, a few days before he left office, he prodded Congress into adding $20 to the monthly pay of all Army officers—regardless of grade.

Davis scored his greatest coup on 3 March 1855, when Congress created four new regiments for frontier service—the 9th and 10th U.S. Infantry and the 1st and 2nd U.S. Cavalry. This act elevated the Army's troop ceiling to a maximum of 18,000.

The Davis reforms made an immediate impact. Between March 1853 and December 1855, the Army's strength grew from 10,745 to 15,753 officers and men. Yet none of the wonders Davis worked could cure the ongoing desertion epidemic. In 1856 alone, 3,223 soldiers took 'French leave,' as desertion was then called. Of the first 500 men to join the 10th Infantry in 1855, 275 deserted before their five years were up. While campaigning in southern Kansas in May 1857, Company E of the 6th Infantry lost nine of its sixty-one rank and file to desertion in fourteen days.

Davis could not be blamed for these losses, but he had his critics. Some Army leaders took exception to his policy on officer appointments. To line up political support for his expansion program, Davis filled 116 officer vacancies in 1855 and 1856 with civilians—undoubtedly a sop to key congressmen. At that time, the U.S. Infantry had 351 officers—236 products of West Point, thirteen promoted from the ranks, and 102 appointed from civil life (sixty-one in 1855 and 1856 alone). Career officers resented seeing political pets

placed in grades equal or superior to their own. Nonetheless, a good share of the civil appointees were Mexican War veterans or West Pointers who had failed to graduate, and they blended in well with the rest of the officer corps.

Despite the existence of political preferment, by the mid-1850s nearly three-quarters of the Army's officers were West Point graduates. Though they did not yet dominate the Army's upper echelons, the gentlemen from the Military Academy fostered continuing progress within the military by imposing their notions of professionalism on the company, battalion, and regimental level.

Without disparaging their valuable contributions, it must be said that West Pointers were not always a blessing on the frontier. The Military Academy in-

An unidentified second lieutenant of the 10th U.S. Infantry, circa 1855. The dark blue Model 1851 dress cap is adorned with a light blue pompon, an eagle and a bugle embroidered in gold, and a silver regimental number. An infantry officer's epaulette consisted of a light blue strap edged with gold lace, with a solid gilt crescent and gold bullion fringe at the outer end. A circle of light blue cloth bearing the owner's regimental number in gold and a border of embroidered silver was placed within the curve of the crescent. Note also the lieutenant's crimson sash, white leather gauntlets, and Model 1850 sword.

A charming daguerreotype of an unidentified second lieutenant of the 8th U.S. Infantry and his pretty young wife, circa 1853–5. This reversed image shows the lieutenant wearing his shoulder straps on his epaulettes. Though not sanctioned by regulations, this style was adopted by other American officers in the 1850s.

Proudly displaying their new 1851-regulation frock coats, two freshly graduated West Pointers, Brevet Second Lieutenant George Crook, 4th U.S. Infantry (left), and Brevet Second Lieutenant John Nugen, 2nd U.S. Infantry (right), pose with an unlucky classmate, Philip H. Sheridan, in the summer of 1852. Sheridan was suspended for a year for menacing a superior Southern cadet with a bayonet in 1851, and did not graduate until 1853. The small ante-bellum regular army did not possess enough officers' vacancies immediately to accommodate every product of the Military Academy. Newly graduated cadets were designated brevet second lieutenants until a permanent slot opened in some regiment.

structed young men in the intricacies of military engineering and conventional warfare. Indian fighting was not part of the curriculum. Hence, many a green subaltern headed west with little knowledge and less respect for the American Indian. Some officers learned from their field experience and became first-rate Indian fighters. Some remained invincibly ignorant. One West Pointer denied a chance to profit from his mistakes was Brevet Second Lieutenant John L. Grattan, Class of 1853.

On 19 August 1854, the commandant at Fort Laramie sent Grattan with an interpreter, two non-commissioned officers, twenty-seven privates of Company G, 6th U.S. Infantry, and two 12-pound guns to a nearby encampment of 4,000 Sioux. Grattan's assignment was to arrest a Miniconjou brave accused of slaying a cow belonging

PLATE 17: IN THE FIELD IN THE '50s
Background figures based on a contemporary Harper's Weekly engraving of the Utah Expedition.

56. Private, 1st U.S. Infantry, Mounted Service, 1853: *An officer's wife on the Texas frontier described the men of the 1st's mounted detachment as clad in shirts of a 'dark blue check material.' The old 1839 forage cap saw service well into the 1850s. This private holds a Model 1842 smoothbore percussion musket.* **57. Private, 6th U.S. Infantry, Campaign Dress, 1857:** *Frontier foot soldiers often campaigned in civilian clothes. As Sergeant Eugene Bandel of the 6th wrote on 18 May 1857: 'You should see us here in our prairie outfits. . . . Every man is wearing a broad-brimmed hat, each of a different color; white trousers of rough material [tent canvas]; a woolen shirt of red, green, blue, or brown . . . , usually open in the front and worn like a coat; the shoes (we still have shoes, though who knows how soon we may have to wear moccasins) with the uppers slashed wherever they might chafe in marching. . . . The bayonets of the privates are with the baggage; my sword, too, is in the wagon, for there is no such thing as hand-to-hand combat with the Indians. Every man carries a long hunting knife in his belt, and some a five or six-shot revolver. A gun over the shoulder completes the soldier.' Note the Model 1855 rifle musket and Colt Model 1851 .36-caliber Navy revolver.*

58. Quartermaster Sergeant, 5th U.S. Infantry, Campaign Dress, 1858: *The doughboys assigned to the Utah Expedition wore 1839 forage caps and uniform jackets normally issued to the Army's mounted regiments. Green facings reveal this jacket was made originally for the Regiment of Mounted Riflemen. The boots are non-regulation. Note the Model 1855 rifle musket and Model 1840 non-commissioned officer's sword. The brass hook securing one of the knapsack straps has dug into the waistbelt, thus hiding itself from view.*

56. Private, 1st U.S. Infantry, Mounted
Service, 1853

58. Quartermaster Sergeant, 5th U.S.
Infantry, Campaign Dress, 1858

57. Private, 6th U.S. Infantry, Campaign
Dress, 1857

to a passing emigrant. The disparity in numbers between his detachment and the Indians did not worry the fire-eating shavetail. He had once bragged that he could whip the entire Sioux nation with twenty doughboys and a howitzer. He now had a chance to prove that boast. Instead of surrendering the cow-killer, some Sioux tried to surround the soldiers. Grattan's response was to fire his two cannon at the encampment, but the guns were poorly aimed and the balls flew too high to do any damage. The enraged Indians were on top of the troops before the whites could reload. Only one private escaped the slaughter, but he was so badly wounded that he died soon after regaining Fort Laramie.

For every reckless fool like Grattan, there was an officer like Second Lieutenant Edward L. Hartz of the the 8th Infantry. In July 1857, Hartz set a cunning trap for Apaches who were raiding traffic along the El Paso road in southwestern Texas. He loaded two infantry companies into some supply wagons at Fort Lancaster. With the troops hidden beneath the canvas covers, the bogus provisions train rolled westward. When Hartz's caravan was forty-five miles from the fort, the Indians pounced. Much to their surprise, they ran into brisk musketry from eighty doughboys. A lively contest ensued, but the Apaches got the worst of it and were finally routed.

Not every successful officer in the 1850s earned his reputation by killing Indians. Climaxing an exhausting pursuit, Lieutenant Colonel Dixon S. Miles and 300 3rd Infantrymen cornered nearly the entire Mescalero Apache tribe in a New Mexican canyon on 2 April 1855. With escape impossible, the chiefs waved a white flag and begged for peace. The Mescaleroes were guilty of numerous depredations, but Miles foreswore the glory of certain victory and treated them with mercy. 'What a beautiful chance for a fight,' Miles wrote wistfully. 'The troops will never get such another. But they [the Indians] have met me in faith trusting to my honor.' Another commendable act of humanity occurred in Texas on 23 May 1859, when Captain J. B. Plummer and two companies of the 1st Infantry shielded the peaceful occupants of the Brazos Indian Agency from 250 blood-thirsty white vigilantes.

Though battling Indians was the Army's primary pastime, it aimed its grandest punitive campaign of the 1850s against a white community in Utah, namely the Mormons of the Salt Lake Basin. Reluctant to take direction from anyone not of their faith, the Mormons harassed the officials Washington sent to govern Utah, a portion of the Mexican Cession. This obdurance aroused the ire of President James Buchanan, Pierce's successor in the White House, and the Army was called into the picture. On 28 May 1857, Commanding General Winfield Scott ordered the concentration of 2,500

regulars at Fort Leavenworth for operations against the Mormons. In June 1857, the 5th and 10th Infantry, accompanied by two batteries of artillery, began plodding westward. This contingent was followed in September by six companies of the 2nd Dragoons.

Unimpressed by the size of the 'Utah Expedition,' Mormon militia—resorting to guerrilla tactics—slipped past the approaching regulars to destroy seventy-five Army wagons stocked with sixty days' worth of provisions near the Green River on 2 October. Short of food and buffeted by heavy snows, the troops were forced to winter in the Rockies near Bridger's Fort. Reacting promptly to the crisis, the War Department dispatched reinforcements—among them the hard-marching 6th Infantry— and a large supply train to save the Utah Expedition from starvation. The relief parties reached their stranded comrades in May and June 1858, staving off disaster by a slim margin. However, before the Utah Expedition could get into shape for the final

Colonel Edmund Brooke Alexander, 10th U.S. Infantry, circa 1855–60. According to the Regulations of 1851 and 1857, field officers were supposed to wear double-breasted frock coats with seven buttons in each row. Alexander is clutching his Model 1850 staff and field officer's sword.

push to Salt Lake City, the Mormon capital, the rebels backed down and promised to submit to the federal government. An unpleasant incident had been narrowly averted, but an infinitely worse showdown pitting American against American was just three years in the offing.

Jefferson Davis contributed his share to the coming carnage by presiding over a revolutionary change in the Army's primary weapons system. In 1855, the rifle musket replaced the smoothbore musket as the standard arm of the U.S. Infantry.

Rifles had been employed in modest quantities by American forces since before 1775, but their usefulness was limited because they required more time to load than smoothbores. In the age of muzzleloaders, the only way the common lead ball could catch in the rifling once it was fired was to grip the spiral grooves as it was rammed home. In other words, rifle balls had to be a little larger than the bore and literally pounded down the barrel, or

Assistant Surgeon Albert James Myer, circa 1855–6. Myer served in Texas, where he frequently ministered to officers and men of the 8th U.S. Infantry. Like many other frontier regulars, Myer preferred civilian clothing for campaign wear, preserving his uniform for garrison duty. His weapon is a privately purchased Model 1855 Colt-Root percussion repeating rifle.

the rifling would not bite. This laborious procedure retarded the rate of fire. During the War of Independence, for instance, a musketman could load and fire three or four times as fast as an expert rifleman.

Then in the late 1840s, Captain Claude E. Minié of the French Army developed an elongated projectile which made it possible to shoot a rifle as rapidly as a musket. Minié called his invention a 'Cylindro Conoidal ball.' It was actually an oblong bullet with a hollow iron cup fitted at the base. The Minié bullet was slightly smaller than the bore diameter of a rifle so it could easily drop down the barrel, its base coming to rest on a previously inserted powder charge. When the rifleman discharged his piece, the force of the exploding powder drove the iron cup into the bullet, expanding the soft lead enough to 'take' the rifling.

The Minié principle caught on quickly in Europe. It was adopted by Belgium in 1850, followed in short order by France and Britain. The U.S. Army was soon conducting its own experiments with a percussion-lock rifle firing conoidal bullets. In his 1854 annual report, Secretary of War Davis stated that the tests demonstrated 'that the new weapon, while it can be loaded as readily as the ordinary musket, is at least effective at three times the distance.' A few months later, the Army embraced the Minié system. The eight senior infantry regiments received Model 1855 rifle muskets, while the newly formed 9th and 10th Infantry obtained Model 1855 rifles. Both weapons were .58-caliber, with long-range sights and lugs for saber bayonets. But the 1855 rifle was somewhat shorter and a little heavier than the rifle musket.

The Minié bullets distributed to the U.S. Infantry differed in design from the French captain's prototype. A bullet with an iron cap was expensive to manufacture, and it had a tendency to malfunction. Sometimes the cup separated from the bullet and spun off at some crazy tangent as the round exited the muzzle, endangering people standing near the shooter. The all-lead American 'Minié ball' had no cup. It was simply manufactured with a hollow base which expanded with the powder blast to fit the rifle grooves.

American infantrymen were delighted with their new shoulder arms, which far outranged the bows and trade muskets of their Indian opponents. The 1855 rifle and rifle musket had an effective range of 500 to 600 yards (provided the day was clear and the shooter's eyesight was good), and when fired at a massed enemy, could kill at 1,000 yards. Nothing the Indians possessed in the 1850s could come close to that, a circumstance which did wonders for the Bluecoats' morale. Apparently, some effort was expended to furnish the troops with enough practice ammunition so they could learn to aim and fire with effect. 'We could get all the cartridges we wanted,'

Company musicians of the 10th U.S. Infantry at Camp Floyd, Utah Territory, 1858. The regiment's principal musician stands at center wearing an 1839-pattern forage cap and a frock coat decorated with three rows of brass buttons and a pair of sergeant's sky blue chevrons.

Seven of the buglers sport 1854 dress caps—five of them battered out of shape. Four musicians have their frock coats adorned with sky blue lace set in the distinctive 'herring-bone' pattern.

wrote Sergeant Bandel of the 6th Infantry on 24 October 1856. 'The American government is not stingy in this matter. I well remember, when first given a rifle with which to practice, that I used up seventy-five cartridges in one day alone.'

Describing the advance of five companies of his regiment against the Sioux at Ash Hollow in September 1855, Bandel testified: 'We attacked them with our rifles, while their arrows or the bullets from their poor flint-locks could not reach us. They were forced to flee.' At the Battle of Four Lakes, fought on 1 September 1858 in Washington Territory, George Wright, the colonel of the 9th Infantry, engaged up to 700 hostile warriors with less than 600 men drawn from his own regiment, the 3rd Artillery, and the 1st Dragoons. Wright's doughboys and red-legged infantry began knocking Indians off their ponies at a distance of 600 yards. Closing in, the troops easily scattered the tribesmen, killing sixty without sustaining any deaths themselves. In his report, Wright attributed his cheap victory 'to the fact that our long-range rifles can reach the enemy where he cannot reach us.'

While frontier foot soldiers gloried in their temporary advantage, no one stopped to ponder seriously what would happen to American troops if they met a trained foe equipped with Minié rifles. The U.S. Army put that chilling proposition to the test in 1861. The results were not pretty.

PLATE 18: 'HARDEE HATS' AND SHOULDER SCALES, 1858–61

A sunny day at Fort Laramie.

59. First Sergeant, 1st U.S. Infantry, Dress Uniform, 1860: *The Army adopted a felt dress hat for the regular infantry on 24 March 1858. Originally, all ranks looped up their brims on the left side. On 13 March 1861, the U.S. War Department directed officers to loop up their brims on the right. Enlisted men attached brass shoulder scales to their frock coats for dress occasions. The issue of coats with pleated skirts ceased in 1858. Early that same year, the Army changed the color of the trousers of both officers and men to dark blue; non-commissioned officers sported sky-blue stripes along the outer seams. This veteran of fifteen years holds his musket at the 'Guard against Infantry' position from the Army's 1855 drillbook, Rifle and Light Infantry Tactics by Major William J. Hardee.*

60. Bugler, 6th U.S. Infantry, Dress Uniform, 1860: *An infantryman adorned his 'Hardee' hat with a brass bugle, regimental number, and company letter, a worsted cord, and one ostrich feather. In the second half of the 1850s, it became the custom to decorate the breast of an infantry musician's frock coat with a gridwork of sky blue lace known as the 'herring-bone' fashion.* **61. Lieutenant Colonel, 7th U.S. Infantry, Dress Uniform, 1861:** *An infantry officer's hat cord was gold with acorn tips. His hat insignia was a gold embroidered bugle and a silver regimental number on a ground of black velvet. A field officer wore three ostrich feathers on his hat; a company officer had two. The versatile frock coat was worn with epaulettes as part of the dress uniform and with shoulder straps for service. Note the sky blue welt on the trousers (a distinction proper to all infantry officers) and the Model 1850 staff and field officer's sword.*

59. First Sergeant, 1st U.S. Infantry, Dress
Uniform, 1860

60. Bugler, 6th U.S. Infantry, Dress
Uniform, 1860

61. Lieutenant Colonel, 7th U.S. Infantry,
Dress Uniform, 1861

7 The Slaughter of the Innocents
1861–5

On 6 November 1860, the Republican Party, a new Northern-based political coalition dedicated to the containment and eventual eradication of slavery, succeeded in electing Abraham Lincoln President of the United States. Fear and anger swept the states below the Mason/Dixon Line. Despite Lincoln's assurances to the contrary, many Southerners believed the new President meant immediately to dismantle their 'peculiar institution' and the system of white supremacy it supported. Rather than risk the loss of their slave 'property' or bow to a government increasingly dominated by Northerners, citizens of the Deep South embarked upon a radical course. Between 20 December 1860 and 1 February 1861, South Carolina, Mississippi, Florida, Alabama, Georgia, Louisiana, and Texas declared themselves out of the Union. Delegates from the seceded states met at Montgomery, Alabama, on 4 February to form a new Southern republic—the Confederate States of America.

On 6 March 1861, five days before it adopted a national constitution, the Confederate Provisional Congress created an army. It authorized a regular force comprising a corps of engineers, a corps of artillery, six regiments of infantry, and one of cavalry. The new Confederate President, Jefferson Davis, was also empowered to call out 100,000 twelve-month volunteers. Volunteer regiments were to be raised by state governors and then turned over to national authorities. The pay of infantry and artillery privates in the Confederate service was set at $11 a month.

Only a few regular companies ever came into being, but volunteer outfits blossomed all over the South along with the spring flowers. By mid-April, the Confederacy had an army of nearly 67,000. As each state seceded, the federal forts, arsenals, court houses, and customs houses within its borders were occupied by local militia and volunteers. In a matter of weeks, only two installations of any consequence in the Confederacy still flew the Stars and Stripes—the offshore coastal forts at Pensacola,

A sergeant of the crack 7th New York State Militia, which reached Washington, D.C., on 25 April 1861, soon after the fall of Fort Sumter. The 7th wore a gray uniform with black facings. Gray-clad Union regiments were not uncommon during the first year of the Civil War, which led to much confusion on the battlefield. Note the distinctive non-commissioned officer's sword and the Model 1855 rifle musket.

Florida (Fort Pickens), and Charleston, South Carolina (Fort Sumter).

With 183 of its 198 infantry, artillery, and cavalry companies dispersed among seventy-nine frontier posts, the U.S. Army was in no position to oppose the secession movement. Even if the 13,000 to 16,000 blue-clad regulars could have been concentrated rapidly, there were not enough of them to subdue even one Southern state. The Army's effectiveness was further compromised by the resignation of 313 active-duty officers who sided with the Confederacy, leaving 767 to serve the Union. With so few troops on hand, it is no wonder the Lincoln Administration sought to avoid violence in its initial handling of the secession crisis.

The Confederates turned the crisis into a war on 12 April 1861 by unleashing a two-day bombardment on Fort Sumter, forcing the surrender of the tiny Union garrison. On 15 April, President Lincoln appealed for 75,000 state militia to enter federal service for ninety days to suppress the Southern rebellion. The militiamen were to be organized into infantry regiments containing 781 officers and men. Rather than move against their sister slave states, Virginia, Arkansas, North Carolina, and Tennessee joined the Confederacy. The lines were now drawn for the Civil War, the bloodiest conflict in American history.

In the majority of the states still loyal to the Union, the militia systems were so decrepit that many of the units to answer Lincoln's call had to be raised from scratch. Massachusetts proved an exception. Governor John Andrew had been drilling his state militia companies since early January. By nightfall on 17 April, Andrew had four fully-equipped regiments heading southward. Elsewhere, Northern officials matched Andrew's enthusiasm, if not his foresight and efficiency. Five companies of Pennsylvania militia reached Washington on 18 April carrying only thirty-four muskets and no ammunition. Ohio formed twenty-three ninety-day regiments, ten above its quota. The War Department asked New York for seventeen militia regiments, but the Empire State raised thirty-eight infantry regiments boasting 37,000 men—every one enlisted for two full years, not merely three months.

Throughout the North, politicians and private citizens predicted a quick end to the rebellion, but professional soldiers were not as impressed with the raw militiamen flooding into Washington and other rendezvous centers. William Tecumseh Sherman, a West Pointer destined to make a name for himself in this war, huffed, 'You might as well attempt to put out the flames of a burning house with a squirt-gun.'

A similar thought must have crossed Lincoln's mind. Invoking his emergency powers as Commander-in-Chief, the Union President issued a proclamation on 3 May 1861 calling for 42,034 long-term volunteers, 22,714 additional regulars, and 18,000 more sailors. All of these men were to serve three years, unless discharged sooner. The next day, the War Department directed that the volunteers be organized into forty regiments—thirty-nine infantry and one cavalry. Originally, the regular army was slated to receive eight new regiments of infantry, one of cavalry, and one of artillery, but that formula was soon changed to nine infantry regiments and one cavalry regiment. All three-year recruits for the regular and volunteer services received a $100 federal bounty.

Eager to outdo the enemy, the Confederate Congress approved legislation on 8 and 13 May allowing Jefferson Davis to raise as many as 400,000 three-year volunteers. Men could still serve for periods as short as six or twelve months, but only as members of state home-guard units—not the Confederate Army. By early August, the Confederacy had a reported 210,000 troops in the field. Another 200,000 Southerners clamored to get into uniform, but the Davis government did not have weapons for them.

This private of the 6th Virginia Infantry Battalion ('Old Dominion Rifles') typifies the gaudily attired volunteers who sprang to the South's defense in the spring of 1861. His gray hat, jacket, and trousers have green trim.

Six privates of the 4th Michigan Volunteer Infantry in camp near Washington, D.C., in the summer of 1861. The 4th's uniform consisted of dark blue kepis or knit Canadian caps with tassels, sack coats and trousers of the same color as the headgear, and russet leather gaiters. The unit first took the field with Model 1842 smoothbore muskets.

During the first half of 1861, Confederate forces seized 160,000 firearms at federal arsenals and other public repositories in the seceding states, but no more than 20,000 of these were rifles. The rest were smoothbore muskets, many of them antiquated flintlocks converted to the percussion system. The South lacked the industrial capacity to arm its own armies, so the Rebel government sent agents to Europe to buy surplus smallarms. By early 1863, the Confederacy had imported over 80,000 excellent Enfield rifles and 21,000 acceptable smoothbore muskets from England, 27,000 Austrian rifles, and 2,020 Brunswick rifles, with 53,000 more shoulder arms awaiting shipment from London and Vienna. However, Confederate soldiers found that their most reliable source of modern firearms was the Union Army, which they thrashed with such regularity in the first two years of the war. During the major campaigns of 1862, Rebel forces captured over 100,000 Yankee guns. As the second year's fighting drew to a close, most Southern doughboys were toting reliable rifle muskets.

Like the Confederacy, the Union experienced an initial weapons shortage. The 13th New York Infantry, organized at Brooklyn in May 1861, had to leave 200 of its 650 men at home for want of muskets. As late as the summer of 1862, the 24th Iowa Infantry drilled with

PLATE 19: UNION VOLUNTEERS, 1861: THE GAUDY GLORY HUNTERS

62. Corporal, 14th New York State Militia '14th Brooklyn' 1861: In 1860, this proud outfit adopted an elegant chasseur uniform, complete with baggy red trousers, and insisted on keeping the fancy costume throughout its three years of federal service. A red 'button' was added to the blue field on top of the forage cap sometime after 1861. Corporals and privates wore an oval brass belt plate bearing the initials 'SNY' ('State of New York'). During the war, the 14th carried Enfield and Springfield rifle muskets. **63. Private, 83rd Pennsylvania Volunteer Infantry, 1861:** In November 1861, as a reward for its skill on the drill field, this organization received leather shakos with black feather plumes and chasseur uniforms imported from France. **64. Private, 1st Regiment, Rhode Island Detached Militia, 1861:** Commanded by Colonel Ambrose E. Burnside, this ninety-day regiment arrived at Washington, D.C., clad in 'Hardee' hats, long blue flannel shirts worn as blouses, and gray trousers. The Rhode Islanders fought at the First Battle of Bull Run (21 July 1861) with Model 1855 rifle muskets (seen here), Model 1855 rifles, and Burnside carbines. Some men carried privately purchased revolvers. **65. Sergeant, 69th Regiment, New York State Militia, 1861:** Although it wore frock coats with the red facings of the artillery, this regiment of Irish-Americans served as infantry at First Bull Run. The regimental color was a gift from citizens who approved of the 69th's refusal to march in a parade honoring the Prince of Wales during his 1860 visit to New York City.

63. Private, 83rd Pennsylvania Volunteer
Infantry, 1861

65. Sergeant, 69th Regiment, New York
State Militia, 1861

62. Corporal, 14th New York Militia ('14th
Brooklyn'), 1861

64. Private, 1st Regiment, Rhode Island
Detached Militia, 1861

Colonel Micah Jenkins, a blue-blooded plantation aristocrat, gained distinction at the First Battle of Bull Run leading the 5th South Carolina Infantry, and in the Peninsular Campaign with the Palmetto Regiment of Sharpshooters. In conformity with Confederate dress regulations, his gray double-breasted frock coat has a light blue collar and cuffs. His rank is designated by three gold stars on each side of the collar, plus three braids of gold lace set in loops on his coat sleeves and kepi.

Lieutenant Colonel John W. Kimball, 15th Massachusetts Volunteer Infantry, circa 1862, in a uniform prescribed by the U.S. Army's 1861 dress regulations—a double-breasted frock coat with gilt buttons and dark blue trousers with light blue cords adorning the outer seams. Kimball's black Hardee hat sits on a stand at left, with its ostrich feathers, gold hatcord, branch badge (a gold embroidered bugle with a silver regimental number within the bow—both set on a black velvet ground), and brim adornment (a gold embroidered eagle on black velvet). Kimball's light blue shoulder straps have gold borders and a silver leaf at each end.

wooden rifles while it awaited the delivery of guns that could shoot.

These shortcomings were not long-lasting. The North possessed the means and the know-how to equip its armies. In 1860, it was already producing thirty-two times as many firearms as rural Dixie. Nevertheless, it took time to place the section's impressive manufacturing resources on a full wartime footing. In the interim, Washington and the loyal states imported over 1,000,000 rifles and muskets—nearly half of them English Enfields. By 1863, Northern industry had geared itself up for the struggle, and the Union Army was drawing the bulk of its armaments from domestic sources. Before the war's close, federal armories and private factories under government contract turned out more than 2,500,000 smallarms, including 1,700,000 of

the standard, single-shot, muzzleloading Springfield rifle muskets and 340,000 breechloading rifles and carbines.

Unfortunately for the North, her generals were not as able or imaginative as her captains of industry. On 21 July 1861, a Union army of 30,000—largely half-trained militia and volunteers—was disgracefully routed by a slightly smaller and equally green Confederate force at the First Battle of Bull Run. Yankee hopes for a quick end to the rebellion evaporated as panic swept the boys in blue.

The Bull Run battlefield was just twenty-five miles south of Washington, and the Union Congress responded promptly to the setback on 22 July by authorizing the greatest citizen army thus far in American history—500,000 three-year volunteers, most of them infantrymen. A week later, Congress endorsed Lincoln's proclamation of 3 May, raising the statutory strength of the regular army to 42,000 with the addition of ten new regiments. For some strange reason, the Lincoln Administration prescribed three different tables of organization for Union infantry regiments—two for the regular service and one for the volunteers.

The legislation of 22 July stated that each volunteer infantry regiment 'shall have 1 colonel, 1 lieutenant colonel, 1 major, 1 adjutant (a lieutenant), 1 quartermaster (a lieutenant), 1 surgeon and 1 assistant surgeon, 1 sergeant major, 1 regimental quartermaster sergeant, 1 regimental commissary sergeant, 1 hospital steward, 2 principal musicians, and 24 musicians for a band, and shall be composed of 10 companies, each company to consist of 1 captain, 1 first lieutenant, 1 second lieutenant, 1 first sergeant, 4 sergeants, 8 corporals, 2 musicians, 1 wagoner, and from 64 to 82 privates.' This structure was altered over time. By 6 September 1862, regimental bands were forbidden, but each regimental staff was now entitled to one chaplain and a second assistant surgeon. At peak strength, a volunteer regiment constituted thirty-nine officers and 986 enlisted men. During the Civil War, the Union raised 1,696 such outfits, as well as 272 cavalry regiments and seventy-eight artillery regiments.

In the regular army, the ten senior infantry regiments were also single-battalion units with ten companies apiece, but regular companies had no wagoners. The nine new foot regiments, the 11th through 19th Infantry, were much larger organizations with three battalions each—an innovation borrowed from the French Army. Two of the battalions were intended for field operations, and the third was to man a regimental depot and train incoming recruits. Besides a colonel and a lieutenant colonel to oversee the running of the entire unit, a regiment had spots for three majors—one per battalion. Each battalion was divided into eight companies instead of ten and had a total strength of 656 to 807. Theoretically, one of these monster regiments could contain as many as 2,452 officers and men. In reality, regular outfits spent the Civil War with their ranks partially full. Given a preference, most Northern men chose to soldier with friends and neighbors in volunteer units. The 12th, 13th, 14th, 17th, and 19th U.S. Infantry never even tried to organize more than two battalions. The 11th, 15th, 16th, and 18th Infantry each had a third battalion, but none of them managed to form all their companies.

Confederate volunteer infantry regiments were organized much like their Northern counterparts. They usually had ten companies, with anywhere from sixty-four to 125 privates per company. During the war, the Rebel Army fielded 642 regiments, nine legions, 163

Lieutenant Colonel George E. Chamberlin, 11th Vermont Volunteers, shortly after his promotion from major in the summer of 1864. Field officers fought on horseback, so Chamberlin's leather gauntlets are sensible accessories. Note also the non-regulation sword belt with the shoulder attachment to take the weight of the Model 1850 staff and field officer's sword. Organized as infantry in September 1862, the 11th Vermont was converted into heavy artillery that December and spent eighteen months safe behind the defenses of Washington. On 12 May 1864, the 1,500-man regiment was transferred to the Army of the Potomac to serve as infantry. Winning commendations for his gallantry at Spotsylvania and Cold Harbor, Chamberlin was mortally wounded in the Shenandoah Valley on 21 August 1864.

An unidentified corporal of Company A, 6th Wisconsin Volunteer Infantry, one of the original regiments of the famed Iron Brigade. After he assumed command of the brigade in May 1862, Brigadier General John Gibbon outfitted his men with smart new uniforms consisting of Hardee hats, dark blue frock coats, light blue trousers, white leggings, and white cotton gloves. The short musket and sword bayonet seen here are photographer's props. The 6th Wisconsin began service with Belgian muskets, switching later to various models of the Springfield rifle musket.

separate battalions, and sixty-two unattached companies of infantry. About three-quarters of all 'Johnny Rebs' were doughboys.

Spurred on by a surge of patriotism and a determination to stamp out the shame of Bull Run, hordes of Northerners jammed the recruiting stations in the summer and fall of 1861. Succumbing to an unaccustomed spell of generosity, Congress upped an infantry private's pay from $11 to $13 a month on 6 August. On 1 December, the War Department disclosed that the Union Army had swollen to 640,000 volunteers and 20,000 regulars. Because few of the volunteers were subjected to proper physical examinations, a surprising number of the underaged, the overaged, the unfit, and even a few women made their way into the ranks. But in the main, the 'Boys of '61' represented the cream of Northern manhood. 'Never perhaps has a finer body of men in all respects of *physique* been assembled by any power in the world,' observed William H. Russell, a correspondent for the London *Times*, 'and there is no

PLATE 20: ZOUAVE SPLENDOR: NORTH AND SOUTH, 1861–5

Many Civil War volunteer units took the field in flamboyant costumes inspired by the dress of the elite light infantry battalions raised for the French Army in North Africa. **66. Private, 146th New York Volunteer Infantry Regiment, 1863:** *Formed in 1862, the 146th received uniforms copied from those of the French Army's* Tirailleurs Algériens *in June 1863. Two recently discovered photographs show privates wearing checked shirts in place of the prescribed light blue vests with yellow trim. Such a shirt was also found with the uniform of Sergeant Chauncey Smith of the 146th, which is now owned by the Rochester Museum and Science Center. For dress parades, a white turban was wound around the fez. This private is grabbing a cartridge to load his Model 1861 rifle musket.* **67. Private, 1st Special Battalion, Louisiana Infantry ('Wheat's Tigers'), 1861–2:** *The blue jackets issued to this command of Irish roughnecks and wharf rats from New Orleans faded to brown after several months in the field. Trousers were made of mattress ticking. One company wore broad-brimmed hats decorated with anti-Yankee slogans. The battalion carried Model 1841 'Mississippi' rifles.* **68. Corporal, 5th New York Volunteer Infantry ('Duryee Zouaves'), 1862:** *Recruited in the spring of 1861 in New York City, this first class regiment carried Model 1842 muskets, Springfield and Enfield rifle muskets, Sharps rifles, and Spencer repeating rifles at various times in its career. The men's scarlet sashes were edged in medium blue. While wrapping his sash around his waist, this corporal got it twisted so that the blue border does not show along the bottom—a gaffe that occasionally appears in period photographs.* **69. Sergeant, 11th Indiana Volunteer Infantry ('Wallace's Zouaves'), 1863:** *Organized by Colonel Lew Wallace (who later wrote Ben Hur), the 11th first wore red forage caps with blue bands and gray uniforms with red braid. In December 1861, the regiment received a new uniform consisting of regulation sky-blue trousers and black jackets with light blue trim and dark blue false-vest fronts. As the war progressed, officers and men took to wearing blue caps. Figure 69 is loading a Model 1855 rifle.*

66. Private, 146th New York Volunteer
Infantry Regiment, 1863

67. Private, 1st Special Battalion,
Louisiana Infantry ('Wheat's Tigers'),
1861–2

68. Corporal, 5th New York Volunteer
Infantry ('Duryee Zouaves'), 1862

69. Sergeant, 11th Indiana Volunteer
Infantry ('Wallace's Zouaves'), 1863

A gray-clad private of the 18th Tennessee Volunteer Infantry bravely displays his Mississippi rifle and single-shot, bar-hammer pistol. Note the brass 'US' belt plate. Rebels commonly equipped themselves with items taken from federal arsenals and Yankee casualties.

reason why their morale should not be improved so as to equal that of the best troops in Europe.'

Union volunteer units were ordinarily raised by the states and then mustered into federal service. Most of the men in a given company—often an entire regiment—came from the same town, city, or county. Congress prescribed unit elections as the only legal way to fill officers' vacancies, but Northern governors frequently doled out commissions to political supporters, provided these pets helped recruit the companies and regiments they were named to command. Yet whether a volunteer officer owed his appointment to personal popularity or political patronage, chances were he knew no more about soldiering than the men he led. The more trustworthy among the volunteer officers devoted long nights to cramming from drill manuals to keep at least one lesson ahead of the common soldiers. The Confederate Army also suffered the effects of officer elections, although strong evidence exists to suggest that Southern governors took care to present commissions to graduates of West Point and private military academies.

On account of the prevailing democratic ethos, the type of training Civil War soldiers received depended on the caliber of their officers. Private Elisha Stockwell,

who joined the 14th Wisconsin Volunteer Infantry on 25 February 1862, complained: 'We drilled some while . . . , but I was in the awkward squad yet and don't remember being on company drill until after the Battle of Shiloh [6-7 April 1862].' On the other hand, a veteran remembered the taxing regimen instituted by Brigadier General John Gibbon, a regular artilleryman temporarily assigned to the volunteer service, once the latter took command of the 2nd, 6th, and 7th Wisconsin and the 19th Indiana in May 1862: 'There were early morning drills, before breakfast, forenoon drills, afternoon drills and night drills, beside guard mounting and dress parades.'

In July 1861, the Union Congress approved an examination policy to weed out incompetent volunteer officers, but many bunglers held onto their shoulder straps for two years or more. Nevertheless, by 1863 most promotions were being awarded on the basis of merit. Many worthy fellows who began the war as privates ended it as company and field officers. These seasoned veterans made first-rate combat commanders.

Though they usually left home with 1,000 men or more, the rigors of campaigning and the privations of camp life speedily trimmed Union infantry regiments to far below their starting size. Battle losses were often horrendous, and disease killed off twice as many Yanks as Rebel bullets. While simply traveling to the front from 29 August to 8 October 1862, the 24th Michigan dwindled from 1,030 to 898 officers and men. In a letter dated 26 May 1862 from the Shiloh battlefield, Private James K. Newton of the 14th Wisconsin described the common attrition process as it affected his outfit: 'Our Regt is falling away pretty fast, they send off between 40 & 50 every ten days. There is about 300 of us left to do duty & one quarter of those are not able to do the duty that we have to do. We bury from one to three almost every day. We have not lost any that I know of from our Co[mpany] unless some of those that we sent off have died since. When you remember that a little over two months ago we numbered 980 good sound men & now we do not number over three hundred men that are able to do duty, it seems that we have been going down hill pretty fast.'

For much of the war, the typical Union foot regiment took 400 muskets into battle, although that average varied according to the newness of the units involved, the theaters in which they operated, and their exposure to combat (see Table 5). After a battle or two, a regiment might shrink to less than 200 effectives. Similar conditions prevailed in the Confederate Army.

The Union Army's unwise replacement system hardly ameliorated the sorry plight of veteran regiments. Instead of channeling the bulk of their post-1861 recruits into what William Sherman called 'old and tried regiments with their experienced officers on hand,' the Northern states preferred to form brand new volunteer outfits. This practice allowed governors to extend their patronage powers by naming more officers, but it saddled Union generals with a succession of green units that had to be broken in before they were truly dependable. Wisconsin was the only Northern state to make more than a half-hearted effort to maintain the strength of existing regiments, prompting Sherman to quip that one Wisconsin regiment was the equal of an ordinary Yankee brigade (see Table 6). The Confederate Army did a much better job of feeding fresh troops into depleted outfits, but since the South possessed smaller manpower reserves, the size difference between Yankee and Rebel regiments grew less noticeable as the struggle wore on.

Table 5. Average Strengths of Union Volunteer Infantry Regiments, 1862–5

Shiloh	6–7 April 1862	560
Fair Oaks	31 May–1 June 1862	650
Chancellorsville	1–5 May 1863	530
Gettysburg	1–3 July 1863	375
Chickamauga	19–20 September 1863	440
The Wilderness	5–7 May 1864	440
Sherman's Atlanta Campaign	May 1864	305

Once in the field, Civil War infantrymen were grouped together in brigades of four or more regiments. Because of the provincialism of Southerners, Confederate brigades normally contained regiments from the same state. Three or more brigades constituted a division, and, on 17 July 1862, the Union Congress permitted President Lincoln to combine divisions into corps. The Rebels also adopted the corps system.

As 1862 approached, Southern officials were worried that their Army was about to disintegrate. The Confederacy counted 209,852 troops present for duty as of 1 January 1862, but 148 of its regiments were composed of twelve-month men due for discharge in May. As there were only about 1,000,000 white males of military age (eighteen to forty-five) in the South, one-fourth as many as those available to the North, the Rebel Army could not afford to lose too many soldiers in one

Private Henry Moulton joined Company D of the 16th New Hampshire Volunteer Infantry, a nine-month regiment, on 3 October 1862, only to die in Louisiana on 14 May 1863. Moulton's uniform is typical of those issued to many New Hampshire infantrymen. The top of his forage cap is decorated with various brass insignia—a company letter, infantry bugle, regimental number, and the initials 'NHV' (New Hampshire Volunteers). Moulton grasps a converted Belgian musket.

Table 6. Replacement Statistics for the Union's Iron Brigade, Army of the Potomac, 1861–5

Regiments	Date Organized	Original Enrollment	Replacements	Total Enrollment
2nd Wisconsin	June 1861	1,048	137	1,288
6th Wisconsin	July 1861	1,048	798	1,906
7th Wisconsin	August 1861	1,106	685	1,704
19th Indiana	July 1861	1,046	219	1,273
24th Michigan	August 1862	1,030	216	1,246

fell swoop—especially with 527,204 Yankee effectives poised for renewed onslaughts in the upcoming campaign season. On 11 December 1861, the Confederate Congress offered a $50 bounty and a sixty-day furlough to any one-year man re-enlisting for two or three years, provided the war did not end sooner. Short-term veterans dissatisfied with their present leaders or comrades received the right to organize themselves into new companies, battalions, and regiments and to elect new officers—on the condition the men agreed to a second hitch. When this reward system failed to encourage enough re-enlistments, the Davis Administration turned to coercion.

On 16 April 1862, Congress passed an 'Act to Further Provide for the Public Defense,' better known as the Conscription Act. Henceforth, every able-bodied white male aged eighteen to thirty-five could be drafted into the Confederate Army. Furthermore, those persons of draft age already in the service were to remain there for three years from the date of their original enlistment. By blocking the discharge of the one-year men, the Conscription Act allowed the Rebel Army to survive the war's second year, and the law's continued operation helped the Confederacy fend off destruction until 1865.

Initially, the Rebel government softened the impact of conscription by permitting draftees to hire substitutes to serve in their stead. On 21 April and 11 October 1862, Congress also passed two acts which exempted large segments of the male population from military service. Among the privileged classes were Confederate and state officials, government clerks, ministers, mail carriers, almost anyone involved in transportation, factory owners, certain craftsmen and artisans, and one white man on every plantation with twenty or more slaves. That last provision, the notorious 'twenty-nigger law,' was resented by lower and middle-income whites, who owned few or no slaves, and it inspired complaints about 'a rich man's war but a poor man's fight.'

The meatgrinder tactics of the Civil War spent lives quickly, and the Confederacy had repeatedly to strengthen her conscription laws. Substitution was abolished in December 1863. The draft age was boosted to forty-five on 27 September 1862 and broadened again to seventeen and fifty on 17 February 1864. On the latter occasion, Congress also ruled that all Rebel soldiers had to stay in the Army for the duration of the war, a decision preventing the discharge of the three-year volunteers of 1861. 'The conscription is now being pressed mercilessly,' wrote a Southern official on 25 September 1864. 'It is agonizing to see and hear cases daily brought into the War Office, . . . and *all* disallowed. Women come there and weep, wring their hands, scold, entreat, beg, and almost drive me mad. The iron is gone deep into the heart of society.'

These desperate measures prompted Ulysses S. Grant (by March 1864 a lieutenant general commanding all the Union armies) to quip that the Rebels were robbing the cradle and the grave for troops. Yet the majority of those ragged 'gray jackets' kept fighting with the desperate ferocity of cornered tigers long after they realized their cause was lost. Reflecting on Grant's cradle-and-grave jest in November 1864, Major General George Gordon Meade, the leader of the North's hard-luck Army of the Potomac, exclaimed, 'If that is the case, I must say their ghosts and babies fight very well!'

Nonetheless, Southern valor cost Southern lives, and by 1864 recruiters were scraping the bottom of the manpower barrel. On 13 March 1865, the Confederate Congress swallowed its racist pride and approved the enrollment of 300,000 slaves as soldiers. This law came too late to avert defeat. The contest ended before any black regiments were organized.

PLATE 21: UNDER FIRE WITH THE ARMY OF THE POTOMAC, 1862–5

Union infantry regiments carried national colors bearing stars of silver or gold—the latter color apparently the most popular. These flags were often surrounded by gold fringe. **70. Private, 1st Regiment, U.S. Sharpshooters ('Berdan's Sharpshooters'), 1862:** *Photographs in the Michael J. McAfee collection reveal that this regiment's enlisted men wore dark green frock coats with emerald green piping cut in the regulation style—not the officer's coat favored by modern illustrators. Originally, the regiment received sky blue trousers, but later issues were dark green. Note the ostrich feather on the cap, the leather leggings, and the Prussian knapsack. The sharpshooters took the field in the spring of 1862 with Colt revolving rifles, but exchanged those erratic weapons for .52-caliber Sharps breechloading rifles a few months later. Although both saber bayonets and the socket variety were issued, sharpshooters favored the latter. Being lighter, it made aiming easier.* **71. First Sergeant, 88th New York Volunteer Infantry ('The Irish Brigade'), 1863:** *The Irish Brigade's enlisted personnel wore chasseur-pattern forage caps with red shamrocks, fatigue blouses with green facings, and gray trousers. Brigadier General Thomas F. Meagher armed the 63rd, 69th, and 88th New York with Model 1842 smoothbore muskets by early 1862 to encourage his Irishmen to place their reliance on the bayonet instead of marksmanship.* **72. Captain (Oliver Wendell Holmes, Jr.), 20th Massachusetts Volunteer Infantry, 1862:** *Note the single-breasted frock coat prescribed for company officers. Contrary to the Regulations of 1861, many Union soldiers preferred sky blue trousers to dark blue. The future U.S. Supreme Court justice is armed with a Model 1850 foot officer's sword and .44-caliber Model 1860 Colt Army revolver.*

73. Private, 37th Massachusetts Volunteer Infantry, 1865: *Stripped of their brass shoulder scales, frock coats sometimes served as campaign wear. A photograph of the 37th's Charles A. Taggart (a Medal of Honor winner) shows him in a coat with three small buttons on each cuff, rather than the regulation two. In 1864, the regiment received .52-caliber Spencer rifles, seven-shot repeaters.*

71. First Sergeant, 88th New York
Volunteer Infantry ('The Irish Brigade'),
1863

73. Private, 37th Massachusetts
Volunteer Infantry, 1865

70. Private, 1st Regiment, U.S.
Sharpshooters ('Berdan's Sharpshooters'),
1862

72. Captain, 20th Massachusetts
Volunteer Infantry, 1862

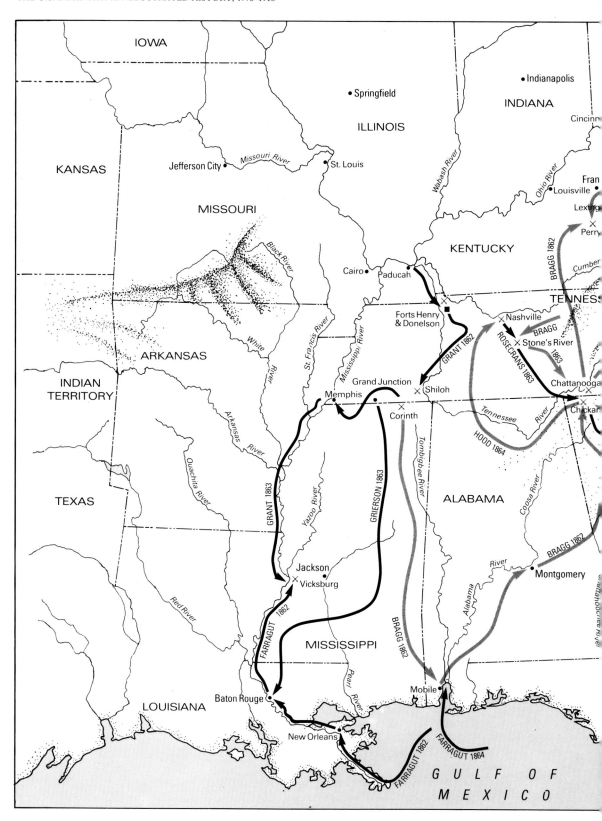

• Columbus

OHIO

PENNSYLVANIA

NEW JERSEY

LEE 1863 ✕ Gettysburg

MARYLAND

DELAWARE

Potomac River Harper's Ferry•

WEST VIRGINIA

• Charleston

JACKSON 1862

Kanawha River

✕ Antietam
Bull Run ✕
BEAUREGARD 1861

LEE 1862

• Washington

Chancellorsville ✕
✕ Fredericksburg
The ✕ Wilderness
✕ Spotsylvania

Shenandoah

VIRGINIA

James River

Richmond •

Cold Harbor
✕

Appomattox •
GRANT 1864-65

Roanoke River

Seven ✕ Days

McCLELLAN 1862

Petersburg

• Danville

Norfolk

xville
GSTREET 1863

Yadkin River

Catawaba River

LONGSTREET 1863

Raleigh •

NORTH   CAROLINA

Goldsboro •

ut Mountain,
ionary Ridge·

Broad River

SHERMAN
1865

Cape Fear River

SOUTH   CAROLINA

Wilmington •

Savannah River

NGSTREET 1863

nta

• Columbia

Santee   River

A T L A N T I C   O C E A N

TERRY 1865

N
• Milledgeville

con •

1864

Oconee River

Ocmulgee River

Altamaha River

Charleston •
Fort Sumter■ ✕

DUPONT 1861

• Savannah

GEORGIA

hassee

Jacksonville•

Suwannee River

FLORIDA

PRINCIPAL MILITARY CAMPAIGNS
OF THE CIVIL WAR
1861-1865

Union Forces ⟶   Confederate Forces ⟶

Major Battles ✕

0   50   100
MILES

Five stalwart youngsters of Company F, 44th Massachusetts Volunteers, another nine-month militia unit formed in the latter half of 1862. Two men (seated at center and at right) wear sack coats and the other three wear frock coats. All five have English equipments with 'snake' buckles and Enfield rifles.

An estimated 800,000 men—four-fifths of the South's eligible white males—served at one time or another in the Confederate Army. This incredible accomplishment in army-building was made possible in part by a reliance on black slave labor, which freed more whites for soldiering. Conscription not only kept veterans in the service, but it also produced about 120,000 draftees and 70,000 substitutes—20 per cent of the Rebel Army. Few nations have achieved such success at mobilizing their military population.

The second year of the Civil War did not go particularly well for the Lincoln Administration. In the Eastern Theater, General Robert E. Lee's Army of Northern Virginia squashed every Northern offensive. The Yanks made some gains in the Western Theater, but they paid dearly for every advance. And whether they presided over victories or defeats, most blue generals whined endlessly for reinforcements for their thinned ranks.

On 2 July 1862, Lincoln solicited the loyal states for 300,000 more three-year volunteers, assigning each state

PLATE 22: UNION VOLUNTEERS IN THE WEST, 1862–5

74. Corporal, 30th Ohio Veteran Volunteer Infantry, 1864: In 1863, Ohio issued shell jackets to the 30th and some other of its infantry regiments. The sky blue chevrons with red edging sewn to the lower sleeves marked a man as a 'veteran volunteer.' Corporals had dark blue trouser stripes half an inch wide. The 30th Ohio received .577-caliber Enfield rifle muskets in 1863. *75. Sergeant, Mississippi Marine Brigade, 1863: Early in 1863, the Union Army detailed six companies of infantry, four of cavalry, and one of artillery to protect naval vessels on the interior waterways. Some of these 'marines' wore unique caps trimmed with green bands and gold lace. Brigade sharpshooters carried Spencer carbines. Soldiers often added extra buttons to their fatigue blouses to improve their appearance. Sergeants wore dark blue stripes one-and-a-half inches wide along the outer seams of their trousers.* *76. Private, 21st Ohio Volunteer Infantry, 1863: Introduced in 1858, the unlined, four-button fatigue blouse served as campaign wear in all branches of the Union Army. Many Yanks preferred modified 'Hardees' or slouch hats for use in the sunny South. Armed with Colt revolving rifles, the 21st Ohio made a valiant, rear-guard stand at the Battle of Chickamauga (19–20 September 1863). In five hours, the 535 Buckeyes fired 43,550 rounds at their shocked Rebel opponents.*

75. Sergeant, Mississippi Marine Brigade, 1863

74. Corporal, 30th Ohio Veteran Volunteer Infantry, 1864

76. Private, 21st Ohio Volunteer Infantry, 1863

a quota based on population. Despite the attendant hoopla and heartfelt appeals, news of Northern setbacks and the mounting casualty lists put a damper on recruiting. Responding boldly on 4 August, Lincoln's War Department ordered a draft of 300,000 militiamen to serve for nine months in the Union Army. The main purpose of this draft was to stimulate volunteering. Any three-year man enlisted by a state above its July quota would count as four militiamen. Draftees were not eligible for the $100 federal bounty paid to volunteers, a strong incentive to step forward of one's own accord. Finally, conscription was popularly considered a blot on an individual's honor and a community's patriotism. 'It is better by far to enlist voluntarily than to be dragged into the army a conscript,' a Vermonter declared on 18 August. 'Nothing to me would appear more degrading.' To avoid the onus of a draft, towns, counties, and cities offered supplementary bounties ranging from $10 to $450. These gratuities served their purpose, but they injected a mercenary flavor into Union recruiting which worsened over time. Under the calls of July and August

1862, the Yankee Army received 421,465 three-year volunteers and 90,000 nine-month men. But this latest drive for soldiers virtually extinguished the North's volunteer spirit.

Borrowing a lesson from their Southern colleagues, Union congressmen embraced conscription with the Enrollment Act of 3 March 1863. All able-bodied male citizens and aliens seeking naturalization between the ages of twenty and forty-five were liable for military duty, and the President was empowered to draft troops as they were needed. Aside from the physically and mentally unfit, and the sole supports of orphans or infirm parents, few classes were exempted. However, conscripts could evade their country's call through substitution or a practice called commutation—the payment of a $300 fee to the federal government.

The North held four drafts in the second half of the

A North Carolina infantryman killed at Spotsylvania, 19 May 1864. Note this veteran's gray jacket, uncovered tin canteen, and Model 1853 Enfield rifle musket.

Private Louis Troutman, Company F, 118th Infantry Regiment, U.S. Colored Troops, a unit raised in Kentucky in 1864. As this and numerous other images testify, the Union's black soldiers took great pride in their appearance. The 118th U.S.C.T., like so many other Union commands, carried Enfield rifles.

Civil War (July 1863, March 1864, July 1864, and December 1864). Each time, the President initiated the process by issuing a call for troops and assigning quotas to the loyal states. Every congressional district had a grace period (normally fifty days) to fill its quota with volunteers. If so, it escaped the shame of conscription.

Consequently, Northern communities engaged in periodic but furious scrambles to nab volunteers for the Union Army. Localities vied with each other in offering the most lavish bounties. In some areas, the bidding soared from $100 to $300, $400, $500, and even $600! The federal government succumbed to the frenzy, raising its bounty for three-year men to $402 late in 1863. By July 1864, a New York district was paying volunteers $1,060 apiece in federal and local funds. One Illinois district advertised $1,055.95 a head. During the final troop call in the winter of 1864–5, anyone enlisting in Philadelphia stood to garner $1,100 in bounties, more cash than a frugal laborer could save in three years. Congress appealed further to the mercenary spirit by increasing a private's monthly pay to $16 on 20 June 1864.

While cultivating crass materialism, the Enrollment Act also lent itself to corruption and fraud. The new recruitment system fostered the rise of two types of parasites—'bounty brokers' and 'bounty jumpers.' Bounty brokers were enterpreneurs who collected hefty commissions by supplying recruits to districts experiencing difficulty in meeting their quotas. Devising an ingenious array of tricks, brokers customarily disguised drunks, derelicts, old men, and boys as acceptable cannon fodder. They also practiced kidnapping on occasion to satisfy their clients' needs. Bounty jumpers were rascals who enlisted in one regiment, collected the bounty, and then deserted, often re-enlisting over and over in other outfits for more easy earnings. In December 1864, ninety-seven out of 300 newly enlisted bounty men leaped from a moving train between Columbus and Cincinnati. That same month, Thomas Ryan was executed in Indianapolis for jumping bounty thirty times. The self-admitted record holder was John O'Connor, sentenced to four years in a New York county prison in March 1865 for thirty-two jumps.

So long as commutation remained intact, the Enrollment Act brought in more money than soldiers. Of the 133,000 men held to service by the first two drafts, 85,000 discharged their obligation by paying the $300 fee. On 4 July 1864, Congress virtually abolished commutation, restricting the privilege solely to conscientious objectors. This well-intentioned amendment simply ripped the ceiling off the price of substitutes and threw the burden of military service more heavily on the poor. Now sunshine patriots had to cough up $500 to $1,000 to keep out of uniform. The North witnessed a

Principal Musician William Witbeck, 93rd New York Volunteer Infantry, attired in a non-regulation dark blue frock coat with unusual sky blue chevrons and dark blue trousers. Principal musicians were entitled to a red worsted sash and a sword.

proliferation of 'substitute brokers,' offering a selection of human refuse to men of means too craven to serve their country.

To be sure, conscription elicited a disturbing degree of opposition and sordidness from Southerners, but the adverse reactions seen in certain parts of the North topped anything experienced in Dixie. In June 1863, 420 Union soldiers had to be sent to Holmes County, Ohio, to disperse 1,000 armed draft resisters. Anti-draft riots rocked New York City, Troy, and Boston that July. Northerners also battled conscription individually. Thousands refused to report for duty or deserted at the first opportunity. Others resorted to every imaginable dodge to be excused from duty—feigning infirmities, mutilating themselves, and bribing draft officials. Bounty men, substitutes, and conscripts were commonly conveyed to their regiments under armed guard—just like common criminals.

At first glance, the Enrollment Act was a dismal flop. Out of a total of 776,829 names drawn, 161,244 men did not report, 315,509 were exempted, 86,724 commuted, 73,607 hired substitutes, and only 46,347 were actually drafted. Yet the draft was not a failure. Its primary purpose was to revive recruiting, and in that it succeeded. While conscription was in force, over 1,000,000 men volunteered for the Union Army.

The severest judges of the draft were the hard-fighting volunteers of '61 and '62. Veterans were shocked and disgusted by the declining quality of the reinforcements that began to reach the front in the summer of 1863. A member of the 13th Massachusetts Infantry labeled a batch of replacements delivered to the regiment that August as mostly 'thieves and roughs.' 'I don't believe in

PLATE 23: BANDSMEN AND MUSICIANS, 1862–5
Many infantry units on both sides possessed brass bands to inspire the troops by playing in camp and on the battlefield. Robert E. Lee said, 'I don't believe we can have an army without music.'
77. Fifer, 54th Massachusetts Volunteer Infantry, 1863:
Company musicians in this crack black regiment wore two types of short jackets—a plain, single-breasted model and a fancier affair festooned with worsted lace. **78. Bandsman, 26th North Carolina Volunteer Infantry, 1862:** *Members of this regimental band, reputedly Robert E. Lee's favorite, wore frock coats of cadet gray wool or jeans and trousers of the latter material. Note the coat's unusual piping. The instrument pictured is a brass over-the-shoulder saxhorn.* **79. Drum Major (Henry S. Peck), 20th Connecticut Volunteer Infantry, 1862:** *Peck's non-regulation chevrons, peculiar to this regiment, featured bottom borders of gold fringe. With the publication of the Regulations of 1851, infantry officers and non-commissioned officers above the rank of corporal were supposed to wear rectangular belt plates (gilt for officers and brass for non-commissioned officers), bearing the 'Arms of the United States' and wreaths in silver or German silver. Corporals and privates received oval 'US' belt plates.*

77. Fifer, 54th Massachusetts Volunteer Infantry, 1863

78. Bandsman, 26th North Carolina Volunteer Infantry, 1862

79. Drum Major, 20th Connecticut Volunteer Infantry, 1862

Three company officers of the 32nd Massachusetts Volunteer Infantry (left to right: a second lieutenant, a captain, and a first lieutenant) posed for a photographer near Hagerstown, Maryland, on 9 July 1863 during the Army of the Potomac's ineffectual pursuit of Robert E. Lee's Army of Northern Virginia following the Battle of Gettysburg. All three Yankees wear four-button sack coats—comfortable campaign garb—as well as black 'false boots' of rubber or patent leather, which fit over their ankle-high bootees. Note the Model 1850 foot officer's swords, the non-regulation sword belts, the dark blue welt on the captain's sky blue trousers, the two different cap badges displayed by the lieutenants, and the absence of sashes for field duty.

recruiting another man!' Lieutenant Colonel Theodore Lyman, a staff officer with the Army of the Potomac, wrote home in August 1864. 'Now we pay huge bounties to every sort of scoundrel and vagabond and alien. These men will *not* fight and you can't make 'em fight.' There was also considerable jealousy on the part of soldiers who had fought two years for a $100 bounty toward late arrivals who enlisted for eight, nine, or ten times as much money. During the preparatory stage for a Union assault on Petersburg, Virginia, late in September 1864, five fresh Pennsylvania regiments were halted on the same road with the veteran 13th New Hampshire Infantry. Reportedly, some of the neophytes had received bounties as high as $1,500. 'Do you suppose we . . . will be ordered into battle?' a nervous Pennsylvanian asked a New Hampshireman. 'No indeed,' joshed the old soldier. 'They won't put you in— you cost too much to be risked in a battle; we didn't cost anything—so they stick us in everywhere.'

Just as the Union Army was being inundated with inferior replacements, it was threatened with the loss of its best troops. Ignoring the Confederate precedent, the North balked at forcing veterans to extend their enlistments. Instead, the Lincoln Administration played upon their patriotism and greed. During the winter of 1863-4 the federal government promised a $402 bounty to every soon-to-be-discharged three-year man who signed on for a second three years. Such stalwarts were entitled to a thirty-day furlough, the right to wear a special chevron on their jacket sleeves, and the title of 'veteran volunteers.' Furthermore, if two-thirds of the men in the same regiment re-enlisted, their unit would not be disbanded, it would have the word 'veteran' added to its name, and its members could all take their furlough together.

In a tremendous display of comradeship and national devotion, some 200,000 Yanks—nearly half of those eligible—became veteran volunteers before the war's close. Nonetheless, the veterans who departed for home were sorely missed, especially as their places were taken by products of the draft and bounty system. Since a veteran was worth two recruits, the Union Army's personnel situation helps explain why Confederate forces performed so well against overwhelming odds in 1864 and 1865. As Lieutenant Colonel Lyman snarled: 'I wish these gentlemen who would overwhelm us with Germans . . . and the offscourings of great cities, could only see—only *see*—a Rebel regiment, in all their rags and squalor. . . . They would know that these men are like wolf hounds, and not to be beaten by turnspits.' However, even the finest soldier can be slain by a knave, and the North possessed more than enough men—both good and bad—to grind the Rebel Army into the dust.

In its unceasing quest for soldiers, the Union

acquiesced in the revolutionary notion of exploiting Afro-Americans. At the war's outset, abolitionists and free black leaders argued that emancipation was a fitting way to punish Southern Rebels and that enlisting former slaves would hasten the demise of the Confederacy. But Abraham Lincoln, fearful of alienating the loyal slave states (Delaware, Maryland, Kentucky, and Missouri), inflaming the prejudices of Northern whites, and creating an issue that would only stiffen Rebel resistance, reiterated that his sole object was to restore the old Union—complete with slavery. By the summer of 1862, however, Lincoln was convinced that the 'peculiar institution' was too important a prop to the enemy war effort to leave undisturbed. Moreover, recent Union defeats disposed the President to wield every weapon within his reach. Already, isolated Yankee commanders in Kansas and occupied sections of Louisiana and South Carolina were forming black regiments. Lincoln issued no orders to stop them. As he later asserted: 'The colored population is the great available, and yet unavailed of force for restoring the Union. The bare sight of 50,000 armed and drilled black soldiers upon the banks of the Mississippi would end the rebellion at once. And who doubts that we can present that sight if we but take hold in earnest.'

Toward the end of August 1862, the War Department quietly sanctioned the recruitment of 5,000 runaway slaves on on the South Carolina Sea Islands. Subsequent to the promulgation of the Emancipation Proclamation on 1 January 1863, the Union Army launched a vigorous campaign to recruit blacks. Officially, 7,122 officers and 178,895 men served in the 'United States Colored Troops.' The Union raised 166 black regiments, 145 of infantry, seven of cavalry, twelve of heavy artillery, one of light artillery, and one of engineers.

On top of all the miseries that befell white soldiers, black troops endured various forms of discrimination. Under fire, U.S.C.T. units behaved no worse (and sometimes much better) than white commands of comparable experience, but many high-ranking officers remained certain that Negroes were fit for nothing more than garrison and fatigue duty. Numerous white enlisted men adopted a more pragmatic view. A member of the 55th Pennsylvania Infantry, a white regiment stationed with the black 1st South Carolina on Port Royal Island, said this of his ebony comrades in April 1863: 'They've as much right to fight for themselves as I have to fight for them.' Such toleration stemmed in part from the Lincoln Administration's shrewd policy of staffing the commissioned ranks in black regiments almost exclusively with white junior officers and enlisted men. Improved prospects for promotion led white veterans to shed their bigotry and accept blacks as comrades. A Wisconsin boy with Major General William Tecumseh Sherman in

The first sergeant of Company G, 77th Infantry Regiment, U.S. Colored Troops, 1864, proudly attired in his regulation full dress uniform, complete with Hardee hat, frock coat, brass shoulder scales, and Model 1840 non-commissioned officer's sword. Raised in 1863 as the 5th Infantry Regiment, Corps d'Afrique, the 77th was composed of Louisianans. Louisiana provided thirty-seven black regiments for the Union Army, more than any other state.

South Carolina admitted in March 1865: 'If I get a chance to get a commission by going in a Black Regt I am a going.'

It required extra courage to join the U.S. Colored Troops. Rebel officials warned that captured black soldiers would be reinslaved and their officers treated as war criminals. Union threats of retaliation prevented the uniform enforcement of this draconian policy, but vengeful Rebs cruelly murdered black prisoners on more than one occasion. The added danger only drew the officers and men in U.S.C.T regiments closer together. Many of the former became advocates of equal rights for Afro-Americans. Colonel Thomas Morgan, the commander of a Negro brigade at the Battle of Nashville (15-16 December 1864), left this tribute to the black man's role in winning the War of the Rebellion:

'Colored soldiers had fought side by side with white troops. They had mingled together in the charge. They had supported each other. . . . All who witnessed their conduct gave them equal praise. The day we longed to see had come and gone, and the sun went down upon a record of coolness, bravery, manliness, never to be

PLATE 24: THE LOOK OF JOHNNY REB, 1861–5
80. Sergeant Major, 17th Regiment, South Carolina Volunteers, 1862: *The Confederate dress regulations of June 1861 authorized double-breasted frock coats with light blue collars and cuffs for all enlisted infantrymen. However, the coats South Carolina issued to some senior non-commissioned officers had gray collars and cuffs with light blue piping. In 1861, eight of the 17th's ten companies received Pattern 1842 'Brown Bess' muskets, smoothbores imported from England.* **81. Second Lieutenant (John A. Bethell), 7th Florida Volunteer Infantry, 1862:** *Based on an ambrotype in a private collection. Government regulations allowed Confederate officers to display their rank in two ways. The first was a gold badge attached to their collars: three stars indicated a colonel; two stars, a lieutenant colonel; one star, a major; three horizontal bars, a captain; two bars, a first lieutenant; and one bar, a second lieutenant. The other insignia was the number of strands of gold lace embroidered on the kepi and in the 'Austrian knots' bedecking their lower coat-sleeves: field officers sported three braids; captains, two; and lieutenants, one. Enlisted men of the 7th Florida had dark blue caps with light blue trim.* **82. Captain (Houston B. Lowrie), 6th North Carolina Volunteer Infantry, 1862:** *The cadet gray frock coats of North Carolina officers were identical in style to those worn by their counterparts in the Union Army. Infantry officers from this state had black shoulder straps and trouser belts. As regimental adjutant, Lowrie (who fell at Antietam on 17 September 1862) draped his sash over his right shoulder. A British observer attached to the Army of Northern Virginia related that the jaunty Rebels 'wore their brushes like roses in their button-holes.'* **83. Corporal, 6th–7th Arkansas Volunteer Infantry, 1864:** *To conserve dwindling stores of gray cloth, the typical Confederate infantryman wore a short jacket. As supply problems intensified, many 'Johnny Rebs' were reduced to wearing jackets and trousers made of 'butternut' (light brown) wool. The regimental color shown here is preserved at the Old State House Museum in Little Rock, Arkansas.*

81. Second Lieutenant, 7th Florida
Volunteer Infantry, 1862

83. Corporal, 6th–7th Arkansas Volunteer
Infantry, 1864

80. Sergeant Major, 17th Regiment, South
Carolina Volunteers, 1862

82. Captain, 6th North Carolina Volunteer
Infantry, 1862

unmade. A new chapter in the history of liberty had been written. It had been shown that marching under the flag of freedom, animated by a love of liberty, even the slave becomes a man and a hero.'

From 1861 to 1865, roughly 2,100,000 men—just over half of the North's military population—put in some time with the Union Army. War Department records disclose that 359,528 Yankee soldiers died during the war, 249,458 of accident or disease. The 110,070 who perished from battlefield causes broke down into 104,893 white volunteers, 143 officers (most of them white) and 2,751 men from the black regiments, and 2,283 regulars. Not counting draft dodgers, approximately 200,000 men deserted from the Union Army. Only 267 Yankees were officially executed by federal authorities, 141 for desertion. The sparing use of capital punishment in wartime accounts in part for the widespread incidence of desertion.

Exact figures for Southern losses are harder to come by, as many records were lost with the fall of the Confederacy. The best estimates place the number of Johnny Rebs killed by wounds, illness, and mishaps at 258,000. A Confederate soldier stood twice as much chance of dying as his blue-clad opponent. At least 104,000 'Butternuts' deserted, particularly in the closing stages of the struggle.

On 13 December 1864, John L. Hostetter, a surgeon with the 34th Illinois Infantry and a participant in Sherman's devastating march across Georgia, blurted: 'There is no God in war. It is merciless, cruel, vindictive, un-Christian, savage, relentless. It is all that devils could wish for.' The Civil War was possibly the most terrible war the American soldier has ever known. More Americans fell in this conflict than in any other in history.

The Civil War was an infantryman's war. Eighty per cent of the Union Army and 75 per cent of the Confederate Army were doughboys. Infantrymen inflicted and sustained 80 to 90 per cent of the battle casualties. And, thanks to the rifle musket, the American foot soldier was deadlier than ever.

Though the U.S. Army adopted the rifle musket a good five years prior to Fort Sumter, the full destructive potential of the weapon was unappreciated by American military thinkers and professional soldiers. Troops armed with the rifle musket could deliver an accurate, rapid fire at three to four times the range of the old smoothbore. An eyewitness to the Battle of Spotsylvania (8-12 May 1864) declared that the hail of bullets poured into one sector was so thick that the men there 'were shot to pieces and could only be raised in a blanket.' Recalling a nasty little action in Arkansas, Private John Shepherd of the 33rd Iowa Infantry wrote: 'I look back over the battle of Jenkins' Ferry [30 April 1864] and see the mercy of God in the preservation of my life. I had six or seven holes shot in my blouse and I was not hit. Men were shot down all around and I was spared. . . . Company I had gone into battle with 42 men and lost 21 killed or wounded.' In spite of all this, the tactics of Civil War armies remained firmly rooted in the modes of 18th-century linear warfare.

When the Army embraced the rifle musket in 1855, it replaced its manual of the preceding twenty years, Winfield Scott's *Infantry Tactics,* with Major William J. Hardee's *Rifle and Light Infantry Tactics.* Hardee's system strove to protect its users from the infantry's increased firepower by introducing faster march steps and cutting the time required to maneuver formations and deploy troops in column or line. Where Scott detailed only one company per regiment to function as skirmishers, Hardee wisely recommended that every company be trained to fight in extended order. 'Skirmishers always take advantage of the ground or timber and here where

the woods are thick a skirmisher flits from one tree to another like a bird,' Sergeant Joseph R. Ward, 39th Illinois Veteran Volunteer Infantry, wrote his wife from Virginia in December 1864. 'It is almost impossible to shoot one[,] we have tryed [sic] that and know about how that works.'

Unfortunately, in the days before wireless communications, loose formations tended to derange unit cohesion—particularly in newer outfits. Many Civil War commanders employed skirmish order sparingly, if at all. Like Scott's, the Hardee manual trained companies, battalions, and regiments to deploy in dense lines two ranks deep, the men dressing themselves by touching elbows. Thus Civil War soldiers frequently strode into battle in essentially the same formations as their forebears in the Revolution, the War of 1812, and the Mexican War. Colonel John B. Gordon of the 6th Alabama witnessed a typical Yankee advance at the Battle of Antietam (17 September 1862):

'The men in blue . . . formed in my front, an assaulting column four lines deep. The front line came to a "charge bayonets," the other lines to a "right shoulder shift." The Brave Union commander, superbly mounted, placed himself in front, while his band in [the] rear cheered them with martial music. It was a thrilling spectacle. . . . The banners above them had apparently never been discolored by the smoke and dust of battle. Their gleaming bayonets flashed like burnished silver in the sunlight. With the precision of step and perfect alignment of a holiday parade, this magnificent array moved

Company F, 13th Regiment, Pennsylvania Volunteer Reserve Corps, also known as the 42nd Pennsylvania Volunteer Infantry, circa 1862–3. Members of the 42nd were called 'Pennsylvania Bucktails' because they decorated their forage caps with strips of deer hide. The men wear frock coats and fatigue blouses, and display .52-caliber Sharps breechloading rifles.

Private Ira Lackey, 35th Ohio Volunteer Infantry, in a distinctive dark blue shell jacket adorned with white braid. That garment was issued to Lackey's regiment early in 1863. Lackey enlisted in the 35th on 15 August 1861, was promoted to corporal on 1 May 1863, and was mustered out of the service on 26 August 1864.

to the charge, every step keeping time to the tap of the deep-sounding drum.'

Against troops holding rifle muskets, such methods—even when buttressed by courage and steel discipline—were suicidal. Gordon let the 'Bluebellies' close to within a few rods of his position and then bawled: 'Fire!' 'The effect was appalling,' he recalled. 'The entire [enemy] front line went down in the consuming blast. Before the rear lines could recover, my exultant men were on their feet, devouring them with successive volleys.'

The slaughter was not all one-sided. At Malvern Hill, Corinth, Gettysburg, Franklin, and other places, Southerners marched to their deaths in the same stately and senseless fashion. As subalterns and captains in the Mexican War, many Union and Confederate generals had seen linear tactics succeed time and time again. They clung obstinately to the belief that bayonet charges could win battles long after improved weaponry had rendered such gallantry foolhardy.

There were some stabs at tactical improvisation. Commanders commonly shielded their advancing lines by throwing out clouds of skirmishers to distract and disorder the enemy. Seasoned troops came to realize that parade-ground smartness was not half so important as passing through zones of fire without delay. The adjutant of the 3rd Delaware Infantry recounted how his regiment entered a tussle near Petersburg on 30 September 1864:

'Now people at home think we advance in a beautiful line and fire off our guns. . . . No. No. Down we lay in a field[,] the shells whizzing over and around us. Up rides an aid[e] to [the] brigade commander[,] whispers a few words & dashes away. Attention 3d Brigade. Forward and away we go, come to the briars, go through head long over stumps, bushs [sic] & all not in a nice line of battle but like a big flock of stray sheep—officers shouting, men halloing [sic] & growling, "Swing up that left back on right. Keep by those colours." "Hold on . . . , two men are enough to carry off that man, Steady men["] and so we go till we reach the edge of the woods. "Halt! Officers form your companies!" Again we form a decent line. "Fix bayonets" *We* know what that means. "Forward" "Yell boys" Yeh! Yeh-Yeh! Double quick

The color guard of the 8th Wisconsin Volunteer Infantry (the 'Eagle Regiment') near the Big Black River Bridge soon after the fall of Vicksburg, Mississippi, in July 1863. The private in the sack coat holds the perch for 'Old Abe,' a domesticated bald eagle and the 8th's mascot. The obverse side of the perch's escutcheon was painted red, white, and blue to resemble a U.S. flag. The 8th Wisconsin received Enfield rifles in 1862.

and away we go shouting as loud as we can and, you may not believe it, but the cheering is half the battle when we charge.'

Yet given a clear field of fire, steady troops could peel away a skirmisher screen in short order and mow down charging foes no matter how quickly they moved or how loudly they cheered. After the Battle of Cold Harbor (1-3 June 1864), where 12,000 Yankees were bowled over while mounting useless frontal assaults, Colonel Emory Upton, a brilliant Union infantryman, ranted: 'I am disgusted with the generalship displayed. Our men have, in many instances, been foolishly and wantonly sacrificed. . . . Thousands of lives might have been spared by the exercise of a little skill.'

In the main, Civil War generals were not stupid men; the majority simply were overwhelmed by their responsibilities. Officers appointed from civilian life felt they accomplished enough if they mastered Hardee or another drill manual. That they should come up with a new tactical system was inconceivable to all but a handful. Likewise, most generals with previous experience in the regular army (where they had commanded no more than two or three companies at a time) were too busy learning how to feed, equip, shelter, train, transport, and maneuver the mass citizen armies abruptly entrusted to their care. They had no leisure time to dabble with changes in tactical doctrine. Besides, the regular service of the 1850s was not much concerned with the ramifications of recent trends in military technology or with warfare on the grand scale. 'What would you expect,' an 1845 graduate of West Point exclaimed to an inquisitive Union volunteer officer, 'of men who have had to spend their lives at a two-company post, where there was nothing to do when off duty but play draw-poker and drink whiskey at the sutler's shop?'

The incredible thing about the Civil War was that hundreds of thousands of boys in blue and gray willingly faced such fearful carnage without flinching. At the Battle of Gaines's Mill (27 June 1862), the 1st South Carolina Rifles lost 319 out of 537 men while charging a Yankee battery. At Gettysburg on 2 July 1863, the 1st Minnesota Infantry, 262 officers and men, took on 3,000 Rebels in a desperate holding action. Only forty-seven Minnesotans exited the fray on their own two feet; fifty were killed and 174 wounded. Every battle produced dozens of examples like these. Years later, writers and ageing veterans would ascribe such dauntless bravery to love of country, love of freedom, or Christian fervor, but at the time few common soldiers spoke of their conduct in such flowery terms. Writing home five days after his baptism of fire at Shiloh, Private James K. Newton of the 14th Wisconsin said simply: 'The order was then given for us to advance & then we found out what it was to fight a battle. . . . All that I remember for

a while after that was that I loaded as fast as possible and where I saw a Secesh [Reb] I shot at him, & that was what every one there did.'

The geographic basis of the volunteer regiments contributed to their members' steadfast courage. After World War II, social scientists determined that soldiers behave most nobly under trying circumstances when surrounded by men they know, like, and respect. Civil War regiments, which were recruited from the same localities, consisted of longtime friends and neighbors, men who had grown up together. Such ties bound them together in battle. Abandoning one's comrades when the going got tough seemed unthinkable to most of these men. After watching the punishment of a 14th Wisconsin man for 'Cowardice before the enemy,' Sergeant James Newton scribbled on 10 August 1864: 'If it had been my case I think I would rather have been under ground, than to have been branded as a coward before the whole Reg't.' Soldiers who shrank from danger also knew that word of their behavior would spread all over their home towns, disgracing themselves and their loved ones. As an Ohio veteran in the Western Theater revealed, such pressures stiffened a man's backbone. 'Many a time, if not every time while we were waiting and expecting to be pushed into an engagement, would I have given almost anything to be out of it, back at the rear in some safe place. But despite such sensations, I always had enough strength of will and valued my reputation too much, to shirk—so was enabled to collar myself and compel myself to face the danger.'

Despite such resolve, repeated exposure to rifle fire taught veterans the value of cover. Lieutenant Colonel Lyman of the Army of the Potomac hit the mark when he said: 'Put a man in a hole and a good battery on a hill behind him, and he will beat off three times his number, even if he is not a very good soldier.' In 1862, some officers started taking advantage of whatever features a battlefield offered—a ditch, a rail fence, a stone wall—to shelter their men. In the following year, field works were increasingly prominent at Chancellorsville, Vicksburg, Gettysburg, Chickamauga, and Chattanooga. In 1864, the opposing armies seemed to dig in at every opportunity. Grant's Richmond Campaign and Sherman's Atlanta Campaign became exercises in trench warfare. In the words of an Illinois corporal with Sherman:

'Old soldiers know the value of protection[;] even a little protection is much better than no protection. We commence to dig as soon as we come in front of the enemy—often we use fence rails or timber—anything that will stop balls. A little protection Saves many lives and often wins a Battle.'

In a letter dated 18 May 1864, Lieutenant Colonel Lyman described the pattern followed by Lee's Army of

A sergeant (at left) and two privates of the 7th Illinois Volunteer Infantry, circa 1864. Illinois troops were often issued dark blue jackets in lieu of frock coats or fatigue blouses. These three dandies unbuttoned their jackets to show off their sky blue vests. The half-chevron on the lower left sleeve of the private at right marks him as a 'veteran volunteer.' The 7th Illinois was armed with Springfield and Enfield rifle muskets at various times in the war.

Colonel Robert Nugent of the 69th New York Volunteer Infantry was the last commander of the Army of the Potomac's renowned Irish Brigade. His no-nonsense campaign uniform consists of a dark blue jacket and trousers, a checked flannel shirt, a gold hatcord worn as a tie, and oversized dark blue shoulder straps with gold borders and silver embroidered eagles.

Northern Virginia as it endeavored to halt Grant's inexorable drive on Richmond, the Rebel capital:
'The great feature of this campaign is the extraordinary use made of earthworks. When we arrive on the ground, it takes . . . considerable time to put troops in position for attack, . . . then skirmishers must be thrown forward and an examination made for the point of attack. . . . Meantime what does the enemy? Hastily forming a line of battle, they then collect rails from fences, logs and all other materials, and pile them along the line; bayonets with a few picks and shovels, in the hands of men who work for their lives, soon suffice to cover a man kneeling, and extending often a mile or two. When our line advances, there is the line of the enemy, nothing showing but the bayonets, and the battle-flags stuck on top of the work. It is a rule that, when the Rebels halt, the first day gives them a good rifle-pit, the second, a regular infantry parapet with artillery in position; and the third a parapet with an abattis in front

and entrenched batteries behind. Sometimes they put this three days' work into the first twenty-four hours.'
A Wisconsin surgeon with Sherman saw Yankee troops display the same dexterity in battles around Atlanta:
'It was surprising to see the rapidity with which men will intrench themselves under fire—a few rails piled up in a twinkling, then dirt thrown upon them with numberless tools, bayonets, frying pan, bits of board, bare hands, anything to move dirt and it is not long before a protecting mound rises sufficiently to cover men lying behind it and as the digging proceeds, the ditch deepens as fast as the mound rises until in an almost incredible space of time an intrenchment has been thrown up sufficient to protect from cannon shot as well as rifle balls.'
A captain of the 20th Ohio Infantry, another veteran of the Atlanta Campaign, expounded on how entrenchments changed the complexion of combat:

Colonel Edward H. Ripley, 9th Vermont Volunteer Infantry, spring 1864. For field wear, Ripley favored an enlisted man's sack coat adorned with shoulder straps, a dark blue vest, dark blue trousers with sky blue welts, and high-topped riding boots. He also carried a Model 1860 light cavalry saber, a better cutting weapon than the flimsy field officer's sword.

A one-armed second lieutenant of the 1st Regiment, Veteran Reserve Corps, 1863–5. Created in April 1863, the corps accepted partially disabled Union soldiers and discharged veterans no longer willing to engage in combat. These men guarded transportation facilities, government property, prisoners of war, and conscripts, or worked in military hospitals. A total of twenty-four ten-company regiments and 188 independent companies were raised for the Veteran Reserve Corps. The lieutenant's uniform includes a sky blue coat with dark blue velvet cuffs and collar, plus a pair of sky blue trousers with dark blue double stripes along the outer seams.

'This war has demonstrated that earthworks can be rendered nearly impregnable . . . against direct assault. An attack on fortified lines must cost a fearful price, and should be well weighed whether the cost exceed not the gain. This, then, is what an assault means—a slaughter-pen, a charnel-house, and an army of weeping mothers and sisters at home.'

But the North could not win the war by staying on the tactical defensive. Victory lay in the conquest of the South, and that meant offensive warfare. Union generals felt compelled to fling their troops at Rebel earthworks time after time, throwing away thousands of lives for trifling results. Fortunately for the Yanks, many Confederate generals believed the best defense was the offense. Loath to surrender the initiative, Robert E. Lee preferred attacking to defending. John Bell Hood wrecked the Army of Tennessee by attacking whenever he could. Private Elisha Stockwell told how the 14th Wisconsin helped repel a Rebel assault near Atlanta in the

summer of 1864:

'We took up a position on quite a high ridge in an open field in the rear. We were on reserve. We stacked arms and carried rails up to the line in front, and they too were digging mighty lively, for they could see the Rebs preparing to charge. They charged three times that day, but our boys had a fair line of breastworks by the time they charged the last time, and the dead Rebs were thick in front.'

Such aggressiveness cost the outnumbered Confederate Army more troops than it could afford to lose. By squandering too many lives in too many battles, Rebel generals ensured that the superior manpower and material resources of the North would eventually prevail. The tragedy of the Civil War is that it took four blood-drenched years for that to happen.

8 Policing the Nation
1865–98

At the end of the Civil War, the United States ranked as one of the world's mightiest military powers. As of 1 May 1865, the victorious Union Army had swollen to 1,000,516 officers and men, many of them veterans of fearsome battles and onerous campaigns. But the awesome Northern war machine was not destined to outlive the conflict that called it into being. As soon as the Confederacy collapsed, her conquerors started clamoring for leave to doff their uniforms and go home. Over 800,000 Yankee volunteers were mustered out by 1 October 1865, and almost all the rest returned to civilian life within the next nine months.

The enduring American tradition of rapid postwar demobilization deposited the burden of defending the nation's sprawling land area back on the shoulders of the regular army. Those shoulders were a little larger in 1865 than they had been four years before. Thanks to the additions sponsored by the Lincoln Administration, the standing army's organizational chart listed six cavalry regiments (twelve companies apiece), five artillery regiments (twelve companies apiece), and nineteen infantry regiments (ten regiments with ten companies apiece, and nine with twenty-four companies). Unfortunately, the regular army had remained a skeleton organization throughout the Civil War. Northern boys largely preferred the higher bounties and laxer discipline offered by the volunteer service. Sixty-seven thousand regulars were recruited following Fort Sumter, but 16,365 deserted and 5,465 died in combat and from other causes. Of the 448 companies allowed by law, only 295 were organized before the war's close. By April 1865, the regular army contained 22,310 officers and other ranks, 20,000 short of its legal size.

It was imperative that more regulars be raised without delay. Much work awaited them—especially in two violence-prone quarters of the republic.

Some authorities saw an urgent need for regulars to keep ex-Rebels in line while the old Confederacy underwent Reconstruction. Prevailing over President Andrew Johnson in a series of bitter and complex political skirmishes, a Republican-dominated Congress utilized the Army to support a crusade aimed at transforming the South's political system and granting newly freed slaves the fundamental rights of American citizenship, including adult male suffrage. From 1867 to 1877, roughly 36 to 25 per cent of the regular army was posted in Dixie for Reconstruction duty (see Table 7). 'Our

Table 7. The Regular Army and Reconstruction, 1867-77

Year	Total in Regular Army	Federal Troops in the South
1867	56,815	20,117
1868	50,916	17,657
1869	36,774	11,237
1870	37,075	9,050
1871	28,953	8,038
1872	29,214	7,368
1874	30,520	7,701
1876	26,312	6,011

soldiers hate that kind of duty terribly,' stated William Tecumseh Sherman, the Army's commanding general from 1869 to 1884, 'and not one of our officers but would prefer to go to the plains against the Indians rather than encounter a street mob, or serve a civil process.'

As Sherman indicated, federal troops were also needed in the West after Appomattox to relieve volunteers garrisoning frontier forts and to quell a new wave of Indian uprisings. The Civil War failed to staunch the flow of emigrants who came to the Great Plains and the

PLATE 25: A NEW LOOK FOR THE DRESS UNIFORM, 1872–81

Before the limestone blockhouse at Fort Hays, Kansas.
84. Musician, 5th U.S. Infantry, Dress Uniform, 1875: *Under the uniform regulations of July 1872, company musicians continued to wear sets of 'herring-bone' lace on their dress coats. An enlisted man's Model 1872 full dress cap sported a white worsted pompon; the officer's version came with a plume of white cocks' feathers.* **85. First Lieutenant (Adjutant George William Baird), 5th U.S. Infantry, Dress Uniform, 1876:** *The 1872 regulations gave all regimental officers double-breasted coats. Field officers wore nine buttons in each row; company officers had seven. A regiment's adjutant was marked by an elaborate gold aiguillette draped across his chest.* **86. Colonel (Nelson A. Miles), 5th U.S. Infantry, Dress Uniform, 1873:** *Field officers displayed 'three double stripes of gold braid' on their cuffs, while subalterns rated two. Field officers had gold sword belts. Sky blue silk stripes were woven into the belts of junior officers. All regimental officers had dark blue stripes one-and-a-half inches wide on their trousers.* **87. Sergeant, 9th U.S. Infantry, Dress Uniform, 1876:** *On 19 November 1875, a pair of crossed rifles replaced the bugle as the cap badge of the U.S. Infantry. The red borders on the lower service stripes denoted 'service in war.' A sergeant's 1872-pattern trousers had dark blue stripes one inch wide. This veteran's waistbelt and 1874 infantry ('Palmer') brace system support a pair of Model 1874 McKeever cartridge boxes.*

85. First Lieutenant, 5th U.S. Infantry,
Dress Uniform, 1876

87. Sergeant, 9th U.S. Infantry, Dress
Uniform, 1876

84. Musician, 5th U.S. Infantry, Dress
Uniform, 1875

86. Colonel, 5th U.S. Infantry, Dress
Uniform, 1873

lands beyond to seek their fortunes. The Far West's white population grew by 1,000,000 souls in the 1860s, and by 2,500,000 more before 1880. As pioneer numbers increased, so did the pressure to deprive the region's 270,000 uncaged Indians of their precious hunting grounds. Finally awakening to the enormity of the white threat, some tribes submitted peacefully to the trespassing hordes. Others fought with a desperation that made their earlier resistance seem tame by comparison. From 1865 to 1898, the U.S. Army conducted 938 combat actions against hostile warriors, encounters resulting in the deaths of 919 Bluecoats and the wounding of 1,025 more. For a quarter of a century following the Civil War, Indian fighting was again the primary mission of the American regular. A 13th Infantryman who battled recalcitrant natives in the early 1870s summed up the Army's frontier experience in these words: 'We were bewhiskered savages living under canvas.'

All through the second half of 1865 and the first half of 1866, Army officers labored feverishly to construct an adequate regular force to replace the departing volunteers. They had a difficult time. By June 1866, the standing army mustered only 33,490 of all ranks. However, a few recruiting parties enjoyed heartening successes. When the 18th U.S. Infantry journeyed west in the spring of 1866 to man forts situated along key transportation routes, it had its full complement of 2,200

Officers of the 8th U.S. Infantry in their full dress finery on David's Island, near New Rochelle, New York, circa 1870. The regular army retained the styles of the Civil War era until 1872. Instead of the uncomfortable Hardee hat, these officers sport a smart little chapeau with a dented crown and a narrow brim. The first lieutenant at far left, the officer of the day, wears his sash draped over his right shoulder.

men. Nonetheless, the infusion of manpower did not necessarily improve the 18th's combat effectiveness. Except for a nucleus of 300 veterans, all the troops were 'fresh fish' straight from the factory or the farm, and their superiors found no time to train them. W. H. Bisbee, a company officer, later estimated that 200 of these green enlisted personnel fell victim to the Sioux and Cheyennes in 1866 and 1867 because they did not know how to handle their weapons properly.

Exhibiting an uncharacteristic sensitivity to peacetime military problems, Congress hastened to the rescue of the regular establishment. On 28 July 1866, President Johnson signed an 'Act to increase and fix the Military Peace Establishment of the United States.' Although the U.S. Artillery stood pat with five regiments, the U.S. Cavalry expanded to ten regiments and the U.S. Infantry to forty-five. Four of the new infantry regiments (the 42nd, 43rd, 44th, and 45th) constituted a 'Veteran Reserve Corps,' drawing its members from Union soldiers wounded in the late war. The Veteran Reserve Corps was intended exclusively for garrison duty, freeing fitter troops for field service. In keeping with the current Congress's enlightened views on race, six other regiments (the 38th, 39th, 40th, and 41st Infantry and the 9th and 10th Cavalry) were formed with black enlisted men and white officers. These were the first regular Negro regiments in the history of the republic. The term of service was now three years for infantry and artillery and five years for cavalry. Furthermore, the Army was empowered to enroll as many as 1,000 Indian scouts.

On the negative side, the Army Act of 1866 was not actually as generous to the U.S. Infantry as it might appear. The branch was reorganized into forty-five ten-company, single-battalion regiments. The nine over-

sized regiments created during the Civil War lost their second and third battalions. The twenty-seven separated battalions each received two new companies and became full regiments in their own right. For example, the 2nd Battalion, 18th Infantry, was redesignated as the 27th Infantry. Thus, only 134 fresh companies had to be formed to complete the congressional expansion plan—not 260.

The law stated that an infantry regiment should have 'one colonel, one lieutenant-colonel, one major, one adjutant, one regimental-quartermaster, one sergeant-major, one quartermaster-sergeant, one commissary-sergeant, one hospital-steward, two principal musicians, and ten companies.' A company was entitled to one captain, two lieutenants, one first sergeant, one quarter-master sergeant, four sergeants, eight corporals, two artificers, two musicians, and one wagoner. Congress left the exact number of privates in the regular army to the discretion of the President. Each infantry and cavalry company was allowed fifty to 100 privates, and artillery companies could have as many as 122. Johnson fixed the strength of 620 companies (all the infantry and cavalry and almost all the artillery) at sixty-four privates. The only exceptions were the Army's ten light artillery companies (two per artillery regiment), which were permitted 122 privates apiece. These arrangements gave the U.S. Army an official complement of 54,302. In the following year, Johnson decreed that every company assigned to the frontier should have 100 privates, and by September 1867, the Army totaled 56,815 officers and men. The regular service had never known such health between wars.

Besides the welcome increase in size, the U.S. Infantry benefited enormously from the Army's adoption of an improved shoulder arm. The Civil War proved the

worth of certain commercial breechloading weapons. Despite a few defects, breechloaders were easier to handle and gave a faster rate of fire than the standard muzzleloading rifle musket. In 1864, the economy-minded Ordnance Department began exploring the possibility of converting Springfield rifle muskets into practical breechloading infantry rifles. The winning design, the brainchild of Master Armorer Erskin S. Allin of the government's Springfield Arsenal, was incorporated in the manufacture of the Model 1865 and Model 1866 U.S. rifles. The latter was delivered to frontier garrisons in significant numbers in 1867. Doughboys affectionately rechristened their gleaming new arms 'Long Toms' and 'trapdoor Springfields.' The Model 1866 Springfield could fire a dozen rounds in one minute—three times the rate of fire of the discarded muzzleloader—and its range was twice as far. Subjected to several minor modifications over the years, the single-shot trapdoor Springfield reigned as the standard arm of the U.S. Infantry until the early 1890s.

Allin's invention came as a rude surprise to the Plains Indians. Mounted warriors had learned to charge after white infantrymen fired their first volley, secure in the knowledge that there was time to unloose a shower of arrows or even strike home with a lance or war club before the Bluecoats could reload their clumsy muzzle-loaders. Such a scenario must have fueled the hopes of

Alexander Gardner's camera caught six soldiers of the short-lived 38th U.S. Infantry serving as escorts on a stagecoach belonging to the United States Express Company at Hays City, Kansas, in October 1867. The standing sergeant wears a slouch hat and four-button fatigue blouse. The other troops are attired in forage caps, frock coats, and brass shoulder scales. An officer in a frock coat and broad-brimmed hat peers from the coach door.

A company of regular infantry-men in their 1872-regulation dress uniforms on the parade ground at Fort Lyon, Colorado, circa 1877. Two musicians, their coats decorated with strips of sky-blue lace arranged in a 'herring-bone' pattern, stand at far left. The two officers and all the enlisted men seen here wear white gloves.

1,000 Sioux braves on 2 August 1867, when they trapped two officers and twenty-six soldiers of the 27th Infantry and four civilians within a rude corral of fourteen wagon boxes five miles west of Fort Phil Kearny on the bloody Bozeman Trail. Some of these warriors had massacred eighty men from the fort's garrison nine months earlier, and they doubtlessly expected another easy victory. But the exulting natives did not know that the Bluecoats crouching behind the wagon boxes clutched recently issued Model 1866 U.S. rifles. As the Sioux bore down on the corral, Captain John W. Powell, the white commander, shouted: 'Take your places men! Here they come! Shoot to kill!' The troops were not completely familiar with their new breechloaders, but the hostiles obligingly closed to pointblank range. Working their weapons frantically, the whites threw out an impene-trable ring of rifle fire, fending off the Sioux for four hours until a relief force arrived from the fort. With a loss of six killed and two wounded, Powell's steadfast band hit as many as 180 Indians. Nearly sixty Sioux died as a result of their wounds.

The Wagon Box Fight taught the Sioux the folly of mounting a massed charge against white infantry, a lesson many took to heart. Red Horse, a Sioux chief,

PLATE 26: THE 'WALK-A-HEAPS': INDIAN HUNTERS ON FOOT, 1865–90

88. Private, 27th Infantry, Winter Field Dress, 1867: *Aside from his Model 1866 ('Allin Conversion') breechloading rifle and Model 1866 cartridge box, this winter picket is dressed just as he would have appeared in the Civil War.* **89. Sergeant, 14th U.S. Infantry, Campaign Dress, 1876:** *Based on the famous Stanley Morrow photographs of Brigadier General George Crook's infantry in the Sioux War of 1876. For hot summer marches, troops shed their blouses in favor of civilian shirts or the 1874 issue pattern of gray flannel. Note the Model 1873 Springfield rifle, the privately procured hat and 'thimble belt,' and the rolled-up rubber blanket (a versatile item that served as a ground sheet, shelter half, and raincoat).* **90. Private, 8th U.S. Infantry, Campaign Dress, 1886:** *Twenty picked men from the 8th Infantry joined in the first leg of a grueling, four-month pursuit of Geronimo that began in May 1886. They literally marched themselves out of their uniforms, one participant from the 4th Cavalry recalling: 'Suits of underclothing formed our uniform and moccasins covered our feet.' Note the Model 1885 campaign hat and Model 1879 Springfield rifle.* **91. Corporal, 21st Infantry, Campaign Dress, 1873:** *The Model 1872 fatigue hat came equipped with hooks and eyes so the brim could be held up to resemble a Napoleonic bicorn. The 1872-pattern fatigue blouse was unpopular and soon passed out of use. The corporal's rifle is a Model 1868 Springfield. A Model 1872 cartridge box rests on his right hip.*

89. Sergeant, 14th U.S. Infantry,
Campaign Dress, 1876

91. Corporal, 21st U.S. Infantry, Campaign
Dress, 1873

88. Private, 27th U.S. Infantry, Winter
Field Dress, 1867

90. Private, 8th U.S. Infantry, Campaign
Dress, 1886

claimed that the 2,000 to 4,000 warriors who annihilated George Armstrong Custer's 7th Cavalry at the Little Big Horn in June 1876 retreated at the approach of 200–odd 7th Infantrymen armed with breechloading rifles. 'Indians can't fight walking soldiers,' Red Horse complained, 'they are afraid of them, and so we moved away.'

At the same time as frontier foot soldiers were field-testing the trapdoor Springfield, they were also forced to master a new drillbook. On 1 August 1867, the War Department adopted a manual entitled *Infantry Tactics* by Lieutenant Colonel Emory Upton, 1st U.S. Artillery. An 1861 graduate of West Point, Upton possessed an active intelligence, unflappable courage, and abiding concern for the welfare of his men—sterling qualities which contributed to an extremely promising military career. Rising rapidly to the command of an infantry brigade in the Army of the Potomac by the summer of 1863, he became disgusted with the way his colleagues sacrificed thousands of lives because of their blind reliance on obsolete tactics. Given a free hand at the Battle of Spotsylvania (10 May 1864), Upton arranged twelve regiments in a special assault column that pierced a well-entrenched Confederate line and nabbed 1,000 prisoners. After the Civil War, Upton returned to the Military Academy as instructor of tactics, and he set to work to devise a system of infantry tactics better attuned to the realities of the battlefield.

Upton's *Infantry Tactics* recognized the destructive power of rifled weapons—especially breechloaders. Because the Long Tom's rate of fire enabled troops to hold a broader front, American infantrymen were now taught to fight in one rank as well as two. A thinner battle line presented less of a target to the enemy, but it also made it more difficult for officers to supervise their men. To compensate for the loss in control, Upton advised that each soldier be trained to act as a thinking individual and not merely as a cog in a machine.

Drawing on his Civil War experiences, Upton paid extra attention to the role of skirmishers in combat. He instructed commanders to use skirmishers 'to clear the way for the main body, their movements . . . so regulated as to keep it constantly covered.' In an attack, skirmishers were to dash forward in extended order, halting 150 yards from the enemy to deliver a harassing fire with their rifles. Marching in column to minimize their exposure to unfriendly fire, assault troops would advance behind the shield of skirmishers. As it closed to 200 yards, the column would deploy into line so that every man could bring his rifle to bear—and then charge. If enemy resistance proved tougher than expected, reinforcements could be fed to the skirmish lines and assault columns. Upton seemed to think that if enough men were available to press the attack, any position

could be carried.

The new tactical system was an intelligent response to problems that had baffled America's best military minds since 1861. Although the Army retired Upton's *Infantry Tactics* prior to its next conventional war, his ideas were borrowed by subsequent manuals, and they served the American soldier well into the 20th century.

Between the expansion of 1866 and the work of Emory Upton, the U.S. Infantry seemed destined for a golden age, but the federal government blighted that dream when it reverted to its habit of economizing at the expense of the military. The fiscal ax fell with a vengeance on 3 March 1869 when fickle Congress ordered the elimination of the 26th through 45th Infantry. Officers and men from the twenty unfortunate regiments were absorbed by the surviving twenty-five. The Veteran Reserve Corps disappeared entirely, and the number of black foot regiments was halved. (The 38th and 41st Infantry were amalgamated into a new 24th Regiment, and the 39th and 40th Infantry were com-

Captain Wyllys Lyman, 5th U.S. Infantry, a hero of the Red River War of 1874–5, donned his 1872-regulation dress coat for a visit to the photographer shortly after that taxing campaign. Lyman's Model 1872 chasseur-pattern forage cap, with its gold embroidered bugle badge and silver regimental number, sits on a table.

bined as the 25th Infantry.) The legislators also limited the Army to 37,313 officers and men, and they re-established five years as the term of enlistment for all regulars.

The reductions of 1869 seriously diminished the standing and morale of the U.S. Infantry. In 1867, the branch constituted 62 per cent of the regular establishment; by 1870, the Army was only 50 per cent infantry. Furthermore, many 'web-feet' resented the demise of their old regiments and arbitrary transfers to strange commands. In April 1869, a former 30th Infantryman, unhappy with his new surroundings in the 4th Infantry, vowed that he had 'sixteen months to serve yet, and when that is up they can go to the devil—they won't get this Chile again.'

Budget-cutting politicians shook the Army once more in July 1870, restricting the enlisted contingent to 30,000 men. Four years later, the troop ceiling was lowered to 25,000 rank and file, where it would remain without appreciable change until 1898. The wave of contractions

that washed over the Army from 1869 to 1874 forced the dismissal of 900 officers, many of them able leaders.

The revival of congressional stinginess left the regular army with forty shrinking regiments to garrison more than 200 separate posts spread over the length and breadth of a country with the dimensions of an empire. To meet its weighty responsibilities, the Army fell back into its old role as a national constabulary—broken up into hundreds of one- or two-company detachments. Regiments usually existed in name only, a state of affairs which hampered the Army's ability to respond to major crises. The 12th Infantry was kept dispersed from 1869 to 1887! When the 21st Infantry assembled its ten companies for field maneuvers near Fort Robinson, Nebraska, in 1889, it was the first time they had been reunited in a decade. As in the past, the company became the basic administrative, tactical, and logistical unit in the regular service, the source of a soldier's identity and

First Lieutenant William L. Sherwood of the 21st U.S. Infantry was treacherously slain in April 1873 near the Lava Beds of northern California by Modoc Indians flying a flag of truce. Here he wears his 1872-pattern undress coat, a single-breasted sack coat of dark blue serge. The coat was piped with black braid and decorated on the breast with black 'herring-bone' loops.

In 1874, the U.S. Army replaced the 1872 plaited fatigue blouse with the five-button sack coat modeled here by an unknown private. The infantry version had sky blue piping on the collar and cuffs. The private's black leather accoutrements were designed by First Lieutenant George H. Palmer, 16th Infantry, and adopted by the Army in 1875. Palmer's 'brace system' was inspired by equipments developed by the British.

the focus of his loyalty. An 8th Infantryman who enlisted in the late 1880s testified: 'The company is everything to a soldier.'

The financial constraints of the post-Civil War era robbed the regular army of the power to solve two vexing problems—how to fill its ranks with high-caliber recruits and how to keep men in the service until their enlistments ran out. As John E. Cox, a 1st Infantryman from 1872 to 1877, discovered, a soldier's lot was still as hard as it had been in ante-bellum days:

'There was regular guard duty, drills—the most vigorous of exercise—target practice, frequent inspections, fatigue duties, eternal scrubbings, polishing, cooking, barbering, tailoring, teaming, herding, blacksmithing, carpentering, painting, saw-milling, wood chopping, clerking, escorting, campaigning, etc., etc. . . . The fact is, the Army is one of the busiest bodies of men in the United States. Generally, the soldiers earn their wages by doing downright hard work for the government, in addition to regular soldier duties.'

With peacetime soldiering as unpopular as ever, regular recruiters had no other alternative but to lower their standards. The pickings were best among the urban poor—frequently men devoid of education, job skills, or the semblance of pride. On 18 September 1877, the New York *Sun* categorized America's defenders as 'bummers, loafers, and foreign paupers.' Even hard-boiled, long-service officers were dismayed at the sight of so many unsavory characters wearing their country's uniform. 'No squad of recruits enlisted in New York leaves the city without containing faces familiar to the old city detectives,' fumed Colonel William B. Hazen of the 6th Infantry in 1872. 'We enlist men . . . without knowing their names, residences or anything whatever about them. Is it strange that a third of our Army deserts each year?'

Congress intensified the unattractiveness of military life on 15 July 1870 by instituting across-the-board pay cuts for all enlisted grades. A private's pittance shrank from $16 to $13 a month, and disgruntled soldiers took up the chant: 'A dollar a day is damn poor pay, but thirteen a month is less.' For thousands of Bluecoats, the drop in salary was the last straw, and they retaliated the only way they could. In 1871, the year the pay cut took effect, 8,800 troops—32.6 per cent of the Army's enlisted personnel—deserted. In a lame attempt to make amends, Congress proffered a cheap solution to the desertion scourge on 15 May 1872, establishing a system of longevity pay. Any soldier who served honorably through his third, fourth, and fifth year would receive bonuses totaling $72. But this meager incentive had little impact on the Army's retention rate.

To be sure, desertion had long been the bane of the U.S. Army. The records collected between 1867 and 1891 simply added new contours to a familiar story. During those years, 255,712 men took the enlistment oath, and 88,475—about one-third—deserted. The only force capable of luring large quantities of choice recruits into the regular army and holding them there was economic catastrophe—such as the Depression of 1873-9. As the *Army and Navy Journal* reported in October 1873: 'One result of the financial difficulties . . . is seen in the character of the men now offering themselves for enlistment. . . . Our recruiting officers have never had a better choice of material.'

Much to the surprise of white Americans, the Army's black regiments were spared wholesale personnel turnovers. Though the targets of petty discrimination, including a ten-year exile to the meanest stations in the West—the posts on the Texas frontier—the 24th and 25th Infantry suffered fewer desertions and enjoyed more re-enlistments than most white units. In fact, the 24th boasted the lowest desertion rate of any regular regiment for seven straight years (1880 to 1886). Redfield Proctor, the nation's Secretary of War from 1889 to 1891, identified the primary reason for this sterling record: 'To the colored man the service offers a career, to the white man too often a refuge.' In a society still attached to notions of white supremacy, the Army offered almost the only place an Afro-American could safely assert his manhood. In addition, the faithful conduct of black infantrymen was inspired by a loftier motive than simple self-interest. As G. G. Mullins, the

PLATE 27: INFANTRY FASHIONS, 1881–90

Near the south sally port at Fort Mackinac, Michigan.

92. First Sergeant, 24th U.S. Infantry, Dress Uniform, 1889: *In 1884, the U.S. Infantry dropped sky blue as its facing color, and the new frock coat approved that year came with a collar 'faced with white cloth all around.' In 1888, chevrons of gold lace were authorized for the 'dress-coat.' An enlisted war veteran was entitled to 'a diagonal half chevron' edged all around with 'cloth of the same color as the facings of the arm of service in which the soldier earned the right to wear it.' The scarlet borders on this non-commissioned officer's lowermost service stripes indicate that he was an artilleryman in the Civil War.* **93. First Lieutenant, 15th U.S. Infantry, Dress Uniform, 1882:** *The Model 1881 officer's helmet came with a gilt chain-chinstrap. Beginning with the 1872 regulations, company officers of infantry carried the Model 1860 staff and field officer's sword.* **94. Captain (Frank Heartt Edmunds), 1st U.S. Infantry, Undress, 1889:** *The captain's forage cap is a variation on the smart style first introduced in 1872. The 1889-pattern officer's undress coat was edged with black mohair braid. The two marksman's buttons on each side of the collar testify to the wearer's prowess with the Springfield rifle.* **95. Private, 8th U.S. Infantry, Undress Summer Uniform, 1887:** *This soldier wears a Model 1880 sun helmet and an 1883-pattern sack coat—with a pair of marksman's sterling silver buttons adorning the collar and a marksman's bronze pin on the breast.*

93. First Lieutenant, 15th U.S. Infantry,
Dress Uniform, 1882

92. First Sergeant, 24th U.S. Infantry,
Dress Uniform, 1889

95. Private, 8th U.S. Infantry, Summer
Undress, 1887

The short-handed Indian-fighting Army did not have enough artillerymen for field service, so infantrymen were often detailed as scratch crews for howitzers and Gatling guns. Five 20th Infantrymen posed in 1877 at Fort McKean, Dakota Territory, with the 1-inch Gatling they manned during the ill-fated Little Big Horn Campaign of 1876. Four soldiers display the new crossed rifles cap badge introduced in 1875, but the corporal at far left retains his old bugle insignia.

A company of the 5th U.S. Infantry in winter campaign dress at Fort Keogh, Montana Territory, circa 1877. When Colonel Nelson A. Miles took the 5th into the field to campaign against the Sioux in November 1876, he made sure his men were warmly clothed. They were issued buffalo overcoats and overshoes, fur caps, and mittens. The men fashioned woolen masks to protect their heads and faces and cut up Army blankets to make special winter underwear.

25th's patronizing but well-meaning chaplain, stated in 1877:

'The ambition to be all that soldiers should be is not confined to a few of these sons of an unfortunate race. They are possessed of the notion that the colored people of the whole country are more or less affected by their conduct in the army. The chaplain is sometimes touched by . . . their manly anxiety to be well thought of at Army HQ and throughout the states. This is the bottom secret of their patient toil and surprising progress....'

The discontent that undermined the white soldier's devotion to duty also permeated the regular officer corps. The Army reorganization of 1866 featured a sincere effort to provide places for deserving Union volunteer officers who wished to pursue careers in the military. For most of these heroes, however, a regular commission brought a plunge in status. Former generals took charge of regiments, battalions, and companies as colonels, majors, and captains. Men who had sported eagles or oak leaves on their shoulder straps exchanged them for a lieutenant's insignia. The same thing happened to regular officers who had attained high temporary rank while leading volunteer units against the Confederacy. These Civil War veterans would dominate the Army command structure for the next forty years. After 1866, West Point resumed its function as the regular establishment's main source of 'shavetail' second lieutenants, but hundreds of civilians with political clout

Second Lieutenant John Alex Lockwood, 17th U.S. Infantry, in his full dress uniform, 1884. Lockwood's gold Russian-style shoulder knots have the white cloth pads introduced the year this photograph was taken. The black Model 1881 helmet has a gilt spike, top-piece, chain-chinstrap, eagle device, and side buttons, and the regimental number on the eagle's shield is white metal.

wrote his wife: 'They [certain officers] had rather gamble and drink at a post than serve in the field. During good weather they do well, but in the first rain, they curl up like wet hens and do nothing but growl and whine.'

Whether they preserved their zeal for soldiering or slid into apathy, regular officers stationed on the frontier encountered a lifetime's worth of frustration as they prosecuted the last of America's Indian wars, which spanned the years 1865 to 1890. For men accustomed to the grand, toe-to-toe slugfests of the Civil War, the Indian way of fighting seemed almost cowardly. The warriors of the Far West, masters of hit-and-run guerrilla tactics, chose to strike when the odds were most in their favor. They normally steered clear of large bodies of white and black troops. The red men preferred battles that they could win with little or no loss to themselves. With their fleet ponies and superior knowledge of the country, native braves outran and outsmarted pursuing Army columns with irritating regularity. Such methods turned Indian campaigns into what a first sergeant of the 10th Infantry called 'a war of who could last longest.'

Yet, above all else, the red man was an unpredictable foe. If pressed too closely—or if his family was threatened—or religious omens assured him of success—he could turn and fight with a tenacity equal to that of any crack professional troops in America or Europe. Sergeant Riley R. Lane, 7th U.S. Infantry, one of the first whites to see the remains of the 263 7th Cavalrymen slaughtered at the Little Big Horn, portrayed the perilously fluid nature of Indian fighting in this apt analogy: 'The expedition reminded me of an illustration I saw in one of the papers, of the Prince of Wales' Tiger hunt in India. First the Prince gets a rear view of the tiger; Then a front view, then the tiger gets a rear view of the Prince of Wales.'

The Army doctrine of that era did not credit infantry with a decisive role in crushing Indian outbreaks. Since most hostile tribes were well mounted, it made sense to hunt them with 'pony soldiers.' Doughboys usually accompanied the major field columns, but, theoretically, their main purpose was supportive—guarding supply trains and base depots to free the cavalry for offensive sorties. Infantrymen took umbrage at their continual subordination to the 'sore-asses.' Colonel Miles of the 5th Infantry criticized one general for planning Indian campaigns 'without studying or confidence in anything but cavalry.'

The high command's attitude did more harm to the U.S. Infantry than merely deflate its self-esteem. In the summer of 1876, Congress responded to the Custer Massacre by enlarging each cavalry company to 100 enlisted men. But the legislators also voted to maintain

received lieutenancies without the benefit of a formal military education. Furthermore, 156 persistent non-commissioned officers managed to overcome the rigid Army caste system and enter the officer corps between 1867 and 1892.

Whatever their backgrounds, officers of the post-Civil War Army found themselves stuck in dead-end careers. Seniority determined promotion, and there was not much upward mobility in a small standing force threatened with further decreases. A second lieutenant commissioned in 1877 could expect to wait a minimum of twenty-four years before making major, and as many as thirty-seven years to become a colonel. In 1890, one general stated that 'almost all the captains of infantry' were too old to drill their companies.

As officers aged without advancement, they tended to lose their pride and spirit. In December 1881, Lieutenant General Philip H. Sheridan warned the government that it 'cannot expect officers to strive hard, take risks and perform distinguished service on our frontiers' without offering them tangible rewards. Sheridan's fears arose from hard experience. During the grueling Red River War, Nelson A. Miles, the colonel of the 5th U.S. Infantry, complained that some of his officers were 'worse than useless.' On 24 September 1874, Miles

Company B, 25th U.S. Infantry, at Fort Snelling, Minnesota, circa 1884–8. The dark blue dress coats with their white collars, shoulder straps, cuffs, and piping were authorized in 1884. The black regiments of the Indian-fighting Army enjoyed a remarkably high retention rate, as witnessed by the white half-chevrons bedecking the lower sleeves of so many of these proud warriors. Each chevron was awarded for one successfully completed term of enlistment.

the Army's total troop ceiling at 25,000. Consequently, the U.S. Cavalry could not grow without corresponding shrinkage in the infantry. Every infantry regiment accordingly was confined to a maximum of 375 rank and file, and the proportion of infantrymen in the regular army dwindled to 38 per cent.

Yet even after the reorganization of 1876, the U.S. Cavalry was never big enough to spearhead every Army lunge into Indian country. Doughboys received their share of chances for death and glory in the final stands of the various tribes. For most web-feet, however, an Indian campaign brought nothing more than blisters and exhaustion. 'I cannot tell of all the storms encountered,' Sergeant John E. Cox, 1st U.S. Infantry, recalled of his days on the Northern Plains, 'of hard marches on short rations, and often without water, of camps made without wood for fires; of rivers crossed only with great difficulty; of any disagreeable experiences connected with campaigning in the "bad lands."' It was with good reason that the Sioux called frontier foot soldiers 'walk-a-heaps.'

In those instances where infantry commands brought their quarry to bay, the Bluecoats often ended up wish-ing that the hostiles had gotten away. The life of a typical Indian male centered on hunting, riding, raiding, and horse-stealing, activities which produced a formidable warrior. On the other hand, the men who entered the regular army usually lacked a background in the martial arts, and the shoddy training they received hardly left them proficient at personal combat. In fact, the Army continued to dispense with any sort of uniform basic training until 1881. Recruits were still expected to learn how to soldier after they joined their companies. But most line units were kept too busy with active campaigning and housekeeping chores to maintain respectable training programs.

The chronic indifference to soldier preparation was most noticeable in the state of Army marksmanship. Contrary to the yarns spun by novelists and other mythmakers, the bulk of the regulars who patrolled the Far West in the late 1860s and the 1870s were abominable shots. In January 1879, a worried staff officer commented:

'Our arms can kill an enemy as soon as he becomes distinctly visible to the eye, provided he is hit. And it is just in that inability to hit that the true source of all dissatisfaction with our standard arms . . . is to be found. Our soldiers as a class are not skillful marksmen.'

Poor Army marksmanship owed its existence to two factors—inadequate military budgets and the conservatism of the officer corps. For a long time, Congress simply refused to provide troops with an ample supply of practice ammunition. Beginning in 1872, each soldier was apportioned ninety extra rounds a year—hardly

Seven non-commissioned officers of the 13th U.S. Infantry in New Mexico during the Apache Campaign of 1885–6. They wear privately purchased broad-brimmed hats and bandanas. Six of them are in the Army's 1883 dark blue flannel overshirt, but the soldier standing at far left displays a handsome 'fireman's shirt' with white piping—an item much favored by American cowboys. For field operations, frontier infantrymen preferred to carry their rifle ammunition on looped 'prairie belts' instead of in cartridge boxes.

enough to turn a novice into a crack shot. The annual allotment eventually rose to 240 rounds per man in October 1877—a definite improvement. Unfortunately, the closed minds of certain officers negated much of that modest advance. Commanders fettered to a Civil War past were disposed to believe that all their troops needed to know about shooting was how to fire volleys at targets set at ranges of only 100 to 200 yards. But volleys were of little use against Indians, who liked to fight spread out—usually at far distances and often from covered positions. Nevertheless, many pig-headed white officers adhered to the volley policy because they held that the average regular was too dull-witted to master anything more difficult. Betraying no sense of shame, Colonel John Gibbon of the 7th Infantry admitted to a group of congressmen in 1878:

'I have never, until quite recently, permitted any men at my post to fire at over a hundred yards, for the reason that the vast majority of the men cannot hit [a target] the size [of] a man at a greater distance than that. And my personal experience teaches me that with the vast majority of men it takes a lifetime to attain even ordinary proficiency in rifle-practice. In other words, that at beyond one hundred or one hundred and fifty yards, all the firing of our men is pretty much a matter of chance.'

Despite all its alleged inadequacies and real defects, the U.S. Infantry produced the Army's best all-around Indian fighter of the 1870s and 1880s—Nelson Appleton Miles. Born in Massachusetts on 8 August 1839, Miles was working as a clerk in a Boston crockery store when

the Civil War broke out. With borrowed money, he recruited enough men to obtain a lieutenancy in the 22nd Massachusetts Volunteer Infantry. Over the next four years, this oft-wounded but irrepressible young scrapper scaled the heights of the profession of arms. By the summer of 1864, he was commanding a division in the Army of the Potomac, and he ended his volunteer service as a brevet major general. Deciding to make the Army his life, Miles obtained a regular appointment as colonel of the new black 40th U.S. Infantry in 1866, settling down to Reconstruction duty in North Carolina. In 1869, he transferred to the 5th Infantry and went west to battle Indians.

Nelson Miles assumed command of the 5th Infantry with a determination to transform it into 'the best disciplined, most orderly and easiest controlled regiment in the United States.' His men soon learned that their colonel was a perfectionist who demanded more from them than was the norm in other outfits. A fanatic on the subject of physical fitness, Miles had a gymnasium built for the 5th in the winter of 1873-4—the first such establishment in the U.S. Army—and he added calisthenics and other exercises as part of his soldiers' regular routine. Miles kept the 5th combat-ready by drilling the regiment at every opportunity. The troops came to know their Upton backwards and forwards. They could form a skirmish line, a battle line, and the time-honored hollow square with speed and unvarying smartness. Miles never let these skills grow rusty—even when his command was in transit. On 2 August 1876, while the little steamboat, *E. H. Durfee,* was conveying six companies of the 5th up the Yellowstone to seek out the Indians who had vanquished Custer, Miles wrote his wife: 'At almost every stopping place we have disembarked (in three minutes) and had battalion and scout drill, so that this command at least will be in fine condition and quite strong. The recruits are doing remarkably well.' Three days earlier, the proud colonel had given a fuller description of his training methods: 'The command is in fine spirits and every preparation made to make it efficient. I had drills three time a day on shore and boat and have just had officers' instructions in the cabin. In fact the steamer, ever since we came aboard, has been as busy as a beehive, and I believe the command will be in fine condition when we arrive in the hostile country.'

Miles's insistence on professionalism at every level endowed the 5th Infantry with a prowess and élan that placed it in a class above most other regular organizations of its day. The 5th and its colonel consistently outperformed their peers—regardless of circumstances. Following the Custer Massacre, the regiment won some of its proudest laurels and redeemed much of the Army's honor by chasing Sioux and Northern Cheyennes back and forth across Montana during the brutal winter of 1876-7.

In the fall of 1876, after other white commanders withdrew their troops to distant, permanent forts to escape the ravages of winter on the Northern Plains, Miles found himself alone in the middle of Sioux country—holding the Tongue River Cantonment with only his own regiment and six companies of the 22nd Infantry. The hardy young colonel's mission was to harass hostile Indian bands venturing into the Yellowstone Valley, and he executed his orders with a zeal that surpassed the expectations of his superiors. Outfitting his men with buffalo coats, fur caps, and other warm clothing, Miles sent them out onto the frigid Montana wastes to locate and smash the enemy. Miles gambled that his walk-a-heaps could survive in the high snowdrifts and bone-chilling temperatures which robbed the natives of their mobility. He was right. In epic scouting movements traversing 300, 400, and 700 miles at a crack, elements of the 5th and 22nd Infantry tracked down, engaged, and defeated superior bodies of savages under the direction of such renowned leaders as Sitting Bull and Crazy Horse.

Nelson Miles did more than any single Army officer to chastise the Indians responsible for the Custer Massacre. His relentless hounding left the hostiles with two choices—either surrender or flee to Canada. Miles also proved that there was still a need for infantrymen in the Indian-fighting Army. He was an awful braggart, but no one could contradict him when he told a congressional committee on 13 December 1877: 'A body of infantry troops can walk down any band of Indians in the country in four months.'

For all his pride in his branch of the service, Miles realized that mobility was of crucial importance in any effort to hunt Indians. He also knew that a soldier became more mobile when placed atop a horse. Following his fruitful winter campaign, Miles was reinforced with battalions of the 2nd and 7th Cavalry. He put these pony soldiers to good use in the spring, summer, and fall of 1877, while operating against the Sioux and Nez Percés. Miles also experimented in a brilliant fashion with that venerable frontier expedient—mounted infantry. Overrunning a Sioux village at Muddy Creek on 7 May 1877 with three 2nd Cavalry companies, Miles captured 450 Indian ponies. He had half of the animals killed, but saved the remainder to mount four companies of the 5th Infantry. By all accounts, the web-feet experienced a good deal of trouble in their initial efforts to master the skittish beasts. Many a hapless soldier was flung into the air for a short trip that ended with a sharp jolt on the ground. However, horses and riders soon got used to each other, and the mounted battalion became the pride of the regiment. Miles's converted troopers even called themselves the '11th Cavalry.'

The 5th Infantry's mounted battalion figured prominently in the vicious Battle of Bear Paw Mountain (30 September-5 October 1877), which wrote a close to the heart-breaking Nez Percé War. With obvious satisfaction, Miles described the conduct of the '11th Cavalry' on that occasion in his 1896 memoirs: 'The [mounted] battalion . . . charged forward up to the very edge of the valley in which the Indian camp was located, threw themselves upon the ground, holding the lariats of their ponies in their left hands, and opened a deadly fire with their long range rifles upon the enemy with telling effect. The tactics were somewhat Indian in fashion, and most effective, as they presented a small target when lying or kneeling upon the ground, and their ponies were so accustomed to the din and noise of the . . . buffalo chase . . . that they stood quietly behind their riders, many of them putting their heads down to nibble the green grass upon which they were standing.'

If ambition and good sense taught Nelson Miles the value of thorough training, the humiliation and criticism

A sergeant of Company A, 25th U.S. Infantry, circa 1887. His dapper 'walking out' uniform consists of an 1876 forage cap; an 1883 sack coat with white chevrons; a civilian shirt, cravat, tiepin, vest, and watch chain; and sky blue trousers with white stripes one inch wide down the outer seams.

stemming from the Army's frequently slip-shod performance in the Indian wars steadily converted hundreds of his colleagues to the same faith. During the last two decades of the 19th century, these progressive officers and their civilian allies instigated a string of reforms that changed American regulars into happier and more effective soldiers.

In August 1879, the U.S. Army adopted a scientific system of target practice, complete with a fine manual. Each post was to have an 'Instructor of Musketry' charged with teaching every officer and man to estimate distances and hit targets at ranges between 100 and 600 yards. Standards were upgraded in 1884, and troops were schooled to train their sights on marks set at 800, 900, and 1,000 yards. In 1885, the Army issued an improved target manual and increased the allowance for practice ammunition to $7.50 per man per year. Since brand new rounds cost 2½¢ apiece and reloaded rounds went for less than a penny, an infantryman could expect to fire 300 to 750 practice shots each year. Outstanding performance was rewarded with medals, prizes, and other honors, and a mania for target shooting swept the Army. By 1898, the American soldier was the finest military marksman on the planet.

The drive to teach the regular army to shoot straight was accompanied by a campaign to improve other soldierly skills. In 1881, 'companies of instruction' came into being at the main recruit depots to provide enlistees with four months of basic training before they received unit assignments. Starting in 1884, each new man was issued a copy of *The Soldier's Manual,* a pocket-sized compendium crammed with information and useful advice on military life. In 1889, Congress launched a strict effort to provide all enlisted men with the rudiments of an elementary education.

To ensure that all the extra instruction did not go to waste, the Army stiffened its admission standards. In October 1889, recruiting officers were ordered to obtain a truthful personal history from each candidate and to reject men of dubious background. In 1891, Congress added a basic ability to read, write, and understand English to the list of minimum requirements for recruits. Two years later, the legislators forbade the acceptance in

First Lieutenant Charles Byrne, the regimental adjutant of the 6th U.S. Infantry from 1 April 1890 to 31 March 1894, a position that entitled him to the elaborate gold aiguillette, cords, and tassels seen on the breast of his full dress coat. Like field officers, adjutants of infantry regiments wore dress helmets surmounted by plumes of white buffalo hair.

peacetime of any man older than thirty. Finally in August 1894, Congress restricted recruiting solely to American citizens and immigrants who had already begun the naturalization process.

Complementing its search for a better class of soldier, the regular army sought to boost its retention rate with other timely changes—such as issuing healthier rations and more comfortable uniforms. There were also attempts to placate the rank and file by permitting them legally to shorten their enlistments. On 16 June 1890, Congress passed 'An Act to Prevent Desertion and for Other Purposes.' After one year of service, a soldier could buy his way out of the Army by paying a fee of $120. At the end of his third year, he could apply for a free discharge. The latter option was so popular that in August 1894 Congress simply shortened the official term of enlistment to three years. These humane reforms, along with a new period of economic dislocations, reduced the desertion rate to below 10 per cent from 1890 to 1895.

In 1882, it became mandatory for regular officers to retire at the age of sixty-four, a rule which helped rid the Army of some deadwood and brought a little movement to the logjam in promotions. An 1890 law specified that examinations had to be administered to candidates for ranks below that of lieutenant colonel, a belated move to give merit a place in a promotion system still too dominated by seniority.

The U.S. Infantry grew increasingly formidable in the 1890s when the Ordnance Department began replacing the single-shot Springfield rifle with the .30-caliber Krag-Jörgensen, a bolt-action, magazine-fed, five-shot weapon. Although the Long Tom served the walk-a-heaps well enough in scrapes with small parties of indifferently armed Indians, it became obsolete shortly after its adoption. European armies were quick to adopt repeating rifles firing cartridges loaded with smokeless powder. American officers were not oblivious to these technological advances—nor to the fact that numerous Indians were arming themselves with repeaters. Nonetheless, the conservative Army establishment stuck stubbornly to the rugged trapdoor Springfield until 1892, when the Krag system was finally adopted. By 1897, Krag rifles and carbines were in general use throughout the regular army.

It would be wrong to pretend that everything was sweetness and light for the U.S. Army after 1880. Dozens of Bluecoats fell in Indian battles during the ensuing ten years. Then in 1890, once the power of the Western tribes was forever broken, Congress ordered the deactivation of two companies (I and K) in every infantry regiment. On 9 March 1891, each of the nineteen white infantry regiments west of the Mississippi was authorized to resurrect one of its defunct companies by enlisting American Indians. The rationale behind this short-lived experiment asserted that a tour in the Army would furnish young warriors with a constructive channel for their aggressive instincts and

Officers of the 25th U.S. Infantry at Fort Missoula, Montana, 1894. The chaplain at the left end of the top row (the only black in the group) wears the plain frock coat prescribed by the Regulations of 1888. The others wear 1892 undress coats trimmed with flat black mohair braid. Their forage caps are decorated with silver numerals, gold embroidered crossed rifles, and gold on silver cords.

The first sergeant of Company C, 18th U.S. Infantry, San Antonio, Texas, circa 1895–8. He holds his Model 1895 forage cap in his left hand, and his tailored 1883 sack coat has a pair of markman's sterling silver buttons on the collar and a sharpshooter's sterling silver cross on the left breast. To win the latter, a rifleman had to score an 88 per cent on targets set at 200, 300, and 600 yards, and 76 per cent at 800, 900, and 1,000 yards.

A private of Company C, 21st U.S. Infantry, dressed for cold weather service in his sky blue overcoat, circa 1895. The Regulations of 1881 permitted infantrymen to wear a double-breasted overcoat with a cape lined in dark blue. Though the Army adopted the bolt-action Krag-Jörgensen rifle in 1892, the 21st Infantry was still armed with old Springfield 'trapdoor' rifles in 1895. The men carried their .45–70 black powder cartridges on woven looped belts of blue webbing with brass Model 1883 buckles.

serve to assimilate them into white culture. But the Indians found Army life too confining, and they were all released from the service by 1897.

The passing of Reconstruction in 1877 did not completely curtail the U.S. Infantry's involvement in domestic disturbances. In the latter half of the 19th century, the United States evolved into the world's top manufacturing nation. The spread of industrialization was accomplished through the callous exploitation of the working classes, and America's cities became cesspools of misery. When laborers fought for fair wages, shorter hours, and safer working conditions by staging strikes, the national government, which catered to conservative business interests, frequently dispatched soldiers to defend the status quo. From 1886 to 1895, federal troops responded to 328 calls to disperse disaffected Americans.

The best that can be said of the regulars' strike-breaking activities is that they carried out their orders and normally treated strikers with restraint.

The thirty-three years that elapsed after the Civil War constituted a time of ups and downs for the U.S. Army. In spite of its ridiculously minuscule size, the U.S. Infantry made considerable progress. By 1898, its members were expert riflemen, their ranks stiffened by a respectable cadre of bronzed combat veterans. Indeed, on the regimental level, the entire regular establishment was a well-oiled fighting machine. But as America's third foreign war of the 19th century was about to show, grave weaknesses still existed in the machine's command structure.

9 Pawns of Imperialism
1898–1916

On 25 April 1898, Congress declared war on Spain. No pronouncement from Washington has ever been greeted with more delight by the American people. William Allen White, a Kansas newspaper editor and a keen observer of the heartland, captured the patriotic frenzy gripping his countrymen as they sent their sons to battle: 'Everywhere over this good, fair land, flags were flying. Trains carrying soldiers were hurrying from the North, from the East, from the West, to the Southland; and as they sped over the green prairies and the brown mountains, little children on fences greeted the soldiers with flapping scarfs and handkerchiefs and flags; at the stations, crowds gathered to hurrah for the soldiers, and to throw hats into the air, and to unfurl flags. Everywhere it was flags: tattered, smoke-grimed flags in engine cabs; flags in buttonholes; flags on proud poles; flags fluttering everywhere.'

The horrors of the Civil War lay long forgotten. A fresh generation of young Americans, bred to regard war as a noble adventure, strained to prove its manhood. Any excuse for a fight—and any enemy—would do.

Ostensibly, the United States sprang to arms to liberate Cuba, which was being devastated by a revolt against Spanish rule dating back to 1895. Still mindful that their country was born of revolution and shocked by the brutal, indiscriminate tactics of the Spanish Army, Americans voiced growing sympathy for the Cuban rebels, a sentiment that burgeoned into a demand that the federal government use force to eject the Spaniards and establish the tortured island's independence.

To be sure, the motives for America's intervention were not all altruistic. Having tamed the Wild West and attained industrial supremacy, some Americans thought the time had come for their dynamic, wealthy republic to take her place among the world's great powers. In the late 19th century, such an ambition was pursued along the path of imperialism—seizing colonies to serve as safe markets for a nation's trade, springboards to additional markets, and bases for her navy. Several American politicians hoped the war with Spain would provide the United States with opportunities to enhance her status while aiding the downtrodden Cubans.

As relations with Spain neared the breaking point, the U.S. Army mobilized. On 15 April 1898, the War Department ordered twenty-two infantry regiments to assemble at three ports on the Gulf of Mexico. Six cavalry regiments and most of the artillery were directed to a camp in northern Georgia. The regulars reacted with a businesslike alacrity that impressed the journalists who swooped down on the rendezvous points to sniff for stories for the hero-hungry public. From Tampa, Florida, Poultney Bigelow of *Harper's Weekly* reported: 'I have been camping with regulars, living their life, eating their food, and noting their courage and discipline. . . . In all the armies of Europe there are no better soldiers, man for man, than those of the United States Infantry, and nowhere have I known officers who command more cheerfully the respect and obedience of their men.'

Richard Harding Davis, the country's top war correspondent, wrote that the sight of the same 'doughboys in

A pair of second lieutenants of the 10th U.S. Infantry, circa 1898. They wear 1895 dark blue undress coats with black mohair braid, gilt collar devices, and gold-and-white shoulder straps; white starched shirt collars; and 1885 campaign hats with crowns crushed into fashionable 'Montana peaks.' The 'shavetail' at right displays a sharpshooter's cross, evidence of the regular army's mania for marksmanship in the 1880s and 1890s.

skirmish line . . . or at guard mounting . . . made you proud that they were American soldiers, and desperately sorry there were so few of them.'

As Davis noted, America's regulars looked formidable—as long as you did not count their numbers. On 1 April, the U.S. Army contained 2,143 officers and 26,040 men, hardly enough to defeat even a third-rate power like Spain. The Spanish Army had already committed 150,000 troops to Cuba to suppress the insurrection and enlisted an additional 80,000 Cuban loyalists as auxiliaries. There were 8,000 more Spanish regulars in Puerto Rico, 26,000 in the Philippines, and 150,000 standing ready on the Iberian Peninsula. Whatever its quality, the U.S. Army needed a quick infusion of manpower to even the odds.

Congress took a tentative step in the right direction on 8 March by authorizing two artillery regiments, the 6th and 7th. A few days later, John A. T. Hull, Republican congressman from Iowa, introduced an administration-backed bill to enlarge the regular army in wartime from 28,000 to 104,000 men. President William McKinley and his military advisers intended to make the approaching conflict an all-regular affair if possible. Militia organizations would be retained at home for coastal defense. But this scenario did not appeal to the nation's citizen soldiers, many of whom commanded considerable political influence. Thanks to their fervid opposition, the Hull Bill never came to a vote.

Oddly enough, the militia had reached its nadir in the years immediately following the Civil War. All that bloodletting temporarily extinguished the martial ardor of most citizens. However, the militia enjoyed a quick comeback in the 1870s as the modernization of America's economy led to labor disputes in manufacturing and mining centers. Invariably, the more privileged classes equated attempts to organize unions with anarchy and socialism. Governors frequently responded to strikes by calling out volunteer militia units to safeguard the rights of property. This service endeared the militia to businessmen, who provided it with more financial aid than the federal and state governments. By 1897, the United States possessed 114,000 duly enrolled citizen soldiers—100,000 of them infantry.

By then, nearly every state was calling its militia by a new name—the National Guard. The change in title symbolized rising aspirations. There was not much glory in strike-breaking, preventing lynchings, and quelling other domestic disturbances. Guardsmen wanted to be seen as real soldiers, not standby riot police. They wanted the National Guard integrated into the nation's military establishment as the primary reserve of the regular army. And more than anything else, in 1898 they wanted a fair chance to fight the Spanish.

Grasping his trusty .30-caliber Krag repeating rifle, an unidentified regular infantryman stands ready for action, circa 1898. The dark blue blouse was removed for campaigning in Cuba, Puerto Rico, and the Philippines, but the first American troops sent to the tropics suffered terribly in their woolen shirts and trousers.

Left with no other choice, the McKinley Administration worked out a compromise with the Guard lobby. On 22 April 1898, Congress empowered the President to call on the states for a limitless number of volunteers. All able-bodied male citizens aged eighteen to forty-five were eligible to serve for two years or the duration of the war—whichever was shorter. Volunteers were supposed to have the same organization, regulations, and pay as regulars, except that state governors could name all regimental officers. Volunteer generals and their staffs would be presidential appointees. One key provision stated that any militia company, battalion, or regiment could enlist as a unit under its own officers—an open invitation to the National Guard to join the volunteer army en masse.

To ensure no one mistook the law's true intent, on 23 April McKinley issued a call for 125,000 volunteers—the approximate strength of the National Guard—to man twenty-two regiments, ten battalions, and forty-six companies of infantry; five regiments and seventeen troops of cavalry; and sixteen batteries of light artillery. Each state received a unit quota based on population. Nearly all the National Guard outfits that turned volunteer were understrength, but none had any trouble bolstering their ranks with new members—even though they rejected half their applicants as physically defective. In little more than a month, the oath of enlistment was administered to 124,776 volunteers, and there were still long lines queuing up outside the recruiting stations.

Congress further augmented the volunteer army on 11 May by consenting to the enrollment of 3,500 engineers and 10,000 infantry raised from the country at large. The latter group was restricted to men 'possessing immunity from diseases incident to tropical climates.' The 10,000 'Immunes,' as they were called, went into ten regiments, the 1st through 10th U.S. Volunteer Infantry, six composed of white troops and four of blacks. The President named the officers for these singular units.

President McKinley released a second and final appeal for volunteers on 26 May. Forty thousand men were required to complete existing outfits and 35,000 for twenty-two new infantry regiments and nineteen new artillery batteries. There were still plenty of patriots in civilian clothes aching to test their mettle against the Spanish. By the end of August, the month the fighting ended, the volunteer army had swollen to 8,785 officers and 216,029 other ranks.

Who were these keen glory-hunters, the boys of '98? A lieutenant in the 6th Massachusetts Volunteer Infantry characterized them as 'men from every walk in life . . . the lawyer, the mechanic, the laboring-man, the college student.' The average volunteer was a native-born white man of working-class background in his mid-twenties. Over 8,000 were Afro-Americans, resolute souls who

had to argue and plead for the dubious honor of risking their lives on behalf of a country that denied them equality. Roughly 40 per cent of the volunteers had no prior exposure to soldiering. Even National Guardsmen knew little more than basic close-order drill. But because they grew up with firearms, recruits from the rural South and West proclaimed themselves natural soldiers. On the subject of the American volunteer, William Allen White wrote with naïve confidence: 'He may not know how to present arms in May, but he can be turned into a clean-cut, well-oiled cog in the fighting engine before snow flies. . . . The American knows how to shoot, and he knows all about the mechanism of a gun.' Marksmen or not, the volunteers were lamentably ignorant about

camp sanitation and slow to learn. Hence, roughly eight-tenths of the Americans who perished in the war with Spain succumbed to typhoid, and the bulk of those victims were careless volunteers.

Once the National Guard was placated, Congress raised the statutory size of the regular army to 64,719 officers and men on 26 April by enlarging units already in existence. Infantry regiments were transformed into twelve-company, three-battalion entities by reactivating their two dormant companies and creating two new ones. The 'War organization' of an infantry company was set at 106 men—one first sergeant, one quarter-master sergeant, four sergeants, twelve corporals, two musicians, one artificer, one wagoner, and eighty-four

privates. Every cavalry troop was allowed 100 enlisted personnel, an artillery battery 173 to 200, and an engineer company 150. Capitalizing on the prevailing war fever to firm up its recruiting standards, the regular army turned away 75 per cent of all applicants for enlistment and was still able to raise its numbers to 58,688 before Spain agreed to an armistice. However, the

War by the book. Company E, 2nd U.S. Infantry, practices defensive tactics on a sandy plain near Tampa, Florida, spring 1898. All ranks are in plain dark blue overshirts, but the officers and non-commissioned officers are identified by white stripes on their trousers. Note the bayonet, mess kit, haversack, and canteen displayed on the little earthwork protecting the private in the foreground.

conflict ended before these promising additions could take the field. The regular regiments committed to the war's most significant land battle in Cuba averaged 556 rank and file apiece.

Thus with a few strokes of the pen, the President and Congress called into being an army of just under 300,000—a much bigger host than America needed to drub Spain. Only a third of the volunteers went overseas, and an even smaller fraction actually heard Spanish rifles fired in anger. A surgeon with the unblooded 12th New York Infantry mourned: 'An army of over two hundred thousand men . . . sweated for four months under a Southern sun [in training camps] under all the tension of expectation and the demoralization of disappointment, only to see the war for them, come to an inglorious end.'

Furthermore, in his anxiety to please special interests, McKinley burdened his War Department with more men than it could efficiently handle. When hostilities broke out, the Army's supply bureaus owned only enough spare clothing for 25,000 new troops and 20,000 extra sets of cartridge belts, knapsacks, and accoutrements. Due to a shortage of Krag repeaters, every volunteer command to sail from the United States—save for one regiment of cavalry—carried obsolete trapdoor Springfields. Firing black powder cartridges, the Long Tom emitted a thick cloud of white smoke that revealed the position of its user every time he pulled the trigger. If that was not enough of a drawback, many of these weapons were worn-out regular army cast-offs. 'The rifling is almost gone and there's no telling where it will shoot,' one volunteer complained about his rifle. 'I don't know but it's more dangerous to be behind it than in front of it.'

The legislation of 22 April delineated the organization of brigades (three regiments each), divisions (three brigades), and corps (three divisions). Altogether, the Army issued orders for the creation of eight corps, but only seven were actually constituted. Although the majority of the generals appointed to head these larger formations claimed regular army backgrounds, their service with the constricted peacetime establishment did not prepare them to handle anything grander than a regiment. In words that might have been written about the Army's leadership at the outset of every previous major war, Poultney Bigelow told his readers:
'We must bear in mind that most of our troops have never since the Civil War been brought together in larger bodies than a few companies at a time. Many colonels of regiments have never until this war seen all their men together on a parade ground. Brigadier generals have been created who have never seen the regiments that are to constitute their brigade. We have for this war laid out a complicated scheme of army organization, and

intrusted the working of it in most instances to men who scarcely know the manual of arms.'

The first sizable U.S. ground force to engage the Spanish was the V Army Corps, which gathered at Tampa under Major General William R. Shafter. A veteran of the Civil War and former colonel of the black 24th Infantry, the sixty-two-year-old Shafter weighed over 300 pounds. William Randolph Hearst, an admirer of the general, called him 'a sort of human fortress in blue coat and flannel shirt.' Despite Shafter's unimpressive record, seniority elevated him to head the Army's elite corps—eighteen infantry regiments, five cavalry regiments, and an artillery battalion from the regular line, plus nine of the best prepared volunteer regiments, an aggregation of 25,000. It was a promising mix, but Shafter lacked both the time and facilities to conduct large-unit maneuvers and weld V Corps into a cohesive team.

At the end of May, the U.S. Navy blockaded the main Spanish fleet in the harbor at Santiago, the capital of Cuba's easternmost province. If those trapped vessels were destroyed, Spain could neither threaten America's shores nor succor her Caribbean possessions. Shafter received immediate orders to proceed to Santiago and cooperate with the Navy in eliminating the enemy fleet. Less than 12,000 Spanish troops defended the port. More than 20,000 others were scattered throughout eastern Cuba, but they could not concentrate at Santiago for fear of surrendering the countryside to the 15,000 insurgents lurking in the vicinity. The absence of decent roads, the debilitating effects of tropical disease, and a fatalistic resignation to defeat prevented Spanish forces in central and western Cuba from reinforcing the imperilled city.

Shafter had his troubles too. The thirty-one transports sitting off Port Tampa could not accommodate his entire corps. Ultimately, 819 officers and 16,058 men jammed themselves aboard, but most of the volunteers and cavalry horses, many wheeled vehicles, and tons of baggage were left behind. Between 22 and 26 June, a truncated V Corps disembarked on Cuba's southern coast at points seventeen to nine miles east of Santiago. Covered by 1,000 native guerrillas, the landings went unopposed.

Taking time to sort out his tangled regiments, set up a rickety line of communications, and scout the enemy's defenses, Shafter scheduled an assault on Santiago's eastern approaches for the morning of 1 July. Brigadier General Henry W. Lawton's 2nd Division and an unattached regular brigade were directed to seize El Caney, a fortified village to the north controlling the city's water supply and zone of cultivation. Once he secured this preliminary objective, Lawton was to fall in with the rest of V Corps—Brigadier General Jacob F. Kent's 1st Infantry Division and the horseless Cavalry

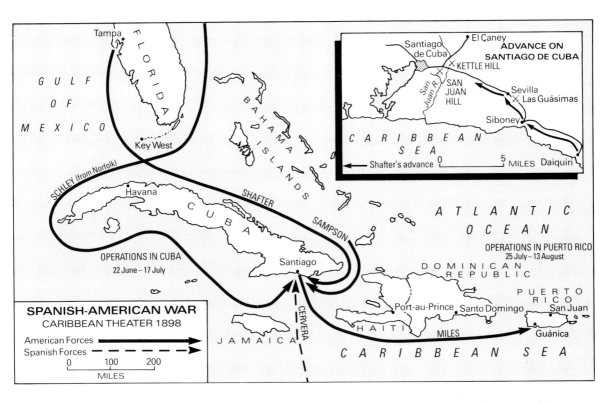

SPANISH-AMERICAN WAR
CARIBBEAN THEATER 1898

American Forces ▬▬▬▶
Spanish Forces ▬ ▬ ▬▶

0   100   200
MILES

OPERATIONS IN CUBA
22 June – 17 July

ADVANCE ON
SANTIAGO DE CUBA

Shafter's advance ◀   0   5 MILES

OPERATIONS IN PUERTO RICO
25 July – 13 August

Gaunt and hollow-eyed 7th Infantrymen survey Santiago de Cuba from a trench on the San Juan Heights, 9 July 1898. Daily rains, searing heat, wool uniforms, and shortages of food, drinking water, camp equipage, and medicine accounted for the bedraggled appearance of these troops and the epidemics of malaria and dysentery that swept their ranks.

Division—for a 10:00 a.m. advance on the San Juan Heights overlooking Santiago.

Shafter's plan unraveled the moment V Corps attempted its execution. Prostrated by gout and the tropical heat, the obese general lost touch with the day's events. At El Caney, 520 Spanish riflemen, holing up in trenches, blockhouses, and a stout stone fort, fought with desperate courage. According to Shafter's time-table, the village was supposed to fall in two hours, but the Spanish tied up Lawton's 5,400 effectives for eight. Finally, with close artillery support, the 12th U.S. Infantry surged into the stone fort, the main enemy stronghold, at 3:00 p.m. Mopping up the last pockets of resistance consumed another two hours.

In the meantime, Kent's doughboys and the cavalry plodded through maddening 100 degree heat to their jumping-off positions below the San Juan Heights. The line of march took them down a narrow jungle trail swept by Spanish rifle fire and shrapnel. Leading one of Kent's brigades, the 71st New York Volunteers broke under the hail of lead and metal slashing through their packed ranks. Shooing the New Yorkers into the brush, Kent plunged on with his regulars. Emerging from that nightmarish avenue of death, the 8,000 panting, sweat-drenched Americans went into line 500 yards from the heights along the far end of a grassy field. As Richard Harding Davis related, the most trying part of their ordeal had only begun:

'Our men were ordered not to return fire but to lie still and wait for further orders. Some of them could see the rifle pits of the enemy quite clearly and the men in them, but many saw nothing but the bushes under which they lay, and the high grass which seemed to burn when pressed against it. It was during this period of waiting that the greater number of our men were killed. For one hour they lay on their rifles staring at the waving green stuff around them, while the bullets drove past incessantly, with savage insistence, cutting the grass again and again.'

Exasperated by this senseless and nerve-racking pause, the men shouted: 'Show us those sons of bitches! For God's sake don't keep us here to be shot without giving us a show!'

Then, at 1:00 p.m., their officers signaled them forward, and the Americans stumbled toward two fortified elevations fronting the San Juan Heights. As Kent's doughboys neared the slopes of San Juan Hill on the left, three Gatling guns commanded by Second Lieutenant John H. Parker, 13th Infantry, unloosed an accurate, nine-minute stream of .30-caliber slugs on the enemy trenches at 600 yards range, forcing the defenders to duck their heads. In the interval, the 1st Infantry Division clambered to within 150 yards of the Spanish. Led by the 6th and 16th Infantry, Kent's regulars surged

An 1899 photograph of Second Lieutenant George Hyslop Knox, 20th U.S. Infantry, at Fort Leavenworth, Kansas, in a drab campaign hat and an officer's dark blue overcoat. Introduced in 1884, the handsome double-breasted ulster was decorated with black mohair netted frog buttons. Knox's sidearm is the old Model 1860 staff and field officer's sword.

over the crest, a ragged blue line firing as it came. To the right, the Cavalry Division overran Kettle Hill. Abandoning the heights, the surviving Spaniards withdrew to an inner defensive ring on Santiago's outskirts.

The fighting on 1 July cost V Corps 205 killed and 1,177 wounded. Shafter believed his command had tangled with 12,000 Spaniards, but, in truth, less than 2,000 had pinned down the cream of the U.S. Army for most of the day. The defenders paid for their valor; 703 were killed, wounded, or captured—355 at El Caney alone. Nonetheless, Shafter was so chastened by his casualties that he discarded any thought of storming the city.

Lady Luck rescued Shafter on 3 July, when the outgunned Spanish fleet made a break from Santiago Harbor. The waiting American warships blew their opponents to ribbons. Two weeks later, the Santiago garrison formally capitulated. It was not a moment too soon. Tropical diseases were infecting Shafter's regiments, turning them into what their rotund general termed 'an army of convalescents.' By the end of July, nearly 25 per cent of his troops appeared on the sick list, and 75 per cent of the corps suffered from some stage of malaria. To better promote the recovery of the afflicted, the command was evacuated to a quarantine camp at Montauk Point, Long Island. There on 3 October 1898, V Corps disbanded.

As pestilence scourged the conquerors of Santiago, Major General Nelson A. Miles, the Army's current commanding general, undertook the capture of Puerto Rico. In late July and early August, Miles landed 15,000 troops on the island. The expedition included regulars from the 11th and 19th Infantry, but the bulk of the men were volunteer foot soldiers from the Northeast and Midwest. Moving with his customary dispatch, Miles bedeviled the Spanish with a four-pronged offensive, replete with elegant flanking maneuvers, herding the foe back on San Juan. The showpiece campaign ground to an abrupt stop on 12 August, when Spain, disheartened by the disaster at Santiago, agreed to an armistice. Still, Miles's interrupted efforts guaranteed the cession of Puerto Rico to the United States at the coming peace conference.

Half a world away from Cuba, where they were not informed of the armistice until 16 August, American and Spanish riflemen squared off in one last battle. Commodore George Dewey and the U.S. Navy's Asiatic Squadron set the stage for this anticlimactic confrontation by destroying a Spanish fleet based at Manila Bay on 1 May 1898. The commodore possessed enough heavy guns to knock Manila down about the ears of its garrison, but he needed American soldiers to hold the city. When the McKinley Administration learned of Dewey's triumph, it put troop trains in motion for San Francisco, amassing 20,000 men there in May and June for a 7,000-mile, trans-Pacific voyage to the new front in the Philippine Islands. The expedition, ultimately named the VIII Army Corps, boasted a core of 5,000 regulars representing the 14th, 18th, and 23rd Infantry, 3rd Artillery (red-legged infantry), 6th Artillery, and 4th Cavalry. The remainder were volunteers, predominantly infantry from the Western states. The corps commander, Major General Wesley Merritt, was a self-important, sixty-two-year-old ex-cavalryman who had done good service in the Civil War.

From 25 May to 29 June, thirteen transports carrying Merritt and 10,907 officers and men sailed through the Golden Gate and steered west, disembarking their passengers near Manila by 4 August. Upon his arrival, Merritt found 13,000 Spanish troops penned up in the city by an army of Filipino nationalists led by Emilio Aguinaldo. Aguinaldo graciously turned over his trenches south of Manila to the Americans, but Dewey and Merritt coolly spurned his overtures for a formal alliance.

As it turned out, Don Fermín Jáudenes y Alvarez, the Spanish governor-general in the Philippines, proved more than happy to deliver Manila to the Americans—provided they staged a sham battle to satisfy his country's honor and kept the vengeful Filipinos away from his garrison. Glad of the offer, Merritt sent 8,930 troops against Manila's outer works on the morning of 13 August. Ignorant of their commander's arrangements, soldiers on both sides shot to kill. Six Americans were slain and ninety-three wounded as VIII Corps drove the enemy from their blockhouses and through the city's suburbs. The Spanish raised a white flag at 11:00 a.m., but desultory firing dragged on well into the afternoon before all combatants heard of the surrender.

Aguinaldo's insurgents were angered by their rude exclusion from the Battle of Manila, and their displeasure grew when the Americans refused them entry to their own capital. The reason for this odd behavior became obvious in a few months. On 10 December 1898, American and Spanish commissioners signed the Treaty of Paris, which granted Cuba her freedom and ceded Puerto Rico, Guam, and the Philippines to the United States. When news of this reached Manila, the Filipinos turned markedly hostile. They had not risen in revolt to see their independence snatched away by a new set of foreign masters. Another war was in the offing.

As the new year opened, Major General Elwell S. Otis, Merritt's successor, was confined to Manila with 22,312 American regulars and volunteers. As many as 40,000 Filipinos glowered at the interlopers from trenches fringing the city limits, and an estimated 40,000 more insurgents were scattered throughout the 120,000 square miles of the archipelago. Half of the native soldiers lacked rifles, but they all carried bolos, wicked cutting knives that did dreadful damage at close quarters. As tensions mounted along the opposing lines, the Americans succumbed to claustrophobic impatience. Practically every man in VIII Corps hoped for an excuse to teach the 'gugus' and 'niggers' the folly of standing up to their Anglo-Protestant betters.

On the night of 4 February 1899, pickets from the 1st Nebraska Infantry fired on four approaching Filipino soldiers after the latter failed to heed an order to halt. Certain the shots betokened a general assault on Manila, other jittery volunteers in forward positions grabbed their rifles and banged away at shadows. Soon Otis's entire perimeter was blazing. At daylight, VIII Corps sprang from its trenches and brushed the Filipinos away from Manila. Otis lost fifty-nine killed and 278 wounded to gain a little elbow room. Six hundred and twelve dead insurgents fell into American hands, but Aguinaldo's total casualties were probably much higher. On that bloody note, the Philippine-American War (perversely labeled an 'insurrection' by the U.S. aggressors) began.

During the first half of 1899, Otis's brigades and divisions lunged north, south, and west from Manila, ranging across central Luzon to strike at Filipino bases and troop concentrations. The insurgents were no match for the better armed and trained invaders. The Americans evicted them from one fortified position after another. Professing utter contempt for their foes, Otis's men behaved with reckless courage. In an encounter on 27 March, Captain Clayton P. Van Houten of the 1st South Dakota Infantry led his company over a railroad bridge spanning the Marilao River, shooting a Filipino colonel with his revolver on the far side. Returning to the opposite bank for artillery support, Van Houten picked up the 250-pound barrel of a mountain gun and re-crossed the bridge unassisted, followed by four men with the cannon's carriage. Other volunteers performed equally incredible deeds in the spring campaigns, and twenty-five were awarded Medals of Honor.

In June 1899, with the onset of the rainy season, Otis took time to overhaul his army. The ratification of the Treaty of Paris at the start of this new war left all his volunteers and 1,650 regulars in the Philippines serving with their enlistments expired. Taking advantage of the natural lull caused by the change in the weather, Otis shipped these men home by October. Before the rains cleared, an infusion of regulars from the United States, including the 4th, 6th, 16th, 17th, 19th, 20th, 22nd, 24th, and 25th Infantry, replenished the Philippine expeditionary force to above the 35,000 mark. Timely action taken in Washington ensured the speedy delivery of additional reinforcements.

On 2 March 1899, President McKinley placed his signature on a bill to continue the regular army at its wartime strength of 65,000. Each infantry regiment was now allowed 'one colonel; one lieutenant-colonel; three majors; fourteen captains, two of whom shall be . . . adjutant and quartermaster; sixteen first lieutenants; of whom one shall be available . . . as commissary and three . . . as battalion adjutants; twelve second lieutenants; one sergeant-major; one quarter-master-sergeant; one commissary-sergeant . . . ; three battalion sergeant majors . . . ; one band [of twenty-four members], and twelve companies, organized into three battalions of four companies each.' To furnish ample manpower to pacify the Philippines, the bill also sanctioned a force of 35,000 federally controlled volunteers recruited for 'the term of two years and four months.' This clause became the birth certificate for the 26th through 49th U.S. Volunteer Infantry and the 11th and 12th U.S. Volunteer Cavalry. Some of the new outfits possessed special characteristics. The 36th and 37th Infantry contained many veteran state volunteers who elected to stay and finish the fight in the Philippines. The 48th and 49th Infantry were black regiments. The 33rd Infantry, raised in Texas, gained a reputation for marksmanship. The Army had acquired a good supply of Krags since the spring of 1898, so every regiment of U.S. Volunteers departed for the Far East packing plenty of modern firepower.

Otis resumed active operations in the Philippines in October 1899. Intent on capturing Aguinaldo and crushing the main insurgent army, columns of American infantry, cavalry, and artillery raced into northern Luzon, while an amphibious force landed at Lingayen Gulf behind the Filipinos. On 12 November, Aguinaldo—threatened on all sides and in imminent danger of being taken—ordered his troops to abandon conventional warfare, disappear into the hills, jungles, and rural villages, and re-emerge at the earliest opportunity as guerrillas. As organized resistance ceased, the Americans, their numbers in excess of 56,000, fanned out across Luzon and beyond—occupying nearly every important island in the archipelago.

Once the insurgents went underground, senior American officers noted the war's resemblance to their earlier bouts with the Indians. To control the countryside, Major General Arthur MacArthur, who relieved Otis as military governor in April 1900, constructed an extensive network of posts. By 1 September 1900, the Americans were manning 413 stations. Parceled out in driblets, the blue-shirted soldiers kept up a constant round of patrols, pursuits, and skirmishes.

While undoubtedly effective, MacArthur's strategy exposed his troops to constant attack. Danger and death stalked the Americans almost everywhere they turned.

The color party of the 14th U.S. Infantry photographed in Manila in 1901 following the regiment's return from China, where it fought heroically to quell the Boxer Rebellion. Two of the men wear khaki blouses with standing collars, which were adopted by the Army in August 1898. The other two have khaki blouses with falling collars, which were sanctioned by the Quartermaster General on 9 June 1899. A color sergeant, identified by a pair of blue-and-white 1892-pattern chevrons, holds the national color. A sergeant grasps the regimental color.

In May 1900, Sergeant Ray Hoover of Company I, 43rd U.S. Volunteer Infantry, wrote his mother from Catbalogan on Samar Island: 'I have been in several skirmishes since I wrote you from Paranas. They keep harassing the outpost every night, and yesterday they made an attack on the town, burning nearly every house, but our boys ran them into the hills.'

Hoover was fortunate compared to his comrades at nearby Catubig. On 15 April 1900, 600 insurgents cornered thirty-one 43rd Infantrymen in the town convent, which doubled as the volunteers' barracks. The Americans held the place for a day and a night, losing one man to the enemy's bullets. Early on 16 April, the guerrillas set the convent on fire. Forced out into the open, fifteen Americans were cut down, but the other fifteen dug in behind the blazing barracks for an unyielding, two-day stand. When a relief party entered Catubig, it discovered thirteen of the steadfast little garrison still alive and the corpses of 150 insurgents littering the town.

On and on it went. The Filipinos would materialize from out of nowhere, kill and run, and then wait for a chance to kill again. In December 1900, the U.S. Army's strength in the Philippines peaked at 69,420 officers and men, but the war was far from over. That same month, Sergeant Hoover wrote from Leyete Island:

'My Co. and a detachment from "D" had what I would call a real fight Dec. 14th. Met the insurgents . . . about 100 riflemen and 5 to 6 hundred Bolomen. Four times they charged but each time our little band sent the lead jackets into them so fast they went back faster than they came . . . with the boys in khaki following them. It was a running fight from three until dark.'

As indefatigable as bloodhounds on a hot scent, the invaders tracked down the guerrillas, making some impressive catches. In March 1901, a company of American officers and native scouts nabbed Aguinaldo, and on 19 April, he released a proclamation urging his people to surrender. Thousands of freedom fighters obeyed. Others vowed to resist to the death. On the morning of 28 September 1901, hundreds of bolo-wielding Filipinos burst without warning into the plaza at Balangiga, a town on Samar, surprising Company C, 9th Infantry, as it sat down to breakfast. Dozens of Americans were hacked to pieces before they could reach their rifles. The survivors, many spattered with their own blood, gunned down 250 insurgents and got away in small boats. Forty-two of the seventy-four doughboys sustained fatal injuries. A mere four escaped without a scratch.

Incensed by the 'Balangiga Massacre,' the American military pulled out all the stops to stamp out the last pockets of native resistance. Finally, on 4 July 1902, President Theodore Roosevelt announced an end to the Philippine Insurrection, lauding the Army for its hard-won victory. In the preceding three-and-a-half years, 126,468 American troops had served in the archipelago at one time or another. They fought 2,811 separate engagements, suffered 4,234 slain and 2,818 wounded, and claimed 16,000 insurgents killed in action. But that last figure is too conservative to be credible.

The dirty little war waged in the Philippines was not one of the prouder episodes in the history of the U.S. Army. Like their forebears in Mexico and on various Indian frontiers, American soldiers posted to the archipelago often acted as though they were absolved

Officers of the 30th U.S. Volunteer Infantry photographed in Manila in 1901 after the regiment's seventeen months of arduous service in the Philippine-American War. They wear drab fatigue hats with cords of gold and black silk and khaki blouses of varying shades. Most of the blouses have removable white shoulder tabs, but the two officers seated at far left have the old sky blue shoulder straps.

from observing the rules of civilized warfare. From the very first, the invaders exhibited a barbarism which mocked their presumption of racial and cultural superiority. On 15 April 1899, the *San Francisco Call* published a startling confession from a corporal of the 1st California Volunteers: 'If [the insurgents] fire a shot from a house we burn the house down and every house near it, and shoot the natives, so they are pretty quiet . . . now.' Some months later, a returned veteran of the 20th Kansas told a reporter: 'The country won't be pacified until the niggers are killed off like the Indians.'

Tactics like these became widespread after the contest entered its guerrilla phase. The Americans systematically tortured natives to extract information; they murdered their prisoners and innocent civilians; they crammed thousands of people into unhealthy concentration camps to separate guerrillas from the general population; and they burned, looted, and raped. As they went about their

PLATE 28: IN CUBA AND PUERTO RICO, 1898
96. First Lieutenant (Palmer Eddy Pierce), 13th U.S. Infantry, Undress, 1898: *In 1895, officers received a new forage cap and undress coat. Both items were trimmed with lustrous black mohair. Officers wore the 1885-pattern dress cape without sidearms.* **97. Sergeant, 2nd U.S. Infantry, Campaign Dress, 1898:** *Note the Krag .30-caliber rifle, woven cartridge belt, cotton duck leggings, and russet brown shoes. Once ashore in Cuba, American troops shed their blouses and fought in their shirtsleeves. The outer layer of the sergeant's blanket roll is a canvas shelter half (part of a two-man 'dog' tent).* **98. Captain (Alexander Greig), 6th Massachusetts Infantry, U.S. Volunteers, Campaign Dress, 1898:** *Midway through the Puerto Rican Campaign, this regiment exchanged its wool uniforms for more practical suits of khaki cotton. The officers' coats were unusual with their low breast pockets and oversized cuff facings. The captain's sidearms are a Model 1896 Colt revolver and Model 1860 staff and field officer's sword. For their postwar victory parade in Boston, the men of the 6th Massachusetts pinned up the brims of their campaign hats with red, yellow, and blue Spanish cockades.*

96. First Lieutenant, 13th U.S. Infantry, Undress, 1898   **97.** Sergeant, 2nd U.S. Infantry, Campaign Dress, 1898   **98.** Captain, 6th Massachusetts Infantry, U.S. Volunteers, Campaign Dress, 1898

'ennobling' work, the boys in blue expressed their feelings in song:

> Damn, damn, damn the Filipinos!
>   Cut-throat, Khakiac ladrones!
> Underneath the starry flag
>   Civilize them with a Krag
> And return us to our beloved home.

Of course, many American soldiers tried to win the hearts and minds of the natives with kind treatment, pursuing pacification through administrative, educational, economic, and public-health reforms. Yet even a humane man could have his heart hardened by the sight of the enemy's atrocities. A 32nd Infantryman decided the Filipinos were 'horrid little people' after he helped retrieve 'two mutilated bodies of American soldiers who had their penises cut off and stuffed into their mouths.' No wonder Americans have preferred to forget their nasty crusade to subdue a far-off people whose only crime was wanting to govern themselves.

The Philippines was not the only trouble spot in the Far East to occupy the U.S. Army's attention at the turn of the century. Early in 1900, the Boxer Rebellion, a rising of nationalists bent on ridding their decayed empire of foreign exploitation, rocked China. As the violent movement spread, Russia, Japan, England, France, Germany, Italy, Austria, and the United States fielded an expedition of 16,000 men, the China Relief Force, to rescue their diplomats trapped at Peking. Included in the 2,000-man American contingent were the 9th and 14th

Infantry, hastily transferred from the Philippines. Both regiments performed well. On 14 August, two companies of the 14th Infantry became the first allied troops to scale Peking's massive, forty-foot outer wall. Pausing a moment to catch their breath, the intrepid doughboys blasted the Chinese defenders off the adjoining ramparts, clearing the way for the relief of the besieged legations by the British.

On 2 February 1901, with the Philippine-American War raging as furiously as ever, Congress remodeled the Army for the second time since the spring of 1898. Instead of raising more federal volunteers to replace the ones slated for release by 1 July, the legislators met their imperial obligations with additional regulars. The U.S. Infantry and Cavalry each received five new regiments. The law allowed the enlistment of 12,000 Philippine Scouts and a provisional Puerto Rican infantry regiment. Congress recast the U.S. Artillery as a 'corps' of thirty field batteries and 126 coast artillery companies. These and other adjustments lifted the Army's maximum strength to 100,619.

Under the 1901 law, every infantry regiment gained a captain, three second lieutenants, and two color sergeants, but lost one first lieutenant. An infantry company would normally contain one first sergeant, one quartermaster sergeant, four sergeants, six corporals, two cooks, two musicians, and forty-eight privates. In an emergency, the President could 'increase the number of sergeants in any company . . . to six, the number of corporals to ten, and the number of privates to one

The non-commissioned staff of the 32nd U.S. Volunteer Infantry in the Philippines, 1901. Left to right: battalion sergeant major, regimental commissary sergeant, battalion sergeant major, chief trumpeter, regimental sergeant major, unidentified, battalion sergeant major, and regimental quartermaster sergeant. They all wear khaki field uniforms, and four have Model 1840 non-commissioned officer's swords.

hundred and twenty-seven.' Predictably enough, as soon as the bloody tumult in the Philippines subsided, Congress let infantry companies and other regular units dwindle to half strength.

For the rank and file doughboy, the Army's personnel policy remained mired in the 19th century. Reflecting on his early service as a second lieutenant with the 30th U.S. Infantry in 1902, George C. Marshall recalled: 'In those far-off days the soldiers of the regular Army got little attention or consideration from the government or the public. . . . Privates got . . . thirteen dollars a month plus ten per cent on foreign service.' A long-awaited pay raise in May 1908 boosted the monthly salary of infantry privates and musicians to $15, a sum still below that earned by soldiers of the same grade at the end of the Civil War! Omar Bradley, who began his military career in 1915 as a shavetail with the 14th Infantry, mused: 'Obviously such low pay . . . seldom attracted higher caliber personnel.'

For the first sixteen years of the 20th century, reformers in and out of uniform schemed to purge the Army of obsolescent ideas, procedures, and equipment. They dreamed of a modern force in readiness—one capable of shielding the continental United States and her overseas possessions. Cost-conscious congressmen and self-appointed upholders of tradition piled up irritating obstacles at the slightest mention of constructive change, but the visionaries and iconoclasts won enough rounds to save the Army from stagnation.

Throughout its history, the Army stumbled whenever it sought to field formations larger than brigade size.

Enlisted men of Company A, 6th U.S. Infantry, model the 1902 dress uniform. Left to right: a corporal, first sergeant, private, field musicians, and sergeant. The men's caps and coats are dark blue with sky-blue trim and brass buttons and insignia. Originally, infantry chevrons and trouser stripes were light blue, but the color was changed to white in 1903. Instead of crossed rifles, field musicians wore brass bugles on their dress caps. Note the service chevrons displayed by the two sergeants. Ordinarily, these were sky-blue, but a white chevron with sky blue piping stood for 'service in war.' The dress belt was of russet leather.

Soldiers of the 35th U.S. Volunteer Infantry gleefully demonstrate the 'water cure,' an excruciating form of torture used to extract information from uncooperative natives during the Philippine-American War of 1899–1902. The troops are dressed in drab campaign hats with sky blue cords, dark blue woolen overshirts, khaki trousers, and brown duck leggings. Curiously, the trumpeter at far left is leaning on a stack of Krag carbines, which indicates that these sadistic soldiers were mounted infantrymen.

Planning officers attached to the new born General Staff (created by Congress in February 1904) realized that as long as the Army remained a disjointed collection of isolated regiments, it could not duplicate the rapid mobilization of armed masses being perfected by European powers—a recognized prerequisite for success in modern warfare. In March 1911, the War Department ordered the activation of a temporary 'Maneuver Division' at San Antonio, Texas. Ten days elapsed before the division's twelve infantry regiments and other units reported for duty—an unacceptably long delay. To avoid a repetition of this embarrassing exercise, the General Staff in 1912 grouped America's ground forces into sixteen permanent divisions—four regular army and twelve National Guard. Until the following year, however, these organizations existed only on paper. Then, between 21 and 24 February 1913, the 2nd Division assembled at two Texas cities with praise-

A first lieutenant of the 18th U.S. Infantry models his 1902 full dress coat, a dark blue garment with a sky blue collar edged in gold lace and a pair of gold shoulder knots. The wearer's rank was indicated by the number of gold braids in the knot on his lower sleeve. A colonel warranted five braids; a lieutenant colonel, four; a major, three; a captain, two; a first lieutenant, one; and a second lieutenant, none. Field officers wore eighteen buttons on their breast (nine per row), and company officers had fourteen.

worthy speed. But the division mustered a mere 11,450 regulars instead of its full complement of 22,565. America's thin olive drab line was still far from being a true army as defined by European standards.

The Dick Act of 21 January 1903 offered encouragement to the National Guard to acquire the same 'organization, armament and discipline' as the regular army within five years. In return for free federal arms, gear, and training officers, Guardsmen were expected to drill twenty-four times a year, attend a five-day encampment each summer, and submit to annual inspections conducted by regular officers. Washington spent $53,000,000 on the militia from 1903 to 1916, but the National Guard's condition barely improved. For all their good intentions, the Dick Act's framers neglected to design a coercive apparatus to ensure compliance by the states. The problem of Guard reform would defy solution until 1916.

Prodded by the self-seeking John 'Gatling gun' Parker, the Army grudgingly tested the utility of the machine gun as an infantry support weapon. On 19 June 1906, the War Department ordered each infantry regiment to detail three non-commissioned officers and eighteen privates to a provisional platoon manning two water-cooled Model 1904 Maxim machine guns. In February 1910, that platoon blossomed into a company

PLATE 29: CIVILIZING WITH A KRAG, 1898–1904

These figures are based on photographs taken during the first six years of the American occupation of the Philippines.

99. Sergeant, 20th Kansas Volunteer Infantry, Field Dress, 1899: *The inability of domestic manufacturers to produce proper khaki cotton material meant that the first troops the United States sent to the Philippines received brown canvas jackets and trousers, although the Americans preferred to fight in their overshirts. Note the red, white, and blue VIII Army Corps pin on the campaign hat. Non-commissioned officers in the 20th Kansas broke a long-standing Army taboo by sewing oversized coat chevrons on their shirts. Due to a shortage of Krags, the outbreak of the Philippine Insurrection found American volunteers still armed with trapdoor Springfields.*

100. First Lieutenant, 18th U.S. Infantry, Summer Field Dress, 1898: *America's first bumbling efforts to garb the guardians of her new tropical empire in suitable uniforms resulted in a bizarre mélange of military fashions. This subaltern sports an 1889-pattern sun helmet (with khaki cover), the khaki coat (with sky blue facings for infantry) authorized for officers only on 9 May 1898, and a pair of white trousers.* **101. First Sergeant, 2nd U.S. Infantry, Mounted Detail, Field Dress, 1901:** *Mounted 2nd Infantrymen rode Filipino ponies and used surplus cavalry equipment. Note the new 1901-pattern khaki cotton overshirt (which lacks chevrons) and the 1899-pattern khaki field trousers.* **102. Private, 23rd U.S. Infantry, Tropical Field Dress, 1904:** *This weary regular models a pair of 1902-pattern tropical service breeches, but he has not yet received a new Model 1903 Springfield rifle to replace his trusty Krag. The crown of his campaign hat has been crushed into a fashionable 'Montana peak.'*

101. First Sergeant, 2nd U.S. Infantry,
Mounted Detail, Field Dress, 1901

99. Sergeant, 20th Kansas Volunteer
Infantry, Field Dress, 1899

100. First Lieutenant, 18th U.S. Infantry,
Summer Field Dress, 1898

102. Private, 23rd U.S. Infantry, Tropical
Field Dress, 1904

with three officers, 108 enlisted men, and six guns (two for every rifle battalion). Despite Parker's exploits at San Juan Hill, his years of proselytizing, and the partial vindication of his theories during the first three years of World War I, his brother officers remained curiously indifferent to the potential of automatic weapons. American soldiers would enter the first great machine gun war with too few of these indispensable arms and no comprehensive doctrine to govern their use.

While the Army withheld its full confidence from the machine gun, it made an impressive stride in rifle development. In 1903, an improved bolt-action rifle produced initially at the Springfield Armory supplanted the Krag as the standard smallarm of the American soldier. Firing a five-round magazine, the 1903 Springfield featured recent advances in weapons technology. It reigned for years as the world's finest combat rifle, serving the American military in one world war and part of another. The Springfield was a marksman's tool, and the Army encouraged its troops to exploit fully the rifle's strengths. Enlisted men who scored well on the firing range earned monthly cash bonuses.

The quest for military preparedness assumed an added sense of urgency in 1914 with the outbreak of World War I, a struggle which threatened to embroil the United States in the worst holocaust humanity had ever seen. Yet even as Europe ran red with blood, the U.S. Army was increasingly distracted by political turmoil originating below the Rio Grande. Known as the Mexican Revolution, this series of upheavals began in 1911 with the fall of Porfirio Diaz, an ageing and corrupt military dictator. Diaz's deceptively easy overthrow ushered in a period of intrigue and bloodletting, as Mexicans resorted to force to settle their disagreements over the country's future. Clashes of personality, factionalism, and conflicting ideologies prolonged and intensified the tragedy. Violence touched every corner of Mexico and threatened to spill over onto American soil. When that happened, Washington alerted the U.S. Army for duty along the border. On two occasions, American authorities felt constrained to place large bodies of regulars in Mexico for extended stays.

The first incursion occurred in April 1914. Seizing on a trivial diplomatic incident to show his contempt for the murderous regime of Victoriano Huerta, a power-hungry general who held Mexico in his grip from February 1913 to July 1914, President Woodrow Wilson directed American naval units to seize the coastal city of Vera Cruz. At the end of the month, the four infantry regiments of the Army's 5th Brigade joined 3,446 U.S. Marines for a peaceful, seven-month occupation of Mexico's queen port.

Pancho Villa, a former bandit chieftain who aspired to rule Mexico, provoked the second American sortie south

Two grizzled veterans of Company L, 16th U.S. Infantry, with Pershing's Punitive Expedition at San Geronimo, Mexico, 28 May 1916. The bearded man in the olive drab sweater is a sergeant. The older man at right displays his first sergeant's chevrons on his 1916-pattern shirt of olive drab cotton. Note the whistle chain dangling from his right breast pocket.

of the border. At 3:30 a.m. on 9 March 1916, 485 of Villa's followers galloped through the border town of Columbus, New Mexico, slaying eighteen Americans and wounding eight. Villa hoped to humiliate the current Mexican government by luring foreign troops into his homeland. He succeeded. The day after the Columbus Raid, President Wilson instructed the Army to dispatch troops 'into Mexico with the sole object of capturing Villa and preventing further raids by his band.' Brigadier General John J. Pershing, a brilliant and exacting officer, took command of the hastily formed 'Punitive Expedition' on 14 March. Placed at his disposal were 192 officers and 4,800 men arrayed in two brigades of cavalry and one of infantry. The main components in the latter were the 6th and 16th Infantry. Once Pershing was well inside Mexico, he received more regular regiments, among them the 17th and 24th Infantry.

The Punitive Expedition was the last hurrah for the American horse soldier. In Europe, the mounted charge had already become a thing of the past, but in the deserts and foothills of Chihuahua, chasing Villistas was still a job for a trooper and his steed. An old 10th Cavalryman, Pershing drove his pony soldiers beyond endurance in his determination to carry out his mission. Pershing consigned his doughboys to less demanding and less glamorous tasks, such as short-range patrols and safeguarding the expedition's base camps. In a chance encounter on 25 May 1916, a private of the 17th Infantry shot and killed Villa's ablest lieutenant, General Candelario Cervantes. The incident was the U.S. Infantry's only taste of glory amid the flies and cactus of Mexico.

Oddly enough, the legitimate Mexican Army caused the Punitive Expedition more trouble than Villa's marauders. Venustiano Carranza, the victor of the power struggle that followed Huerta's fall, demanded the immediate recall of Pershing's command. The American military presence affronted Mexican honor and highlighted the fact that Carranza'a government was still too feeble to police its northern border. When the *gringos* refused to withdraw, Carranzista soldiers started firing on Pershing's mounted patrols. Running the risk of open war, President Wilson shifted additional regular outfits to supporting positions in the American Southwest. On 9 May 1916, he took the precaution of calling out the 5,160 National Guardsmen of Texas, Arizona, and New Mexico.

Egged on by the Mexican crisis and the European war, Congress produced the National Defense Act of 3 June 1916. This opportunely timed and far-reaching legislation laid out a five-year plan to construct a peacetime regular army of 175,000 men embodied in sixty-five regiments of infantry, twenty-five of cavalry, twenty-one of field artillery, seven of engineers, two mounted engineer battalions, 263 companies of coast artillery, eight aero squadrons, miscellaneous support units, and a staff corps. In the event of hostilities, the regular army could fatten its cadres to attain a legal limit of 287,846 men. Congress added a headquarters company and a supply company to every infantry regiment to promote better administration, and it lent official sanction to the existence of regimental machine gun companies. The law also authorized an Officers' Reserve Corps, a Reserve Officers' Training Corps, and an Enlisted Reserve Corps.

The National Defense Act crowned the struggle to upgrade the National Guard by imposing meaningful federal controls over the militia system. Earmarked for a gradual, fourfold build-up, the Guard was duly recognized as an integral part of the 'Army of the United States.' Guardsmen were now required to swear an oath of loyalty to the nation, as well as to their respective states, and to pledge that they would obey the orders of the President. If Congress assented, the President could draft up to 425,000 individuals from the militia for federal service and appoint their officers. Besides keeping up the flow of arms and equipment, Washington would supply Guard units with drill pay,

An artificer of Company B, 16th U.S. Infantry, at El Valle, Mexico, 8 July 1916, during the Punitive Expedition. He proudly displays his Model 1903 Springfield rifle. Note the light blue cord on his campaign hat and the practical bandana—the latter a non-regulation item.

An infantry major attired in the 1911-pattern campaign hat and the English-style, olive drab overcoat approved for officers in 1907. The officer's rank was displayed on the sleeves in the same fashion as on the 1902 full dress coat, but the overcoat's knots were made of black mohair braid.

and commissioned and non-commisioned instructors from the regular army. Guardsmen, for their part, were obliged to double their drill sessions to forty-eight a year and to attend a fifteen-day encampment every summer. States failing to fulfill these terms stood to lose their federal aid.

President Wilson invoked his newly granted powers almost before the ink defining them had time to dry. In mid-June, he federalized the entire National Guard for a show of strength to frighten Carranza. By the end of July, 112,000 citizen soldiers had been transported to staging areas in Texas and Arizona. Close to 40,000 more stood by in reserve at state camps. In many ways, it was an impressive turnout, but the Guard was hardly combat ready. Most units exhibited grave deficiencies, especially a shortage of experienced hands. One-tenth of the militia ignored Wilson's call, and 17 per cent weaseled out of serving by citing family obligations. Of those dutiful chaps who boarded the southbound troop trains, a U.S. senator testified in April 1917: 'When our men went to the border last year, a very considerable percentage—possibly as many as one-half—had never fired a rifle and nearly as large a proportion had never had an hour's drill.' A quarter of the Guardsmen were judged to be physically unfit for active service.

Happily for all concerned, there was no second Mexican-American war. Neither side could afford to goad the other into a serious quarrel. Carranza had his hands full suppressing his domestic foes. He needed no new enemies. Likewise, Wilson discovered that he had something more pressing to worry about than Mexican outlaws. Relations with Germany had sunk so low that it became imperative to disentangle the U.S. Army from what was now an inexpedient sideshow. Besides, the Punitive Expedition had largely served its purpose, exterminating so many Villistas that a repetition of the Columbus Raid seemed unlikely.

On 28 January 1917, the Punitive Expedition began its withdrawal from Mexico, dragging its tail across the American line by 5 February. As they turned their faces northward, Pershing's regulars affected a jaunty air. They were proud of what they had accomplished, relieved to be alive, and glad to leave behind the choking dust and searing temperatures of Chihuahua. But the heat of the Mexican sun could not compare to the man-made inferno awaiting the U.S. Infantry in the trenches of France.

PLATE 30: DRESS BLUES AND OLIVE DRAB, 1903–16
103. Corporal (C. Tucker Beckett), 16th U.S. Infantry, Dress Uniform, 1915: *By 1915, the 1902 dress uniform had fallen into general disuse. At most posts, the men donned their dress blues no more than once or twice a year, usually without the sky blue breast cords prescribed by regulations. Originally, the coat's chevrons were sky blue, but the color was changed to white in 1910. When America entered World War I in April 1917, the Army halted the issue of dress uniforms.* **104. First Lieutenant, 6th U.S. Infantry, Summer Field Dress, 1916:** *This member of the Punitive Expedition sports a Model 1911 olive drab service hat with an officer's gold-and-black cord, a 1916-pattern shirt of olive drab cotton (with the right pocket flap torn back to accommodate a pen), 1912-pattern breeches (of the same material as the shirt), and russet leather strap leggings. His sidearm is a Model 1911 Colt .45-caliber automatic pistol.* **105. Sergeant, 16th U.S. Infantry, Summer Field Dress, 1916:** *Note the goggles on the service hat, the enlisted man's version of the 1916 shirt and 1912 breeches, the Model 1910 cartridge belt of khaki webbing, and the khaki canvas leggings. The sergeant holds a .30-caliber Model 1903 Springfield rifle.*

103. Corporal, 16th U.S. Infantry, Dress Uniform, 1915

104. First Lieutenant, 6th U.S. Infantry, Summer Field Dress, 1916

105. Sergeant, 16th U.S. Infantry, Summer Field Dress, 1916

10 Machinery and Blood

1917–18

On 2 April 1917, Woodrow Wilson appeared before a joint session of Congress to ask for a declaration of war against Germany. The President roundly denounced the 'Imperial German Government' for unleashing its submarines against neutral vessels plying the waters off Great Britain, France, and Italy. 'American ships have been sunk,' Wilson charged, 'American lives taken.' Nevertheless, the President did not invite his countrymen to join him in a war of revenge. Characteristically, he proclaimed his war goals in idealistic terms: 'The world must be made safe for democracy. . . . We have no selfish ends to serve. We desire no conquest, no dominion. . . . We are but one of the champions of the rights of mankind. We shall be satisfied when those rights have been made as secure as the faith and the freedom of nations can make them.'

Eighteen months later, 1,200,000 Americans, the greater part of them infantry, were locked in furious combat with the German Army amid the scarred fields and hillsides of France. Those doughboys constituted the cutting edge of the largest armed host yet raised by the United States. They sailed to Europe imbued with the idea that they were going to protect decency, civilization, and self-government from the barbarism of 'Prussian autocracy.' 'We come from a young and aggressive nation,' said their commander, General John J. Pershing. 'We come from a nation that for one hundred and fifty years has stood before the world as the champion of the sacred principles of human liberty. We now return to Europe, the home of our ancestors, to help defend the same principles upon European soil.'

Like his revered chief, Pershing, Lieutenant Colonel George C. Marshall regarded World War I as the end of one era in America's history and the birth of another: 'Quitting the soil of Europe to escape oppression and the loss of personal liberties, the early settlers in America laid the foundations of a government based on equality, personal liberty, and justice. Three hundred years later their descendants returned to Europe and . . . launched their first attack on the remaining forces of autocracy to secure those same principles for the people of the Old World.'

Henceforth, the U.S. Army would defend America's interests not by simply guarding her borders, but by venturing to the far corners of the globe to intervene in foreign wars and readjust the existing world order.

Whether America's sons truly advanced the causes of equality, liberty, and justice is a matter for debate. In 1917 and 1918, American propagandists called Pershing's soldiers the 'Army of Freedom' and commemorated their exploits in the florid language of 19th century romanticism.

For those 'Yanks' who reached the Western Front in time to behold the repellent face of modern battle, timeworn clichés about valor and glory rang hollow. The conflict that had ravaged Europe since 1914 was a new kind of war—so impersonal, so inhumane, so cataclysmic—that it defied description. George Marshall accompanied the first American division sent overseas as a staff captain, and he summed up his experiences tersely: 'War . . . is mud and rain and cold.' Captain Jesse W. Wooldridge of the 38th U.S. Infantry, who lost 138 out of 189 men while leading a desperate counterattack along the Marne River on 15 July 1918, was even more emphatic: 'There is no romance in modern war. It is a matter of machinery and blood; a concentration of all the great destructive forces of the world.'

Because it imposed such heavy demands on its participants, World War I dramatically altered the U.S. Army. The dispersed police force with a quaint frontier heritage gave way to a large modern army capable of besting troops produced by the most advanced military system in the world. The new Army of Freedom never totally cleansed itself of the amateurism long associated with the American way of war, but it did its part in defeating Germany. Much of the credit for that victory was earned the hard way by the U.S. Infantry. Captain Eddie Rickenbacker, America's leading air ace, gallantly testified: 'I have always maintained that American infantrymen were the heroes of the war.' And a German general paid the doughboys this grudging tribute: 'They may not look so good, but hell, how they can fight.'

In the summer of 1914, as World War I engulfed Europe, Woodrow Wilson counseled his fellow citizens to remain 'impartial in thought as well as deed.' But it was not easy to practice what the President preached. Americans enjoyed close social and cultural ties with Great Britain and France, the senior partners in the Allied coalition. Burgeoning Allied orders for munitions and foodstuffs strengthened those relationships as American export levels climbed to unprecedented highs. Thanks to Teutonic blundering and Allied propaganda, Americans generally blamed Germany, the leader of the Central Powers, for starting the war, and they regarded German soldiers and sailors as merciless brutes who murdered helpless civilians with impunity. Furthermore, Wilson and other American policy-makers worried about the consequences of an Allied defeat. For years, Germany had challenged America's ambitions in the Pacific and the Caribbean. There was no telling what the Germans would do if the restraining force of British naval power was weakened. Thus when Berlin resorted to unrestricted submarine warfare in early 1917 and tried to stir up a second Mexican-American war, it furnished the Wilson Administration and the American people with an excuse to enter the European holocaust. 'I was only seventeen then,' recalled Alphonso Bulz, a Texas lad destined to fight in France with the 143rd Infantry, 'but I thought I'd better go over there and fight so I wouldn't be no slave to any foreign country.' To his protesting father, Bulz announced: 'I want to go to war, [and] show that Kaiser he can't fool around with Americans.'

Germany's warlords knew that an intensified submarine blockade was likely to goad Wilson into hostilities, but they thought they could vanquish the Allies before the United States mobilized sufficiently to affect the outcome of the struggle. At the time, it seemed a reasonable risk. In European eyes, the U.S. Army warranted no consideration as a strategic factor. As of 1 April 1917, America possessed 127,588 regulars. The National Guard numbered 181,620, with 80,446 still in federal service—a legacy of the recent unpleasantness south of the border. On the Western Front, such a force could be annihilated within a matter of weeks and never make a dent in the enemy's well-fortified lines.

To create a respectable army without undue delay, Washington turned almost immediately to conscription. On 18 May 1917, Wilson signed 'An Act Authorizing the President to Increase Temporarily the Military Establishment of the United States,' better known as the Selective Service Act. The law made all resident males aged twenty-one to thirty liable for registration and (except for those exempted under certain conditions) the draft. Conscripts would go into a new organization, the 'National Army.' The regular army and National Guard were authorized to recruit enough men to bring themselves to the war strengths established by the National Defense Act of 1916, and they could receive conscripts to remedy any shortfalls. All soldiers, regardless of category, were subject to the same regulations, pay, and allowances as the regular establishment. Enlistees and draftees were bound to serve for the duration of the emergency. Finally, the President could increase or decrease regular units in response to changing conditions in Europe.

The Selective Service experienced numerous problems and was not always administered with consistency or fairness, but it proved an invaluable asset to the American war effort. Since her birth in battle more than a century earlier, the United States had failed to assemble large armies and maintain them for prolonged periods of conflict without resorting to bribery or coercion. In previous wars, an initial rush of patriotic excitement was often enough to fill the Army's ranks for the first year or so. But as casualty lists mounted and tales of military hardship filtered back to the home folks, the pool of willing recruits rapidly evaporated, causing all sorts of complications for a government in sore need of cannon fodder.

The Selective Service was a sensible response to the demands of total war. It was also flexible enough to meet America's fluctuating manpower requirements. In August 1918, Congress broadened the age limits for conscription to eighteen and forty-five. Altogether, draft officials registered 24,234,021 men and inducted 2,810,296, the Army accepting 2,702,687. Counting voluntary enlistments, the Army came to total 4,271,150 during the war, but its peak strength at any time hovered around 3,700,000 (see Table 8). The U.S. Infantry appropriated about a third of those personnel by expanding to 297 regiments. The Army also created 165 machine gun battalions for service with infantry brigades and divisions.

For most of World War I, men entering the U.S. Army fell into one of three categories: regulars, guardsmen, and draftees (see Table 8). In August 1918, these distinctions were abolished, and the three components were merged into a single 'United States Army.'

Table 8. Regulars, Guardsmen, and Draftees, 1917-18

Category	Strength	Percentage
Regular Army	527,000	13%
National Guard	382,000	10%
National Army	3,091,000	77%

The millions of men who donned Army olive drab in 1917 and 1918 were a mixed lot, representing every segment of American society. The writer Frazier Hunt left this word portrait of the rank and file of the 77th Division, a National Army outfit swarming with New York City boys: 'A score of races, a dozen religions, rich men, poor men, honest men, ex-second story workers, bankers, clerks, street cleaners, bond salesmen, pants makers, but all soldiers in an American army now, wearing the same uniform and drawing the same $30 a month.' An estimated 20 per cent of the Army's draftees were immigrants. Alvin C. York of the 328th Infantry, a Tennessee hillbilly who became the most famous

Privates of the U.S. 1st Division confer during a trench warfare exercise near Gondrecourt on a cold July day in 1917. Doughboys like these joked that France had only two seasons—winter and August. The sloppily packed shelter halves and mud-covered Springfields mark these 'regulars' as two of the thousands of green recruits who filled out the division before it was rushed across the Atlantic. Contrary to this posed propaganda picture, most of the 1st Division's personnel endured their first French winter in summer uniforms—without overcoats.

Corporal C. Thompson of the 369th U.S. Infantry Regiment, painted in Champagne in 1918 by Raymond Desvarreux. Originally known as the 15th New York Infantry National Guard, this crack outfit was recruited in Harlem. Though officially a part of the U.S. 93rd Division, the 369th was assigned to the French Fourth Army in March 1918 and spent the remainder of the war fighting under foreign command. Thompson wears an American uniform, but his rifle and accoutrements are French.

A private of the U.S. 30th Division mans a forward trench in Belgium, circa July–August 1918. The 30th was attached to the British Expeditionary Force for its tour on the Western Front. This man is armed with the Short Magazine Lee-Enfield rifle—either the .303-caliber British version or the mass-produced American copy modified to take .30-caliber ammunition. Note the entrenching tool on the back of the private's pack and his khaki leggings, which belong to the era of the Spanish-American War.

American foot soldier of the war, was dismayed to find himself 'throwed in with a lot of Greeks and Italians.' However, he subsequently learned that his strange comrades made 'right-smart fighters.' Such a transformation was not achieved with ease. 'Some of these Polish lads hadn't been in the country over a couple of years and hardly knew any English,' reported a lieutenant in the 339th Infantry. 'Actually I had to learn Polish from a Polish corporal we had in order to give the commands for the men to do right face and left face.' The foreign-born were not the only ones to encounter training problems. Close to a quarter of the conscripts were illiterate. Native whites averaged less than seven years of education, immigrants less than five, and Southern blacks less than three. All things considered, the vaunted Army of Freedom was not a very sophisticated amalgam.

Under its tables of organization, the War Department required a minimum of 200,000 officers to train and lead 4,000,000 men. When Congress declared war, fewer than 9,000 officers—5,791 regulars and 3,199 National Guardsmen—were in federal service. To its credit, the Wilson Administration established a system of officer procurement based on military professionalism, rather than political privilege. More Guard officers were federalized, the West Point curriculum compressed into one year, and promotions doled out to trusted enlisted men, but these contrivances filled only 24,000 more command slots. At the same time, the Army opened a network of Officers' Training Camps and put qualified applicants through three months of intensive instruction and physical conditioning. These ersatz military academies supplied nearly half of the Army's officers and over two-thirds of those assigned to line duty (see Table 9).

Table 9. Army Officer Procurement, 1917–18

Source of Officers	Number	Percentage
Regular Army	6,000	3%
National Guard	12,000	6%
From the Ranks	16,000	8%
Officers' Training Camps	96,000	48%
Physicians*	42,000	21%
Clergymen (Chaplains)*	26,000	13%
Directly from Civil Life*	2,000	1%

*Most of these men were specialists or technicians with little or no military training.

According to Mark Clark, a 1917 West Point graduate and a captain in the 11th Infantry, the majority of the 'ninety-day wonders' who helped run his company 'were quite good.' They may have been eager and brave enough, but the new shavetails lacked the seasoning that comes from actually exercising command. One of these prefabricated leaders of men, First Lieutenant John C. Madden of the 355th Infantry, admitted: 'Most of the lieutenants were ninety-day wonders, so I guess you could say it was the blind leading the blind.' Less than 1 per cent of the company commanders sent to France boasted a year's prior service.

Career officers dominated the Army's upper echelons more than in any previous war, but few of these men were adequately prepared for the crushing burdens they shouldered with corps, divisional, brigade, or regimental command. A lieutenant with the 310th Infantry reflected on the shortcomings of the regular officer appointed to the colonelcy of his National Army regiment: 'Thirty years in the Army and he'd never been in battle. Before the war started, he'd never had over five hundred men under his command, and all of them had been regulars. Then bang, he has three thousand men, almost all civilian-soldiers.' It may have been a new sort of war, but the Army's leadership problems conformed to a familiar pattern.

Arming 4,000,000 soldiers was no simple task, even for a nation with America's financial and industrial resources. In April 1917, Army stockpiles contained 600,000 Model 1903 Springfield rifles. It was impossible to increase that quantity in a hurry. The Springfield had to be assembled by artisans, and they could turn out no more than 1,000 a day. Fortunately, a number of American factories had been tooled to mass produce a weapon almost as fine as the Springfield, the Lee-Enfield rifle, for the British Army. At a munitions conference in Washington on 10 May 1917, the American high command decided to adopt a version of the Lee-Enfield modified to take .30-caliber ammunition. During the war, American plants manufactured 2,500,000 rifles for the U.S. Army—313,000 Springfields and the rest Model 1917 Enfields.

The problem of procuring heavy weapons was not solved as easily by American ingenuity. In fact, every tank and most of the airplanes, artillery, machine guns, and automatic rifles employed by the U.S. Army overseas were acquired from the French and British. 'We were literally beggars as to every important weapon,' remarked General Pershing, 'except the rifle.' Finally, in July 1918, American divisions embarking for the Western Front were equipped with two outstanding rapid-fire arms made in their own country, the Model 1917 Browning heavy machine gun and the Browning automatic rifle, both .30-caliber. The Brownings were not introduced into action until September, but the United States shipped 29,000 automatic rifles and 27,000 machine guns to France by 1 November. By that time, a third of the American-crewed automatic rifles peppering German trenches and bunkers were Brownings.

On 18 May 1917, the same day the Draft Bill became law, Secretary of War Newton D. Baker disclosed that his country would shortly dispatch a one-division expeditionary force to France. The purpose of this token reinforcement was to show the flag and buoy up Allied morale while the United States developed her military muscle. Four regular regiments fresh from the Mexican border, the 16th, 18th, 26th, and 28th Infantry, made up the nucleus of this hasty concoction, but when the U.S. 1st Division sailed from Hoboken in June, it had lost its seasoned character. At the time of their selection, the four regiments mustered about 700 men apiece, 1,300 short of war strength. Because cadres of experienced soldiers had to be retained in the United States to train future divisions, each regiment lost half of its veteran personnel and was then pumped up to a strength of 2,000 with an overpowering implantation of raw recruits. On 4 July 1917, a week after the division's vanguard tumbled ashore at St. Nazaire, the 2nd Battalion of the 16th Infantry staged a sloppy parade in Paris. Disgusted by the Americans' unsteady formations and bumbling evolutions, a French soldier muttered: 'And they send *that* to help us.' 'We hadn't even been trained in squads left and squads right,' acknowledged Captain Marshall of the division's staff. 'It was vitally essential,' he later wrote, 'that our men be disciplined and the organization reasonably well trained before entering the line.'

Almost a year would pass before Americans could take legitimate pride in the 1st Division. Yet from this sorry start evolved the American Expeditionary Force (AEF), the mighty, ever-growing army group that tipped the conflict's manpower scales in favor of the Allies and extinguished Germany's last hopes for victory. By 11 November 1918, the day an armistice stayed the slaughter, 2,086,000 American troops had crossed the Atlantic, and 1,390,000 of them—more than two-thirds—had fought in France. The AEF encompassed 31 per cent of the soldiers deployed by the Allies on the Western Front, 3 per cent more than the British and only 10 per cent less than the French. Of the forty-two American divisions to land in France before the firing ceased, twenty-nine got into action. By the second week of October 1918, the Yanks were holding 101 miles of front—23 per cent of the Allied battle line—and a greater share than the one entrusted to the much older British Expeditionary Force (BEF).

John J. Pershing, the AEF's strong-willed, square-jawed commander, guided the American army in France through all its assorted growing pains—from its conception to its final gory battles. Born in Missouri in 1860, this uncommon man graduated from West Point in 1886 and received a taste of frontier soldiering with the 6th and 10th Cavalry. He fought bravely in Cuba in 1898. Between 1899 and 1913, Pershing served three tours in the Philippines. There he displayed talent as a diplomat, administrator, and bush tactician, forcing the Moros, semi-civilized Muslim tribesmen, to accept American rule. Pershing functioned as well behind a desk—as a staff officer and an instructor of military science—as he did astride a horse. His handling of the Punitive Expedition made him a logical choice to command the AEF. Fifty-seven-years-old in April 1917, he was the fittest major general in the Army and the last one to control a sizable combat command. On 6 October 1917, with the AEF barely more than 60,000 strong, Congress elevated Pershing to the rank of full general.

In the course of his tenure with the AEF, Pershing acquired a reputation as a sour-faced martinet. Convinced that tight discipline and military courtesy were the cornerstones of battlefield effectiveness, he insisted that his troops observe high standards in their dress and bearing. But Pershing cared more about performance than appearance. He believed that the American soldier was innately superior to the Allies and the Germans, and he wanted his doughboys★ to excel. Pershing demanded much from himself and his subordinates, and he ruthlessly removed those officers who fell short of his expectations. 'He is looking for results,' scribbled one division commander. 'He intends to have them. He will sacrifice any man who does not bring them.'

That Pershing turned irascible on occasion should come as no surprise. The responsibilities he bore would have broken a man of less grit, vigor, and intelligence. His mission was to cross a wide ocean, establish his headquarters in a foreign land, and build a great fighting army virtually from scratch, overseeing its organization, training, and supply. Instructed to cooperate with the British and the French, he was also warned to maintain the AEF as 'a separate and distinct component of the combined forces.' To put it simply, Pershing held the power to choose when, where, and in what strength the AEF would commit itself to battle. If he faltered or exhibited faulty judgment, it could mean the death of thousands of young Americans and the downfall of the Allied cause.

Pershing's decisions governing the organization and training of the AEF were colored by his understanding of the type of war raging on the Western Front. It was a war unlike anything the American soldier had ever seen. The battlefield had grown into a much more dangerous place, and infantry no longer reigned as its king. The rapid-fire weapons perfected by the Industrial Revolution converted the offensive into a seemingly futile exercise which traded meager gains for appalling casualties. Marshal Henri Philippe Pétain, the level-headed commander of the French Army in the latter part

★The venerable sobriquet, 'doughboy,' long reserved exclusively for infantrymen, was applied to all American soldiers in World War I.

of the war, reduced the tactical revolution to a simple equation: 'Firepower kills.' Indeed, the Western Front had been frozen in a trench-bound stalemate since the winter of 1914. Try as they might, neither side could break the deadlock.

All too tragically, many generals, stubborn children of the 19th century, clung to the belief that foot soldiers possessing the moral fortitude to rush blindly into danger could overcome the latest instruments of destruction. Following one senseless assault with another, the brass hats piled a generation of European manhood in tattered heaps before the opposing trenches. A couple of machine guns could level entire battalions in seconds. 'The German machine gunners were almost iron robots,' wrote an enlisted man in the 312th U.S. Infantry, 'judged from the machine-like precision with which they cut down advancing troops. . . . The attacking forces are always at a disadvantage, having to expose themselves fully to the enemy's fire.' A 26th Infantryman noted that the 'Heinies' handled a Maxim machine gun 'like a sickle. And they'd always shoot low.'

Chattering machine guns laid legions of bright-faced boys beneath rows of white crosses, but artillery was the big killer on the Western Front. Massed batteries struck with paralyzing force—often without warning—exterminating men at random or by timetable. 'We cannot fight artillery,' an American draftee raged in August 1918. 'Jerry [a popular nickname for the enemy] is a rotten sport.' Ordinary light fieldpieces tossed high-explosive shells as far as 7,000 to 9,300 yards. The belligerents employed a varied line of heavier ordnance, culminating in some German behemoths with ranges of twenty-nine to seventy-five miles. The amount of ground an infantry division could take or hold depended on the quantity, size, range, and mobility of its supporting artillery. As Marshal Pétain phrased it: 'Cannon conquers, infantry occupies.' Few battle-wise doughboys cared to dispute that verdict. 'You never saw

any heavier fire against infantry than what those Germans put on us,' claimed a captain of the U.S. 1st Division. 'The noise . . . actually blew out one of my eardrums. . . . Hundreds of our men were just blown to pieces. It was a nightmare! The miracle was not that any of us survived but that we could keep moving.'

To function effectively in such a hellish environment, Pershing concluded that the AEF should field divisions at least twice as large as those belonging to European armies. He wanted a division with the wherewithal to absorb considerable pounding without falling to pieces or seeking relief—a division with the power to cross 'No Man's Land,' capture the enemy's trenches, and roll over his rear areas. The War Department translated Pershing's recommendations into new tables of organization, issuing them to the Army in August 1917. Pershing scrapped the 'triangular division' (nine infantry regiments grouped into three brigades), an American fixture since 1898, replacing it with a 'square division.' The latter included two infantry brigades (four infantry

Table 10. AEF Infantry Organization, 1917-18★

'*Platoon*, 58 men, commanded by 2d or 1st lieutenant.
Company, 6 officers and 250 men, by a captain.
Battalion, 4 companies, by a major.
Regiment, 3 battalions and a machine gun company, 112 officers and 3,720 men, by a colonel.
Brigade, 2 regiments and a machine gun battalion, 258 officers and 8,211 men, by a brigadier general.
Division, 2 infantry and 1 field artillery brigades, 1 engineer regiment, 1 machine gun battalion, 1 signal battalion, and trains; 72 guns, 260 machine guns, 17,666 rifles; 979 officers, 27,082 men; by a major general.
Corps, 2 to 6 divisions, by a major general.
Army, 3 to 5 corps, by a lieutenant general or major general.
Group of Armies, 2 or 3 armies, by a general, lieutenant general, or major general.'

★Quoted from *My Experiences in the World War* (1931) by John J. Pershing.

A machine gun crew of the 26th 'Yankee' Division trains with a French Model 1916 8-millimeter Hotchkiss gun in the Vosges, 10 January 1918. Because there was a shortage of American-made machine guns, twelve AEF divisions received the air-cooled Hotchkiss. These lucky New Englanders are warmly dressed with overcoats, sweaters, gloves, and rubber boots.

regiments and two machine gun battalions), a brigade of field artillery (one regiment of 155-millimeter guns and two of 75-millimeter guns), a regiment of engineers, a machine-gun battalion, a signal battalion, a trench mortar battery, and ammunition, supply, engineer, and sanitary trains. At full strength, an AEF division would go into the line with 28,061 officers and men (Table 10).

Although a square division contained five fewer regiments than the triangular variety, the units which remained were enlarged and endowed with greater firepower. The National Defense Act limited an infantry regiment to fifteen companies, but Pershing raised its war strength from 2,061 to 3,832 of all ranks. The twelve rifle companies were each issued sixteen automatic rifles. The regimental machine gun company had its guns quadrupled from four to sixteen. In addition, a machine gun battalion of three companies joined every infantry brigade, and there were divisional machine gun battalions of four companies. Each of these companies was allocated sixteen 'choppers' and 175 men.

The square division was the basic tactical and administrative unit of the AEF, the building block for larger formations, such as corps and armies. Oddly enough, Pershing left his proud new creation undergunned. The oversized American division held twice as many men as its British and French counterparts, but it boasted no more artillery. Like its triangular predecessor, the AEF division possessed only three artillery regiments.

From the moment the U.S. 1st Division landed in France, proper training for the AEF became one of Pershing's overriding concerns. More than half of the division's officers and two-thirds of the men were abject 'rookies.' But the 1st Division was a special case—a rush job—hurriedly slapped together for propaganda purposes. More time and care were devoted to the preparation of later divisions. When the war was over, the War Department computed that the average doughboy logged six months of basic training at a stateside camp or cantonment before he boarded his eastbound troopship.

Nonetheless, Pershing insisted that all new arrivals undergo an extended advanced training program before they went to the front. Because of Allied censorship, Army instructors in the United States knew very little about conditions on the Western Front. The Yanks had to learn about living in the trenches, guarding against gas attacks and nighttime raids, stringing and cutting barbed wire, and defending a position in depth. Infantrymen had to master new weapons in the American arsenal. Besides its Springfield or Enfield rifles, each AEF infantry platoon carried four automatic rifles, six rifle grenade launchers, and a quantity of hand grenades. At the regimental level, a foot soldier might have to handle a

trench mortar or a 1-pounder cannon. Officers and men also needed to know how to advance behind a rolling barrage, operate with tanks and aerial support, conduct trench raids and reconnaissance patrols, and make optimum use of machine guns.

The AEF Staff Training Section devised a ninety-day schedule of instruction divided into three phases. First, a division would spend a month practicing with basic weapons and participating in tactical exercises. Next, the division was split up, rotating infantry battalions and smaller units into the trenches to serve as components of French divisions, supported by French artillery. Finally, the division was reassembled for one month of training with combined arms, especially artillery and aviation. After that, the division was ready to occupy a sector on its own, but only as a member of a French corps. (In the spring of 1918, diplomatic pressure and strategic considerations compelled Pershing to assign ten divisions to the BEF for their training.) The creation of American corps would occur after an adequate number of divisions became accustomed to combat.

In the final months of the war, the rising tempo of the fighting and the accelerating loss in American lives precipitated drastic abridgments in the AEF's advanced training program. The U.S. General Staff reported that the typical doughboy received two months of additional

PLATE 31: OVER THERE, 1917–18

106. Private, 369th U.S. Infantry, Field Dress, 1918: *Farmed out of the AEF on account of white racial prejudice, this irrepressible National Guard outfit from New York City compiled a proud combat record with the French Fourth Army. Logistical considerations forced the 'Men of Bronze' to accept French helmets, Mannlicher-Berthier rifles, and leather accoutrements, but they kept their American-made Model 1912 service coats and breeches.* **107. Private First Class, 28th U.S. Infantry, U.S. 1st Division, Field Dress, 1917:** *While attached to the 1st Division's staff, Captain George C. Marshall witnessed the following on 20 October 1917: 'The men presented a curious spectacle. The overseas cap had not yet been received and the stiff-brimmed campaign hat was out of the question; consequently, each soldier had met the situation as best suited his fancy. Many purchased olive drab kepis of the Belgian type [pictured here] with a gold tassel hanging from the front tip; a large number had cut off the brim of the campaign hat and wore the close-fitting skull piece; a few had fashioned for themselves headgear from bath towels; and some wore dark blue Alpine caps.' The 1st Division faced its first French winter without sufficient stores of shoes and winter uniforms. This man wears the summer version of the Model 1912 service coat and breeches—lightweight cotton garments.* **108. Corporal, 103rd U.S. Infantry, U.S. 26th ('Yankee') Division, Field Dress, 1918:** *In October 1918, the 26th Division received permission to wear its famous 'YD' shoulder patch. Note the British 1917-pattern small box gas mask and the British-style steel helmet. Two gold wound stripes adorn the lower right sleeve of the wool service coat. The gold stripe on the left sleeve stands for six months of overseas war service. Figures 107 and 108 both carry Model 1903 Springfield magazine rifles.*

106. Private, 369th U.S. Infantry, Field Dress, 1918

107. Private First Class, 28th U.S. Infantry, U.S. 1st Division, Field Dress, 1917

108. Corporal, 103rd U.S. Infantry, U.S. 26th ('Yankee') Division, Field Dress, 1918

preparation in France before he went into the line. But tens of thousands received considerably less. During the bloody Meuse-Argonne Offensive (26 September–11 November 1918), the AEF's average training level dwindled to four months per man. Some units were rushed straight to the front from their troopships. Boys drafted in July 1918 went into action in September. Many new replacements had never handled a rifle in their lives—except for a ten-day crash course held immediately upon their disembarkation.

To compensate for the ignorance of stay-at-home American instructors, the French and British detailed 773 officers and non-commissioned officers to training camps in the United States. These trenchwise veterans— proud of their hard-earned expertise, brimming with survival tips—had much to teach America's callow youth. General Pershing, however, grew certain that too much contact with foreign instructors on either side of the Atlantic could be detrimental to his doughboys. After three years of stupendous slaughter, the Allied armies had come to respect the power of the defense. British instructors posted to the U.S. 36th Division in France warned their pupils: 'Love Mother Earth, love Mother Earth, if you want to go 'ome.' And when yuh attack . . . don't try and do it all with one swipe. Go five, ten yards, no more—then go back to Mother Earth and wait a little bit.' Along with more cautious methods, Allied generals had lower expectations. Instead of squandering lives in a fruitless search for a decisive battle to end the conflict in a single stroke, they settled for a war of attrition.

Pershing rejected the revised Allied tactical theory and the underlying assumption that technological developments had altered the fundamental principles of war. 'It was my opinion,' he later wrote in his memoirs, 'that the victory could not be won by the costly process of attrition, but it must be won by driving the enemy out into the open and engaging him in a war of movement.' It was not enough to teach the AEF to survive in the trenches. Pershing believed that American troops could succeed where others had failed—that the men he led could pierce the enemy's deep defensive zones and drive into Germany. Once clear of the German trenches, the Yanks would have to shift into a new mode of fighting. Pershing called it 'open warfare,' and he listed its primary ingredients as 'individual and group initiative, resourcefulness and tactical judgment.' While demanding 'thorough preparation for trench fighting,' Pershing ordered his divisions 'to train mainly for open combat, with the object from the start of vigorously forcing the offensive.'

Nothing irritated Pershing more than what Allied instructors taught American infantrymen about the rifle. 'The armies on the Western Front . . . had all but given up the use of the rifle,' he reported. 'Machine guns, grenades, Stokes mortars, and one-pounders had become the main reliance of the average Allied soldier.' A white captain in the black 369th Infantry made the same discovery: 'The French . . . were great believers in the hand grenade—their rifles seemed more or less something to put a bayonet on.' Likewise, at Camp Custer, Michigan, in early 1918, British instructors informed an audience composed of the 339th Infantry that in actual combat 'there was not too much rifle shooting but lots of bayonet exercise, and the gun was used as a club more than it was shot.' The Allies knew it was foolish for a man to stay out in the open and exchange shots with a protected foe he could not see. When seconds meant the difference between life and death, an attacking soldier's first order of business was to scurry across No Man's Land. If he reached the enemy's trenches, he usually fought at pointblank range—where all men were marksmen and it was often easier to kill with bayonets, grenades, or satchel charges.

To senior American officers, who began soldiering in the 1880s—the time when the marksmanship craze gripped the U.S. Army—Allied tactical doctrine was anathema. Pershing argued that nothing could 'replace

Private John Dafnomiles, Company F, 2nd Battalion, 6th Infantry, U.S. 5th Division, demonstrates how to fire a French V.B 8 rifle grenade from a Model 1903 Springfield. He wears an olive drab overseas cap based on a French design. The AEF adopted this headgear to replace the broad-brimmed campaign hat. Dafnomiles's lower legs are wrapped with British-style puttees. Puttees proved more practical in the trenches than American leggings.

Five lieutenants of the Machine Gun Company, 18th Infantry, U.S. 1st Division, at Petit Freissy, 15 May 1918. General Pershing was so taken with the British brown leather Sam Browne belt that he ordered every AEF officer to procure one. Three different styles of overseas cap are seen here. The chains hooked to the left shoulder strap buttons are for whistles, which were used to signal troops in combat.

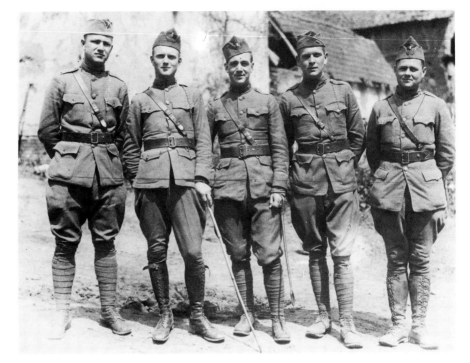

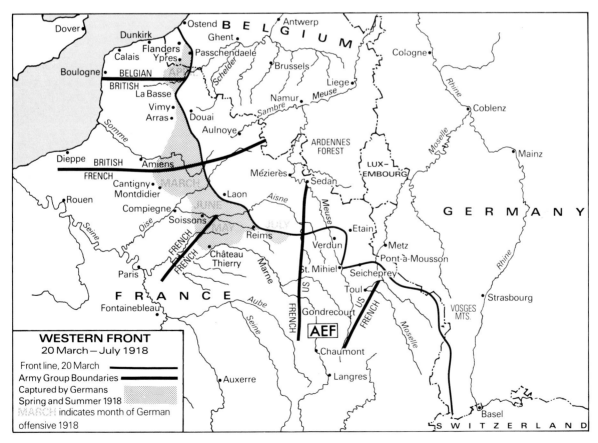

WESTERN FRONT
20 March – July 1918

Front line, 20 March
Army Group Boundaries
Captured by Germans
Spring and Summer 1918
MARCH indicates month of German offensive 1918

the combination of an efficient soldier and his rifle.' The ability of infantry to kill at a distance was vital to his concept of open warfare. Whereas French *poilus* practiced their musketry on 100-yard ranges, Pershing wanted his doughboys to pick off Germans at 600 meters. In discussing recruit training with the War Department, he urged: 'Teach them to shoot straight.' Pershing was sure that an American with faith in himself and his rifle would fight with an aggressiveness that would win the war.

Corporal Alvin C. York, Company G, 328th Infantry, U.S. 82nd Division, epitomized the soldier of Pershing's dreams. On 8 October 1918, York and a sixteen-man patrol ran afoul of a German machine-gun battalion in the maze of trees, slopes, and gullies that made up the Argonne Forest. Nine doughboys fell in the first bursts of enemy fire. Instead of taking cover, York calmly launched an unstoppable, one-man offensive. Armed only with a Model 1917 Enfield rifle and a .45-caliber automatic pistol, the Tennessee farmboy outshot his opponents, killing twenty-five, capturing 132, and putting thirty-five machine guns out of action.

If York represented an ideal, he was also something of an exception. Many doughboys shared the corporal's courage, but not his unerring aim. York had grown up with firearms; he was a crack shot and a skilled hunter long before he marched away to war. Other Yanks who challenged enemy machine guns with their rifles frequently earned themselves nothing but heroes' graves.

Unable to tell the difference between aggressiveness and rashness, the inexperienced Americans fought with an abandon that had long gone out of fashion on the Western Front. They preferred to charge forward blindly and rush German strongpoints, rather than steadily work their way around the enemy's flanks and rear. 'Our men gave better results when employed in a "steamroller" operation,' explained George Marshall. 'Their morale suffered from delays under fire, their spirits were best maintained by continued aggressive action. . . . They bitterly resented casualties suffered while being held in position, without doing any damage to the enemy.' This impatience cost the AEF dearly.

Sergeant Earl Goldsmith, 128th Infantry, 32nd Division, participated in a typical American assault at Juvigny on 1 September 1918:

'The Germans had several machine guns left around the town, and we had to knock them off. There was one . . . that our bunch had to take, and we tried it head on. God, it was a slaughter! They just kept mowing us down. But Lieutenant Harris . . . kept trying to rally us until he was cut in two. Then I had to take over the platoon. . . . Of the forty who started against that damn Maxim, there was only twelve left.'

Sergeant Russell Adams described a similar attack near Château-Thierry, which was mounted a few weeks earlier by the 103rd Infantry, 26th Division:

'There must have been a better way to do it than the one we used, but we were brand new to this . . . way of fighting. . . .

'Anyway, . . . we . . . hit them head-on—first it was to be Company C. . . . Oh those poor devils. . . . They went a-running out of those woods with the sunshine lighting up their bayonets, and those Germans started mowing them down. We [Company B] were to be the second wave, but we hadn't gone very far before we were the first wave—that's how bad . . . Company C had been hit.'

As much as he disparaged his allies' tactics, Pershing failed to devise a better way to move infantry through No Man's Land. Like the British and French, the doughboys went 'over the top' in line, wave after wave, with officers admonishing men to keep their alignment as they slipped into shellholes and tripped over barbed wire. The Germans cut them down like corn under a reaper. Those Yanks lucky enough to escape death or mutilation quickly copied the offensive techniques in vogue among the Allies. 'Crawling foward in twos and threes against each stubborn nest of guns,' recalled Colonel Douglas MacArthur of the 42nd Division, 'we closed in with the bayonet and the hand grenade.'

Repeated exposure to German fire meant heavy casualties, and veteran AEF divisions accepted large increments of rookies to maintain their combat effectiveness. Consequently, an outfit with several battles to its credit could be nearly as green as one fresh from the United States. On 10 October 1918, a seasoned sergeant of the 33rd Division opened his journal and scratched these notes about his infantry company: 'Replacements had been sent to us from National Army Camps, and now it seemed like a new organization, with only a few of the old-timers left.'

PLATE 32: OVER THERE, 1918

109. First Lieutenant, 26th U.S. Infantry, U.S. 1st Division, Field Dress, 1918: With his steel helmet, trench coat, field glasses and case, laced boots, .45-caliber automatic pistol, and cane, this company officer is ready for a tour of the front lines. **110. Private, 26th U.S. Infantry, U.S. 1st Division, Field Dress, 1918:** Woolen overcoats were in great demand in the AEF. **111. Private First Class, 166th U.S. Infantry, U.S. 42nd ('Rainbow') Division, Field Dress, 1918:** For nighttime raids on German lines, troops from this regiment carried automatic pistols and trench knives in addition to their '03 Springfields and bayonets. **112. Sergeant, 166th U.S. Infantry, U.S. 42nd ('Rainbow') Division, Field Dress, 1918:** Hoping to conserve stocks of olive drab material to clothe the expanding wartime Army, on 30 April 1918 the War Department informed the AEF that rank chevrons should be displayed on the right sleeve only, a practice already in force in the British Army and the U.S. Navy.

110. Private, 26th U.S. Infantry, U.S. 1st Division, Field Dress, 1918

112. Sergeant, 166th U.S. Infantry, U.S. 42nd ('Rainbow') Division, Field Dress, 1918

109. First Lieutenant, 26th U.S. Infantry, U.S. 1st Division, Field Dress, 1918

111. Private First Class, 166th U.S. Infantry, U.S. 42nd ('Rainbow') Division, Field Dress, 1918

Although they refused to admit it, Pershing and his generals relied on the meatgrinder tactics of attrition warfare. There was nothing subtle or original about their approach. The AEF simply sought to crush its foes under the sheer weight of numbers. The territory it liberated was bathed in American blood.

Fortunately for Pershing's reputation, quantity counted as much as quality on the Western Front in the latter half of 1918. For each doughboy who perished, there were hundreds to take his place—angry men who dashed forward to avenge their buddies—an inexorable human avalanche burying everything in its path. 'These are great soldiers,' bragged Major William Donovan of the 165th Infantry, a predominantly Irish outfit from New York City, 'they'll take hell with bayonets if they're properly led.' An enemy officer captured by whooping Oklahoma Indians of the 36th Division exclaimed: 'What kind of men are zeze? Zey are vild men; ve can't fight mit vild men!' On 15 July 1918, the German 10th and 36th Divisions tried to force a crossing over the Marne River at a point defended by a lone American regiment, the 38th Infantry. Outnumbered three to one, pounded by eighty-four batteries, and with both flanks dangling in the air, 3,600 doughboys hung

on with rifles, bayonets, and even bare fists, filling the Marne with bodies in gray uniforms. When it was over, one of the chastened German survivors, Gefreiter Earl Recklinghausen, jotted in his notebook: 'Those Americans certainly did clean us up . . . they fight like tigers. . . . If those in front of us are fair specimens of the average American troops and there are as many as they say there are, then good-by for us.'

Recklinghausen had good reason to despair. Even as he wrote, more Yanks were pouring into France at a rate of 10,000 a day. As news of the immense American build-up drifted across the lines, German morale disintegrated. Like his French and British opponents, the German soldier was tiring of the ceaseless slaughter. He had given his all for four cruel years. Now, there was no longer the slightest chance of victory. The meteoric growth of the AEF made the Allies too strong to beat. In due course, an Allied juggernaut, swollen by that unending stream of Americans, would demolish the German Army and ravage the Fatherland. Resolving to spare their people the physical and spiritual desolation of total defeat, Germany's leaders opted to arrange an armistice while their armed forces were still intact.

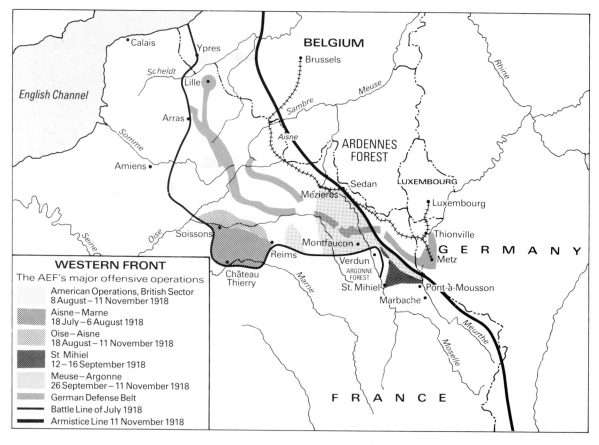

WESTERN FRONT
The AEF's major offensive operations

American Operations, British Sector
8 August – 11 November 1918

Aisne – Marne
18 July – 6 August 1918

Oise – Aisne
18 August – 11 November 1918

St Mihiel
12 – 16 September 1918

Meuse – Argonne
26 September – 11 November 1918

German Defense Belt

Battle Line of July 1918

Armistice Line 11 November 1918

Ironically, as the war lurched into its fourth year, the world wondered if the United States could place enough trained soldiers in Europe to save the Allies from disaster. The tide took a sudden turn in Germany's favor in the fall of 1917. The Bolsheviks seized power in Russia, a key member of the Allied coalition, and agreed to a humiliating peace dictated by the Central Powers. With the collapse of the Eastern Front, the German Army was free to concentrate its still-awesome power against the British and French. Chugging troop trains hauled fifty-two veteran divisions from Russia during the winter lull. By the spring of 1918, 217 German divisions stood poised on the Western Front in grim array for a climactic showdown. For the first time since 1914, the Kaiser's generals in Belgium and France enjoyed an edge in numbers. They outnumbered the Allies by at least 500,000 men; German superiority in riflemen alone exceeded 300,000.

The Allies depended on American reinforcements to offset the enemy's windfall—but instead of a flood, the Yanks arrived in a pitiful trickle. At the end of 1917, eight months after she entered the conflict, the United States had a mere 175,000 troops in France—a dismal showing by any standard. Excluding AEF support

Lieutenant James E. Europe conducts the band of the 369th Infantry—the finest in the AEF—outside American Red Cross Hospital No. 9, Paris, 4 September 1918. Regimental bands were supposed to have twenty-eight members, but the 369th had forty-four bandsmen—many of them the leading black musicians of the day. Europe's olive drab service cap has a russet leather chinstrap and visor and a United States coat of arms insignia of dull finish bronze. The gold chevron on the left lower sleeve of the trumpeter at center signified six months of overseas war service.

troops, Pershing's command amounted to five undermanned divisions. Only one was ready for combat. Three were partially trained, and the fifth was about to be cannibalized to fill out the first four.

There were other contributing factors, but the primary reason for the AEF's stunted growth was the inadequacy of the American merchant marine. With the number of vessels she possessed in June 1917, it would have taken the United States two-and-a-half years to deliver 900,000 doughboys to France. The British might have helped their junior associate, but they protested that they needed every one of their ships to supply their armed forces and civilian population. However, the fall of Russia and the transfer of so many German troops to the Western Front induced the London government to reorder its priorities. Late in January 1918, the British negotiated the first in a series of agreements designed to rush American combat troops to Europe. British tonnage eliminated the AEF's trans-Atlantic transportation bottleneck. During the first thirteen months of America's involvement in the war, 500,000 doughboys reached France. A million-and-a-half more got there in the final six months. Forty-nine per cent of the AEF's 2,086,000 officers and men—1,027,000 in all—crossed the Atlantic in British ships.

London's decision to assist in the AEF's 'Atlantic Ferry' came almost too late to do any good. On 21 March 1918, the Germans unloosed the first in a succession of go-for-broke offensives, staging one a month for five successive months. Their aim was the annihilation of the BEF and the French Army while the AEF was still a toddler. The Kaiser's legions severely mauled their enemies, but the Allies, fighting with their backs to the wall, always managed to repair their buckling lines—with a little help from Pershing. Approximately 90,000 doughboys saw action during the March-July crisis period. Elements of the U.S. 1st Division overran the strategically situated village of Cantigny on 28 May 1918. In prolonged combat around Château-Thierry (1 June-18 July 1918), the U.S. 2nd and 3rd Divisions helped shatter German spearheads thirty-seven miles short of Paris.

Germany staked her all on the proverbial roll of the dice, but luck deserted her. Eight hundred thousand sons of the Fatherland were slain, maimed, or taken prisoner in the great spring and summer drives. Along with those brave men, the German Army lost its offensive capacity, as well as the will to win. Now it was the Allies' turn to seize the initiative and go over to the attack.

As the AEF grew by leaps and bounds in the summer and fall of 1918, American divisions lent increased weight to the hammer blows that drove the Kaiser's troops back on their own frontiers and ever closer to the brink of ruin. Two hundred and seventy thousand

A Catholic chaplain attached to the 104th Infantry, U.S. 26th Division, at Seicheprey, France, 28 April 1918. The Latin crosses on the priest's overseas cap and coat collar are silver. Enlisted men called AEF officers 'Sam Brownes' because they all wore Sam Browne belts.

doughboys joined the French in the Aisne-Marne Counteroffensive to erase the Marne Salient (18 July–6 August 1918). During the AEF's debut as an independent field army, 550,000 Yanks flattened the St Mihiel Salient (12–16 September 1918).

In concert with the grand Allied push that finally brought Germany to terms, Pershing committed 1,200,000 American troops to the maelstrom known as the Meuse-Argonne Offensive (26 September–11 November 1918). It was the greatest battle in the U.S. Army's history, lasting forty-seven gun-blasted, gas-burned, blood-smeared days. Ensconced behind stout defenses—products of a four-year occupation—hardened German veterans treated the AEF to the horrors of modern war, inflicting 120,000 casualties on their assailants. The Yanks took their punishment and refused to quit, clawing their way inch by bitterly contested inch through the most sensitive sector of the enemy's front. The Germans threw in forty-three divisions—roughly 470,000 men—to block the AEF's progress, but to no avail. By 11 November, the day the armistice went into effect, dogged doughboys had killed or wounded 100,000 Germans and taken 26,000 prisoners, 874 cannon, and 3,000 machine guns. When he later analyzed his country's defeat, Field Marshal Paul Von Hindenburg, the German Army's Chief of Staff and supreme commander, offered this conclusion: 'The American infantry in the Argonne won the war.'

In reality, the Allied victory was a joint achievement, made possible by the efforts of many nations. Indeed, when the final casualty figures were tabulated, America's contribution seemed almost insignificant. Between August 1914 and November 1918, the French Army suffered 1,385,300 battle deaths and the British Army 900,000. Russia buried 1,700,000 of her soldiers before she dropped out of the conflict. In contrast, the U.S. Army sacrificed 50,300 lives in combat for the common cause, 50 per cent fewer than even tiny Belgium. However, it must be remembered that the AEF did not assume an active combat role until the last 200 days of the struggle. Moreover, statistics alone cannot convey the tremendous moral impact the eleventh-hour appearance of 2,000,000 fresh American troops had on their friends and foes. It would be fairer to say that the Allies bled the Central Powers and themselves for four long years, and then, in 1918, Great Britain and France stopped Germany from winning the war until the United States could muster strength to administer the *coup de grâce*.

Of course, the doughboys took enormous pride in the part they played, frequently exaggerating their oral and written reminiscences to make it seem that they had vanquished the Kaiser single-handed. Perhaps the proudest and the most boastful of all were the wretches who had done the dirtiest fighting—the common infantry. They had to share their battle honors with gunners, tankers, aviators, and other specialists spawned by the growing complexity of 20th century warfare, but they could still sing with gusto:

> The infantry, the infantry, with dirt behind their ears,
> The infantry, the infantry, that laps up all the beers,
> The cavalry, artillery, the bloomin' engineers,
> They couldn't lick the infantry in a hundred million years.

Nobody knew it then, but a generation later, the sons of those swaggering doughboys would be back in France, writing another chapter in the continuing saga of the U.S. Infantry.

Select Bibliography

Abrahamson, James L. *America Arms for a New Century: The Making of a Great Military Power*. New York: The Free Press, 1981.

Adams, Michael C. C. *Our Masters the Rebels: A Speculation on Union Military Failure in the East 1861–1865*. Cambridge: Harvard University Press, 1978.

Armstrong, David A. *Bullets and Bureaucrats: The Machine Gun and the United States Army, 1861–1916*. Westport, Connecticut: Greenwood Press, 1982.

Ayres, Leonard P. *The War with Germany: A Statistical Summary*. Washington, D.C.: Government Printing Office, 1919.

Bauer, K. Jack. *The Mexican War 1846–1848*. New York: Macmillan Publishing Co., Inc., 1974.

Berg, Fred Anderson. *Encyclopedia of Continental Army Units: Battalions, Regiments and Independent Corps*. Harrisburg: Stackpole Books, 1972.

Coffman, Edward M. *The War to End All Wars: The American Military Experience in World War I*. New York: Oxford University Press, 1968.

Coggins, Jack. *Arms and Equipment of the Civil War*. Garden City: Doubleday & Company, 1962.

Cornish, Dudley Taylor. *The Sable Arm: Negro Troops in the Union Army, 1861–1865*. New York: W. W. Norton & Company, Inc., 1966.

Cosmas, Graham A. *An Army for Empire: The United States Army in the Spanish-American War*. Columbia: University of Missouri Press, 1971.

Cuneo, John R. *Robert Rogers of the Rangers*. New York: Oxford University Press, 1959.

Dufour, Charles L. *The Mexican War: A Compact History 1846–1848*. New York: Hawthorn Books, Inc., 1968.

Dupuy, R. Ernest, and Baumer, William H. *The Little Wars of the United States*. New York: Hawthorn Books, Inc., 1968.

Eaton, Clement. *Jefferson Davis*. New York: The Free Press, 1977.

Elliott, Charles Winslow. *Winfield Scott: The Soldier and the Man*. New York: The Macmillan Company, 1937.

Ferrell, Robert H. *Woodrow Wilson and World War I, 1917–1921*. New York: Harper & Row, 1985.

Foner, Jack D. *The United States Soldier between Two Wars: Army Life and Reforms, 1865–1898*. New York: Humanities Press, 1970.

Fowler, Arlen L. *The Black Infantry in the West 1869–1891*. Westport: Greenwood Publishing Corporation, 1971.

Fox, William F. *Regimental Losses in the American Civil War 1861–1865*. Albany: Fort Orange Press, 1898.

Ganoe, William Addleman. *The History of the United States Army*. Pishton: Eric Lundberg, 1964.

Glatthaar, Joseph T. *The March to the Sea and Beyond: Sherman's Troops in the Savannah and Carolinas Campaigns*. New York: New York University Press, 1985.

Guthman, William H. *March to Massacre: A History of the First Seven Years of the United States Army*. New York: McGraw-Hill Book Company, 1975.

Hamilton, Holman. *Zachary Taylor: Soldier of the Republic*. Hamden: Archon Books, 1966.

Hassler, Warren J., Jr. *With Shield and Sword: American Military Affairs, Colonial Times to the Present*. Ames: Iowa State University Press, 1982.

Hitsman, J. Mackay. *The Incredible War of 1812: A Military History*. Toronto: University of Toronto Press, 1966.

Horsman, Reginald. *The War of 1812*. New York: Alfred A. Knopf, 1969.

Hughes, Nathaniel Cheairs, Jr. *General William J. Hardee: Old Reliable*. Baton Rouge: Louisiana State University Press, 1965.

Hutton, Paul Andrew. *Phil Sheridan and His Army*. Lincoln: University of Nebraska Press, 1985.

Jacobs, James Ripley. *The Beginning of the U.S. Army 1783–1812*. Princeton: Princeton University Press, 1947.

Jacobs, James Ripley, and Tucker, Glenn. *The War of 1812: A Compact History*. New York: Hawthorn Books, Inc., 1969.

Katcher, Philip R. N. *The American War 1812–1814*. Reading: Osprey Publishing Ltd., 1974.

— *The Mexican-American War 1846–1884*. London: Osprey Publishing Ltd., 1976.

— *The U.S. Army 1890–1920*. London: Osprey Publishing Ltd., 1978.

— *Uniforms of the Continental Army*. York: George Shumway Publisher, 1981.

Kennedy, David M. *Over Here: The First World War and American Society*. New York: Oxford University Press, 1980.

Leach, Douglas Edward. *Arms for Empire: A Military History of the British Colonies in North America 1607–1763*. New York: The Macmillan Company, 1973.

Lee, David D. *Sergeant York: An American Hero*. Lexington: The University Press of Kentucky, 1985.

McChristian, Douglas C. *An Army of Marksmen: The Development of United States Army Marksmanship in the 19th Century*. Fort Collins: The Old Army Press, 1981.

McWhiney, Grady, and Jamieson, Perry D. *Attack and Die: Civil War Military Tactics and the Southern Heritage*. University: The University of Alabama Press, 1982.

Mahon, John K. *History of the Second Seminole War 1835–1842*. Gainesville: University of Florida Press, 1967.

— *History of the Militia and the National Guard*. New York: Macmillan Publishing Company, 1983.

Mahon, John K., and Danysh, Romana. *Infantry, Part I: Regular Army*. Army Lineage Series. Washington, D.C.: Office of the Chief of Military History, 1972.

Martin, James Kirby, and Lender, Mark Edward. *A Respectable Army: The Military Origins of the Republic, 1763–1789*. Arlington Heights: Harlan Davidson, Inc., 1982.

May, Robin. *Wolfe's Army*. Reading: Osprey Publishing Limited, 1974.

Millett, Allan R., and Maslowski, Peter. *For the Common Defense: A Military History of the United States of America*. New York: The Free Press, 1984.

Moore, Albert Burton. *Conscription and Conflict in the Confederacy*. New York: The Macmillan Company, 1924.

Murdock, Eugene C. *One Million Men: The Civil War Draft in the North*. Madison: The State Historical Society of Wisconsin, 1971.

Neumann, George C. *Swords & Blades of the American Revolution*. Harrisburg: Stackpole Books, 1973.

Nolan, Alan T. *The Iron Brigade: A Military History*. Madison: The State Historical Society of Wisconsin, 1975.

Peterson, Harold L. *The Book of the Continental Soldier*. Harrisburg: The Stackpole Company, 1968.

Pogue, Forrest C. *George C. Marshall: Education of a General, 1880–1939*. New York: The Viking Press, 1963.

Prucha, Francis Paul. *The Sword of the Republic: The United States Army on the Frontier, 1783–1846*. Bloomington: Indiana University Press, 1977.

Rickey, Don, Jr. *Forty Miles a Day on Beans and Hay: The Enlisted Soldier Fighting the Indian Wars*. Norman: University of Oklahoma Press, 1983.

Sawicki, James A. *Infantry Regiments of the U.S. Army*. Dumfries: Wyvern Publications, 1981.

Sefton, James E. *The United States Army and Reconstruction 1865–1877*. Baton Rouge: Louisiana State University Press, 1967.

Shannon, Fred Albert. *The Organization and Administration of the Union Army 1861–1865*. 2 vols. Cleveland: The

Arthur H. Clark Company, 1928.

Smythe, Donald. *Guerrilla Warrior: The Early Life of John J. Pershing*. New York: Charles Scribner's Sons, 1973.

— *Pershing: General of the Armies*. Bloomington: Indiana University Press, 1986.

Sommers, Richard J. *Richmond Redeemed: The Siege at Petersburg*. Garden City: Doubleday & Company, 1981.

Stagg, J. C. A. *Mr. Madison's War: Politics, Diplomacy, and Warfare in the Early American Republic 1783–1830*. Princeton: Princeton University Press, 1983.

Thompson, Neil Baird. *Crazy Horse Called Them Walk-a-Heaps: The Story of the Foot Soldier in the Prairie Indian Wars*. St. Cloud: North Star Press, 1979.

Todd, Frederick P. *American Military Equipage 1851–1872*. 3 vols. Providence: The Company of Military Historians, 1974–8.

— *American Military Equipage 1851–1872, Volume II: State Forces*. New York: Chatham Square Press, Inc., 1981.

Trask, David F. *The War with Spain in 1898*. New York: Macmillan Publishing Co., Inc., 1981.

Urwin, Gregory J.W., and Fagan, Roberta E., eds. *Custer and His Times: Book Three*. Conway: University of Central Arkansas Press, 1987.

Utley, Robert M. *Frontier Regulars: The United States Army and the Indian, 1866–1890*. New York: Macmillan Publishing Co., Inc., 1973.

— *Frontiersmen in Blue: The United States Army and the Indian, 1848–1865*. Lincoln: University of Nebraska Press, 1981.

Weigley, Russell F. *History of the United States Army*. New York: The Macmillan Company, 1967.

Wiley, Bell Irvin. *The Life of Johnny Reb: The Common Soldier of the Confederacy*. Indianapolis: The Bobbs-Merrill Company, 1943.

— *The Life of Billy Yank: The Common Soldier of the Union*. Baton Rouge: Louisiana State University Press, 1983.

Windrow, Martin, and Embleton, Gerry. *Military Dress of North America 1665–1970*. London: Ian Allan Ltd., 1973.

Wright, Robert K., Jr. *The Continental Army*. Washington. D.C.: Center of Military History, United States Army, 1983.

Illustration Credits

William Gladstone Collection and the U.S. Army Military History Institute pages 7, 110, 133; National Archives pages 5, 75, 80, 90, 93, 117 (top left), 121, 124, 125 (left), 129, 130, 131, 134, 138, 141, 146, 148, 149, 152, 153, 158 (top left), 158 (bottom left); 161, 164, 165, 169, 170; Gary Zaboly Collection page 9; Tim Todish and Suagothel Productions Ltd., pages 11, 12; West Point Museum Collections, United States Military Academy pages 14, 36 (top left), 46 (bottom), 50, 60, 74, 108, 120, 145, 158 (top right); National Park Service 16, 24 (bottom); Prints Division, The New York Public Library, Astor, Lenox, and Tilden Foundations page 18; Georgia Historical Society page 21 (left); Independence National Historical Park Collection pages 21 (right), 22; U.S. Army pages 24 (top), 33, 45; Anne S.K. Brown Military Collection, Brown University Library page 28; Private Collection page 29; National Portrait Gallery, Smithsonian Institution, Washington, D.C. page 36 (centre left and right); Collection of Mrs. George Gammon, photograph courtesy of the Anglo-American Art Museum, Louisiana State University, Baton Rouge page 36 (top right); The New York Historical Society, New York City page 36 (bottom left); The Cleveland Museum of Art, Gift of the John Huntington Art and Polytechnic Trust page 36 (bottom right); Abby Rockefeller Folk Art Collection, Williamsburg, Virginia page 46 (top); Houghton Library, Harvard University page 48; Historic Fort

Snelling, Minnesota Historical Society page 53; South Carolina Library, University of South Carolina page 56 (top); Chicago Historical Society page 56 (bottom); Library of Congress pages 62, 92 (left); U.S. Army History Institute pages 64, 81 (left), 84, 122, 125 (right); Cass County, Indiana, Historical Society page 65; California Historical Society, San Francisco page 69 (left); Massachusetts Commandery Military Order of the Loyal Legion of the U.S. Army Military Institute pages 69 (right), 76, 88, 104; Mrs. James L. Collins, Jr., Collection and the U.S. Army Military History Institute page 77; Herb Peck, Jr., pages 81 (right), 89, 94, 96; U.S. Military Academy Archives, West Point page 82; U.S. Army Signal Corps Museum page 88; Utah State Historical Society page 86; Michael J. AcAfee pages 92 (right), 97, 102, 105, 106, 117 (right); Cliff Breidinger Collection and the U.S. Army Military History Institute page 112; Warren County Historical Society page 113; G.A.R. Memorial Hall Museum, Wisconsin Veterans Museum page 114; Illinois State Historical Library page 116 (left); Roger D. Hunt Collection and the U.S. Army Military History Institution page 116 (right); Custer Battlefield National Monument page 128; Fort Leavenworth Museum pages 133 (bottom), 135 (right), 136, 142, 150, 154; Fort Sam Houston Museum page 135 (eft); George E. Bush, Jr. 137.

Index

Page numbers in italic refer to illustrations. Index main headings are in **bold**. American military units not a part of the U.S. Army (Regulars) are grouped alphabetically by state or territory of origin. In all categories, numbered military units take precedence. Wars are listed in chronological order under the heading, **Wars.**